MW01206533

DIGITAL WORK
in an *Analog World*

Improving Software Engineering
Through Applied Psychology

JOHN R. FOX

Digital Work in an Analog World

Copyright © 2011 by John R. Fox
All rights reserved.

This book is also available in electronic form.

No part of this work shall be reproduced, stored in a retrieval system, or transmitted, in any form, or by any means (electronic, mechanical, photocopying, recording, or otherwise) without the prior written permission of the author. No patent liability is assumed with respect to the use of the information contained herein. Although every precaution has been taken in the preparation of this book, the publisher and the author assume no responsibility for errors or omissions. Neither is any liability assumed for damages resulting from the use of the information contained herein.

ISBN 10: 1466381523
ISBN 13: 978-1466381520
Library of Congress Control Number: 2011917665
Printed and bound in the United States of America

Published by Studio City Media Endeavors
Minneapolis, Minnesota

STUDIO CITY
media endeavors

www.studiocity.me

ALHASSANE,

ALL THE BEST!

Acknowledgements

Several people provided valuable assistance and guidance on this journey.

The entire project would likely not have gotten far without the help of Steve McConnell's experience, encouragement, and insights.

Other key people who provided feedback and encouragement include Andy Powell, my Psychology Coach, who helped point me in the right directions in regard to research. Melissa Worthington provided valuable viewpoints on the overall project, as she always does.

Nelson Fox, Joel Arnold, Ben Aldritt, and Devon Musgrave helped shape and improve the manuscript in many ways.

Special thanks to Dave Steingart and Todd Hauschildt of SWAT Solutions, who afforded me the flexibility to complete this book. In addition, Todd's experience provided many insights that positively influenced the text.

Melissa Arnold of Studio City Media Endeavors, my publisher, was a lifesaver. I'm convinced there's nothing she can't handle.

A huge thanks goes out to my incredible wife Audrey and our two sons, who had to endure endless chatter about software engineering concepts for the past two years. Audrey also attended numerous social functions on her own, as a result of my writing efforts. You're the best!

And finally, I'd like to thank my parents, Gene & Peg, for all that they've done for me and my seven amazing siblings.

Table of Contents

81 PART II
Psychological Factors in Software Engineering

PREFACE

The human mind is capable of incredibly astonishing accomplishments. Do you think it would have been possible to convince someone living in the year 1800, just shortly after America was born, that one day a fellow countryman would actually land and walk on the moon? I highly doubt it. In fact, you would likely have been severely ridiculed. The human race really has accumulated a tremendous number of stellar achievements to boast about.

Our Global Positioning System (GPS), readily available to everyone, is one such example. If you research what it takes to actually implement the GPS system that you have in your car or even on your phone, you would most likely be amazed. Understanding and using GPS systems is a personal hobby. So like most enthusiasts (and technical people) I wanted to better understand how it works and acquaint myself with the design of the system so that I could to use it more effectively. I started researching GPS systems and was not too surprised to find books, of several hundred pages, that described the detailed workings and intricate design of GPS systems. The mathematics involved, particularly the geometry, was fascinating and extremely complex. I have a hard time imagining how this was ever implemented into "production" as we say in our industry and am somewhat surprised how well and consistently the systems actually work. If our government could pull off this implausible feat, couldn't a handful of us software folks build a software system that works consistently and reliably too? Of course, I'm not saying that implementing the first working GPS system was without problems, delays and budget overruns. But if you consider the sheer magnitude of the effort involved in launching the GPS system, it makes building your average software system appear rather trivial in comparison.

There are many other outstanding human achievements of note besides the GPS system: the integrated circuit and the astounding pace of computer hardware development, wireless technology, artificial joints and other human body parts, organ transplants, nuclear power plants, and of course the list of notable human achievement goes on and on. One such feat of the human brain, although not nearly as practical as the GPS system, was the raw display of human memory and mastery of numbers displayed by Daniel Tammet. On pi day (March 14th or 3/14 in reference to the leading pi digits) in 2004, Daniel recited pi (which is an infinite number) to 22,514 digits over the course of about 5 hours to set the European and British record. To put this accomplishment in perspective, try memorizing pi to even 25 digits yourself. What's even more amazing is that Daniel's personal best is not even close to the purported world record of over 65,000 digits!

However, with all of that said, the human mind also has many embarrassing shortcomings and frailties. Our minds can be easily tricked in many situations, even when you already know what's coming. One such example is Anchoring, which will be discussed in the section on software estimation.

Part of what we need to achieve is a deeper understanding of these human frailties and tendencies and see how they might impact the software engineering process so that we can deal with them accordingly. The other part of the equation is to better understand behavior on two major levels – individuals and groups – so we can learn how to get the most out of our development teams. Understanding how people think and behave in different situations and in different cultures is crucial to improving work efforts everywhere, regardless of profession. Learning how to improve our brain functioning and reasoning is imperative and this book will touch on that topic as well.

Throughout this book I will reference many scientific studies, some classics, as well as some of my own theories. My theories will typically be how a particular psychological concept might apply in the software development arena. When I do reference my own theories, without any studies to back them up, I will always distinguish between my theories and official scientific studies.

This book is not necessarily targeted at one specific group within the software engineering discipline. Hopefully this book will be utilized by Project Managers, Developers, DBAs, Business Analysts, QA Specialists, and other management people that participate in software development in one form or another. Some concepts may only apply to a particular group, but on the whole everyone will hopefully find some enlightening ideas to bring home. This book does not set out to proclaim that certain personality types may only perform particular kinds of duties. There is no magic test that can be taken that will tell you what your absolute best fit would be. There are some psychological tests (or instruments as they are called) that may lead you down a particular avenue better suited for you, but there is nothing definitive.

There have not been many research studies done using computer programmers, or other software development professionals, as the only subjects. This book will highlight areas where studies in our field would be useful and perhaps someday, somewhere, enterprising graduate students will organize and carry out these experiments. Applying psychological concepts and principles to the software process might be another way to help our industry move the needle, ever so slightly perhaps, in the right direction. While I do believe that a better understanding of psychology can help us, I'm not suggesting that this is a silver bullet either. In fact, believing in Silver Bullets has been a considerable part of the problem, but more about that later.

This book draws upon three principle areas of psychology: Personality Theory, Social Psychology, and Industrial / Organizational Psychology, also known as I/O Psychology. Several additional branches of psychology are also referenced such as Positive Psychology, Physiological Psychology, Cognitive Psychology, Cultural Psychology and others. The goal is to draw upon some of the well known and well studied principles in addition to some principles that may be a little outside the mainstream. My hope is to link these theories to the non-technical challenges of software development in a continuing effort to improve our field by helping to prevent unwanted behaviors and decisions and substituting those with better alternatives.

A look at how to prevent these problems, once identified, will be explored. However, once you begin to open your mind to some of the ideas presented throughout this book, I'm quite certain that you will see more possibilities to improve your software process and the overall health of your software organization. Of course, getting people to admit that they could actually benefit from some modifications to the way they approach software engineering is a major obstacle for many of us. Admitting that we could benefit from some enhancements or new approaches is sometimes painful and this is something technical people routinely struggle with.

Therefore, one of the major premises of this book is that technical people can improve their development skills and their value to an organization in multiple ways. The obvious one is by accruing more technical proficiency and acumen and this is the one most of us gravitate towards. However, the one approach quite often overlooked is mastering the domain of "soft" skills. How software professionals interact with other members of the organization, their planning abilities, leadership skills, dealing with stressors and emotional topics, and other similar issues. These soft skills, on certain occasions anyway, may actually be more crucial to an organization's overall success than its technical abilities.

Finally, I have not conducted any research experiments or launched any "official" broad based surveys. My hopeful contribution is a result of assembling a vast array of research in specific areas of psychology. I pull data and ideas from a multitude of sources and attempt to link or apply them to our field. Since I have spent many years in this industry, holding nearly every position imaginable, I will strive to offer numerous perspectives to help enlighten readers at all levels. Your comments are welcome at jfox@analogdevelopment.com.

Notice to Readers

Before you delve into the content, a few points need to be made regarding the nature of this book. It may be trying to read at times, because it highlights the challenges many of us in the industry face. But, it's meant to be used as a means to grow and learn about ourselves in order to advance our careers. In typical fashion, those things we find most uncomfortable are those that hit closest to home and are issues we routinely struggle with. It's exactly these issues we should examine closely in our professional lives, because addressing them will yield the greatest improvement.

Many of the challenges featured throughout the text are ones I myself struggle with regularly. However, in order to improve our situation, we must first recognize where our opportunities lie and then take the necessary measures in order to realize these opportunities.

PART I

Lay of the Land

CHAPTER 1

Getting Started

WHY PSYCHOLOGY & SOFTWARE ENGINEERING?

There are several compelling reasons why organizations should consider applying the principles of psychology and improved soft skills to promote better software engineering outcomes. These will be explored here in greater detail.

Dubious Track Record

The most obvious grounds for considering the application of psychology and soft skills in software engineering is our maligned track record. Unfortunately for us, our track record as a profession is rather abysmal. Pick an adjective of your own, make up a new one perhaps, but no matter how you slice it, we're not doing well by anyone's standard. There's a surplus of data available to describe our troubled state of software development.

Project Metrics

According to the *CHAOS Summary 2009* report issued by the highly regarded Standish Group, about one quarter of all projects are cancelled outright or never put into production. Slightly less than half of all software projects are substantially late, over budget, or have been released with reduced feature sets. The remaining projects, about one third of them, are considered successful. These numbers represent a slight decline from previously reported data from the Standish Group. Any other industry that had a track record similar to this might not survive. The laws of economics would eventually intervene and the industry would either have to make substantial adjustments or it would likely become extinct.

However, the numbers that don't show up in reports like those from the Standish Group are the frail software quality metrics. Having spent many years in the software quality business, one quickly discerns a pattern of compressed quality assurance timelines. As development times are inflated, the time remaining for proper testing gets squeezed, but it's rare to see the software release dates adjusted accordingly. This does not necessarily imply that the programmers are tardy though. While developers may be partially accountable there are several other factors, described throughout this book, which may come into play as well. Therefore, even those projects that are delivered on-time and with unabridged feature sets may be substandard. My analysis is that somewhere between 70-80 percent of projects are guilty of compressed QA timelines. This means that the risk of a software defect being missed by the QA team increases as QA cycles get crunched.

Monetary costs are another solemn matter. U.S. businesses are wasting billions of dollars and endless hours on these projects, each and every year. The U.S. government claims that nearly $60 billion dollars was lost on bad software in the year 2000 (See NIST article entitled: Software Errors Cost U.S. Economy $59.5 Billion Annually, June 28, 2002).

And while this data is a bit stale, I'm guessing that it may well be worse today since the more recent CHAOS Report shows some slight deterioration in our progress. This is not just a problem for people in the software industry, but for society at large. Someone actually pays for these failures at some point and that someone is the consumer who buys products and services from companies that engage in software engineering of any kind, as well as constituents of failed government projects.

Another cost is that borne of poor or faulty products or infrastructure that the software in question manages or monitors. There are far too many examples of noteworthy software failures in our society to fully document (but I will share a few to whet your appetite all the same). Some of these failures have been catastrophic, causing loss of life, while others cause human anguish, schedule delays, while virtually all cost money.

Needless to say, we're not setting records in the proper direction and it doesn't appear to be getting any better. Even relatively new programming constructs, like Object Oriented programming, have not seemed to help much. Other techniques such as Agile development may be making some inroads, but the jury is still out here too. This implies that we need to at least consider investigating some of the "soft issues" involved in software engineering to see if we can't find some minor breakthroughs and improvements.

This in itself is one of the problems. Many developers, and technical professionals in general, have a limited desire to focus on improving or acquiring skills outside the realm of technology. Learn a new programming language? Sure, why not? Master AJAX? Absolutely, bring it on, been waiting for that one. But mention discipline, interpersonal skills or planning techniques and the benefits aren't usually as obvious or captivating for most technical people, even though we realize that these are critical skills. For most of us, thinking about these soft skills is not particularly intriguing and we have other, more urgent, problems to concern ourselves with now.

Notable Software Failures

This section probably merits its own volume. Perhaps even several volumes like Knuth's famous set (The Art of Computer Programming). Being in the software quality business myself, at SWAT Solutions, I have documented innumerable incidents of software failures over the past several years. However, there is really no need for me to sort through this vast compilation as I'm offered regular suggestions on a daily basis in the newspapers across the United States. Today was no exception as USA Today featured an article regarding the U.S. Census Bureau's software problems, which are plaguing the 2010 census. It's probably not fair to pick solely on the U.S. government though, after all their software development efforts may actually be better than many corporations. I've spent several years involved in government software development of one kind or another and remain reasonably impressed with their approach and results. The Department of Defense in particular utilizes rigorous standards and processes for developing and deploying software systems in complex environments and with elevated security standards besides.

Late night television host Jay Leno has a segment where readers send in comical or erroneous newspaper headings from across the country. It would be rather easy to collect similar, yet not nearly as amusing, software failure reports as they are much more common than you might realize.

What distresses me about these repeated incidents is just that – they're constantly repeated. High profile new systems and updates to existing systems which end up shutting down or severely crippling some key piece of commerce or infrastructure occur on a frighteningly regular basis around the globe. Remember the PayPal update that hampered ecommerce at eBay for several days? Or what about the student college entrance test scores that were mistakenly lowered a number of years back? Regrettably, this list goes on and on.

Unique Discipline

Developing software is substantially different than most activities normal people perform every day on the job. That's why you probably won't find a book entitled *Psychology and the Welding Process* at your favorite book retailer. There are not many things you can build in this world, of any substance and value, without any planning. But some, usually smaller, software development organizations do just that. They sit down at their computer(s) and start hacking out what they refer to, in good faith no doubt, as a "Prototype." The next thing you know this Prototype has somehow morphed itself into Release 1.0 (and maybe without too many changes) and suddenly you're in the software business. They probably did not intend to build a product without adequate planning, but that was the resulting outcome nonetheless.

I'm not suggesting that every organization building software operates in a haphazard fashion. I've been involved with IT steering committees that required all major software projects be cleared before takeoff. There are many quality software organizations that perform exhaustive detailed planning and analysis before they write the first line of code. But I'm guessing that even those buttoned down, organized shops have had moments when they've built some sort of software utility, on the fly, that they never imagined might become a key component of their system some day. This utility probably caused them some angst at various points along the way and would eventually need to be redesigned and rewritten. At other times, and this is by far the more likely case, some quick and dirty enhancements were made to an enterprise system in order to satisfy a special request from a large customer somewhere. It's difficult to oversee what every department and every development group is doing every day, and the business side of the house is routinely putting intense pressure on development teams for new features, fixes and products on a tighter timeline. The smaller development shops appear to be more prone to building first and defining requirements later as there is typically less structure within these organizations.

Software development, besides having a tendency to succumb to ad-hoc development, is also an abstract activity and this is what occasionally makes it so difficult and cumbersome to manage. There have been several valiant attempts by many talented and knowledgeable groups and individuals in an effort to improve our lot over the decades. There are countless standards, best practices, new development methodologies, and even relatively new language genres (think Object Oriented here) that have sprung up to help our distressed profession. And while these developments have surely improved the situation over the decades, they have not really changed things all that dramatically. This is not to say that those groups and individuals who would adopt all of these improvement techniques would not be better off. They most certainly would be and I'm a huge proponent of software best practices. But, rather, the problem is profoundly rooted in the human psyche and if short cuts are possible people will find ways to justify using them. That's just one small example of the psychology involved in software development. There are many explanations behind the numerous decisions made during a typical software project. These may originate from various stakeholders: as individuals; teams; and organizations at large. These different stakeholders may be influenced by a variety of factors. Even the culture in which one is raised has significant impacts on how software is developed. With more and more software development occurring globally, this is becoming an important issue.

With all that said, there actually are some substantial benefits to building prototypes without exhaustive prior planning efforts. Because we do work in an abstract field, many of the business teams that approve and define requirements for software projects may have a deeper understanding of these efforts when they can actually see something tangible for themselves.

Since software development is usually a team-based activity, with many significant decision points involved (including team selection process), team dynamics and human behavior become essential ingredients in the ensuing outcomes. When you're examining human behavior, there are no absolutes. If that were the case our development problems (and many others) certainly would have been solved long ago. There are countless variables that drive human behavior and if the same individual were to face the same set of circumstances again in the future, he may or may not behave in the same way. There are several possible linkages between the common, non-technical, problems found in the software development process and many of the principles and concepts found within psychology. Determining whether these linkages actually pertain to your circumstances is the real challenge and you are the only one who can decide if that is the case.

Untapped Resource

It's somewhat rare to encounter organizations that have truly made a determined commitment to develop and focus on essential soft skills for technical professionals. Here are some possible explanations why companies appear to devote limited resources to improving the soft skills of their software professionals.

ROI Measurements

Measuring the return on investment of soft skills training is obviously difficult, if not downright impossible. How do you know if the training is working, and even if it is, is there a related positive effect on the overall software effort? For many of these types of questions there is no real apparent way to quantify an answer. You might never actually know if your improved software outcomes were due to enhanced teamwork.

Companies that have difficulty evaluating training investments may avoid them altogether, even if they believe that there are benefits to be realized. Investments in new technical skills are easier to justify, and visualizing the expected results is effortless for most organizations.

Responsibility of the Individual

Some people, and therefore some organizations, believe that the individual is responsible for these matters and it's not the job of HR departments to teach everyone how to get along or do their jobs properly. A related reason for dodging soft skills training is that some managers believe this training will not yield lasting improvements. It takes time and discipline to adopt new personal habits and one-shot training efforts may have little effect.

Not Appreciated

Many soft skills are underappreciated by technical organizations by virtue of the fact that they are soft skills. When you combine the difficulty of measuring results along with the uncertainty of whether organizations are even responsible for this type of training, apathy in regards to soft skills development may result.

Lack of Resources

Many software organizations, due to a multitude of factors, have scaled down to the bare minimum. Software engineering has become an extremely competitive endeavor over the past decade with more and more locations throughout the world coming on-line. When funding is scarce, training of all types tends to decline, especially soft skills training.

Conclusion

Software development is both complex and abstract in nature and noticeable improvements in software engineering have been difficult to attain. Therefore, it is prudent to consider other means for moving the industry forward. Exploring the effects of improved soft skills is one such potential area. And although there are some valid reasons to look the other way, my experience in the software industry along with my research in this field, leads me to conclude that an emphasis on soft skills has a reasonable ability to yield positive long-term results. It has the ability to produce a beneficial impact on employee retention, corporate culture, and overall productivity on a recurring basis. However, the effort must be on-going and just herding everyone off to a two day class once a year will doubtless be insufficient. Technical professionals must be convinced that expanding these skills is worth their time and continued efforts. Supervisors should support these efforts as part of their normal developmental plans for software professionals.

RESEARCH IN PSYCHOLOGY

If you've studied psychology in the past, then this section may be review material for you. However, you might just be surprised about how much you've forgotten from your high school or college psychology courses.

There has been a phenomenal amount of research done in the various fields of psychology over the past 50 years. The research continues unabated to this day. Much of the research that is over 30 years old comes from the countries you'd expect; the United States, Canada, Australia, and Western Europe. Many other countries are now in the midst of a significant uptick in their research efforts. This will help validate, and possibly invalidate, some of the research already started. It is critical, especially as the software field globalizes, that research from other countries on subjects in different cultures, comes forward.

Research Basics

Research in most scientific fields comes about rather slowly. One person builds on the previous person's studies and the next researcher builds upon that, and so on over the years. When I was an undergraduate student in Psychology I remember, to this day, that the point of research was to answer the next logical question posed from the cumulative research to date on any particular topic. Eventually hypotheses and theories are either strengthened or weakened. In the field of Psychology, it's difficult to actually "prove" anything. A preponderance of evidence can be built, but there will usually be some weaknesses in the research supporting the theories. In addition, when a major research claim is confirmed, several researchers will likely refute the claim by finding other possible explanations or accounts for the finding. This was precisely the case when Leon Festinger first laid claim to the theory of Cognitive Dissonance in 1957. It has literally taken decades to further refine and fully shake out this concept, some of which will be featured at greater lengths in chapter six.

One of the weaknesses in psychological research is that much of it is done with college age, female students in the United States. This is obviously quite limiting. Will the results extrapolate nicely to middle aged men in Japan? Maybe not. This is why it is so important to expand research in other countries and with other types of subjects. Also, many of the research experiments I have reviewed during my research for this book, and it numbers in the hundreds, seem somewhat contrived in order to work within the confines of a laboratory where the variables under test may be controlled and observed. However, the major, reputable research journals have strict standards for publishing works and many of them require multiple studies to ensure that the research is valid.

Fortunately more and more research is now being conducted outside the United States. This will allow us to begin determining the cultural impact of many theories previously posited in the U.S. and will yield a clearer picture of the various consequences culture may have on behavior.

Methods of Research

There are several fundamental research methods utilized in psychological research, which are highlighted here.

Observational Method

This is the most obvious method of acquiring new information and while it has limited usefulness, there are some advantages. One of the benefits of observation is that you can watch activities in their normal setting. Many research experiments, as you will learn throughout this book, are artificial in nature so that they may be more easily observed. Subjects are usually duped into thinking the experiment is about one topic when it's really about something entirely unrelated. Does this diminish the value and validity of the research? See the side bar for a more detailed discussion.

There are two primary types of observational research; surveys and case studies. We'll take a brief look at each of these methods.

Surveys

The most direct way to find out about what people are thinking or doing and why, is to just ask them. Survey techniques have become more reliable and elaborate over the decades, which make it possible to determine some general results about certain behaviors and thinking. This assumes that the sample is representative of the general population under study and that the sampling

VALIDITY AND RELIABILITY

One of the primary concerns regarding scientific research is to understand how reliable experimental or test results are and if they are indeed considered to be valid.

Reliability of results determines how consistent the experimental or test results are over time. That is, can the same result in the same situation be repeated? Is the identified measure or result accurate and true? Duplicated measurements, over some elapsed time period, are one way to determine if results are reliable. There are always some discrepancies in experimental and test results because of certain uncontrolled variables, the state of the subjects under test being one. This is referred to as measurement error and statistical analysis is then used to determine error variances in relation to a mean value. Once a result is deemed reliable, it now must be determined if it is actually valid.

Validity is the process of determining whether what you measured is what you intended to measure. Having different measurements or tests available on the same subjects that yield nearly indistinguishable results is a start in determining whether or not a particular construct is valid.

The issues and complexities of reliability and validity are why many psychology experiments and test results are disputed by other researchers. Will you get the same results consistently and are they accurately measuring what they were supposed to measure? If this question cannot be satisfactorily answered then doubts regarding the subject matter will linger.

size is adequate. Most of these issues have been addressed since the early days of surveying. Now surveying has gone to the web, which has complicated things somewhat.

The shortcoming with surveys is that some people may not tell you what they're really thinking or doing, but rather what they think you'd like to hear. It reminds me of the focus group for a particular product in which participants said they preferred the black model and when upon leaving the focus study group they were allowed to take a product home for participating in the study, most members opted for the yellow model. The thinking is that they assumed that most other people would prefer the black model but they themselves preferred yellow.

Case Studies

A case study is a more detailed investigation of some particular event, usually something fairly dramatic such as a mass murder or large Ponzi scheme. Some psychological testing may be involved and events leading up to the tragedy may be examined more closely. In some cases, the culture of the times may be reviewed to determine what led to the event in question.

Correlational Research Method

Many times researchers are interested if two distinct variables are somehow related to each other and if so, how. As programmers we are familiar with variables, however in this case they are characteristics of people that may vary. An example might be a researcher trying to determine whether people who grew up in large families are more generous than those of smaller families. This would be a correlation. The types of correlations are endless. Are men who play video games more likely to be better programmers than those who do not? As you can see, there are many correlations that psychologists would be interested in studying.

Once the variables are selected, they are correlated mathematically to determine how they are related, if at all. This is called a correlation coefficient that has a range of -1.0 to +1.0, where -1.0 and +1.0 are extremely rare conditions referred to as perfectly correlated either negatively or positively. A common positive correlation is between height and weight. The taller people become the more they typically will weigh. In this particular example you might find a correlation of approximately +.7. This would be considered a strong correlation. The reason it is not +1.0 is that some people who are short may be heavy and others who are taller may also be very thin. So in summary, correlations that are close to -1.0 or +1.0 may yield some useful information. Correlations hovering near zero mean that there is little or no correlation between the two variables under review.

One warning about correlations is that people have a natural tendency to assume that because two variables are related, one is the cause of the other. This may or may not be true and more research is usually required to see if indeed one variable is the cause of the other.

Experimental Research

The way that researchers determine whether two variables are indeed related in some way, is to conduct formal experiments where one variable is controlled and modified, called the **Independent Variable**, in order to observe the result on the other **Dependent Variable**. This is why experiments have two or more groups involved. One group is treated differently than the other group(s) to see if the impact on the dependent variable in question is significant based upon the different treatment or condition.

There are several concerns when conducting formal experiments, one of the most prominent being a random assignment of participants to both experimental groups. If you're hoping to extrapolate results to the population at large this is absolutely critical. Once a researcher has found a significant relationship between two variables, other researchers will then usually attempt to replicate the results using slightly different treatments and conditions. After many variations of core research are completed on the topic, the bigger picture will begin to emerge and trends can be anticipated when the general conditions are met. Then it is up to others to determine if and how these tendencies relate to a particular subject area. That is exactly what this book attempts to do for software development.

Meta-Analysis

When many different studies are conducted in the same area of research, there are nearly always at least some minor discrepancies in the results. However, there is a statistical technique called meta-analysis that reviews groups of related studies to determine if the dependent variable is reliably influenced by the independent variable, across multiple studies. This gives us more confidence in the overall results in the case where perhaps comparable studies might yield somewhat different results. The meta-analysis technique essentially provides researchers a tool that can summarize groups of associated experiments.

Other Concerns

There are several additional concerns with psychological research besides those previously mentioned which included the overabundance of college aged subjects and the bulk of the research having been conducted in Western cultures. Probably the most concerning of these is what is referred to as **Experimental Bias**. When a researcher has an idea of what he believes will occur he may have undue influence on the outcome of an experiment or he may perhaps even misinterpret results. Participants also may have certain expectations of how they are expected to act or what they believe the experiment is really about. This is why most experimenters intentionally mislead participants. This way they will not have expectations about the true intention of the research.

Regarding experiments relative to the field of software engineering there are even more problems. Most of the experiments and studies have not utilized software professionals as subjects because psychological research is more generalized by nature.

THE CPU (AKA THE BRAIN)

It all originates from here, so it's quite logical to begin with a discussion of the human brain. It has been relatively recently, at least from a scientific research perspective, that we've begun to really understand the normal brain. In the past, much of what we have learned about the brain has been a result of brain injuries or abnormal brain functioning to a large degree, where risky invasive procedures inside the skull were a matter of life or death.

Most people don't really know how their brain actually functions. Having some basic understanding of our own CPU will help us program it, just as knowledge of a CPU's instruction set allows one to write better, more efficient code. While it is possible to program without knowing the CPU instruction set (via the use of higher level languages which most of us use today) it is certainly beneficial to understand the basics of its operation. After all, those people who have little comprehension of the inner workings of their brain may still be excellent developers. A car analogy works here too. You can drive all you please without knowing too many intricate details of how the engine works, as long as you remember it requires gasoline. Understanding core brain functioning ought to help us better exploit it, just as understanding how a car functions will improve the maintenance and usage of the vehicle.

During the past decade or so extensive research has become more viable due to the advances in non-invasive methods, primarily scanning techniques, also known as brain imaging. CT, PET, MRI and fMRI have become part of the neuroscientist's vernacular and now to some extent the medical community at large, including the patients (see the side bar for more descriptions of these imaging technologies). Scientists have also established connections between brain functioning and our hormonal systems. It's now becoming clear that there are strong connections between certain behavioral tendencies and brain physiology. We're beginning to understand

BRAIN IMAGING TECHNIQUES

There are several brain imaging or scanning techniques that have been developed and refined over the past few decades. These techniques are improving and innovative new approaches are undoubtedly being developed as you read this book.

PET – Positron Emission Tomography (PET) uses small amounts of a safe but short-lived radioactive liquid that eventually makes its way to the brain to map activity. When the injected liquid undergoes radioactive decay a positron is emitted, which can be picked up by the computer to determine the general level of activity in that area of the brain.

fMRI – Functional magnetic resonance imaging, or fMRI, is another technique for measuring brain activity. It works by detecting the changes in blood oxygenation and flow that occur in response to neural activity – when a brain area is more active it consumes more oxygen. To meet this increased demand, blood flow increases to the active area. fMRI can be used to produce activation maps showing which parts of the brain are involved in a particular mental process (Michael Demitri, M.D.).

MEG – Magnetoencephalography (MEG) is an imaging technique used to measure the changes in magnetic fields produced by electrical activity in the brain via extremely sensitive devices known as SQUIDs (superconducting quantum interference devices). This allows researchers to identify the location of neural activity.

NIRS – Near infrared spectroscopy is an optical technique for measuring blood oxygenation in the brain. It works by shining light in the near infrared part of the spectrum (700-900nm) through the skull and detecting how much the remerging light is attenuated. How much the light is attenuated depends on blood oxygenation and thus NIRS can provide an indirect measure of brain activity (Michael Demitri, M.D.).

that various levels of certain hormones may elicit certain behaviors. Too much of one particular hormone and you may have one result, too little and something else may occur.

Scientists have also mapped the brain so that we generally know what regions of the brain are responsible for the wide assortment of activity it monitors and controls. We also know that much of the brain's capacity functions on autopilot and that a minute fraction is involved in controlled thinking or what is happening when you're consciously thinking about a particular problem.

Brain Functioning

While much has been discovered, there is still a great deal that we don't yet know about the human brain. It does appear however to be capable of at least some distributed processing, the full extent of which is not yet known. While slower than your typical CPU (the CPU typically processes data serially, but very fast) the human brain, with many distinct regions, is able to activate multiple areas simultaneously to "solve" problems. You can see a quick comparison of Brain versus CPU in Figure 1.1 below, adapted from Willamette University in Salem, Oregon.

	Processing Elements	Element Size	Energy Use	Processing Speed	Style of Computation	Fault Tolerant	Learns	Intelligent Conscious
	10^{14} synapses	10^{-6} m	30 W	100 Hz	parallel distributed	yes	yes	usually
	10^{8} transistors	10^{-6} m	30 W (CPU)	10^{9} Hz	serial centralized	no	some	not (yet)

FIGURE 1.1

Brain Regions

There are several regions of the brain, but for our purposes the concentration will be primarily on three major components. The first is what the layman knows as the inner brain, also referred to technically as the limbic system. The second area is the outer brain, better known by neuroscientists as the frontal-parietal cortex. The last brain construct reviewed, although it's not really a region, is the left and right brain hemispheres.

Limbic System

The limbic system is the more mature part of our brain, evolutionally speaking. It's the component associated with the classic flight or fight response that supposedly kept us from becoming lunch for a saber-tooth tiger back in the caveman days. It's impulsive in nature and operates to a large degree on autopilot if left unchecked. As man evolved, the outer areas of our brain developed to promote thinking and reasoning and to some degree, in my way of thinking at least, these two regions are in conflict with each other. The beauty of it all is that our brains are mostly wired for single tasks versus multi-tasking. Of course part of our brain constantly and sub-consciously monitors and controls autonomic activities such as breathing, but to actually have two distinct thought processes operating simultane-ously is not really considered to be possible. The reason this is a good thing is that once we get the proper portion of our brain engaged (generally and usually preferably the cortex area) it will shut down the others so we don't get too jumbled up. This is not completely correct either, as the inner brain provides functions required for memory and learning too. The brain is obviously an exceedingly complex instrument and I'm generalizing some-what in order to simplify the concepts as it relates to our subject matter.

Typically we find ourselves in trouble when the inner brain is in control when it needn't or shouldn't be. This causes reactions and behaviors that may not be warranted and we may end up regretting later. Throughout the book references will be made to these different areas of the brain and how we can employ them to our advantage.

Prefrontal Cortex

This area of the brain is our "thinking" center, which is responsible for logical reasoning and planning. Whenever you're consciously thinking about how to solve a problem, your prefrontal cortex is active. However, the prefrontal cortex encompasses more than just technical problem solving; it's also involved in determining appropriate social behavior. This requires thought and planning too.

Studies on people who have practiced meditation for many years have accumulated evidence that shows that the brain can be strengthened and enhanced in weak areas. Brain scans reveal distinct and beneficial differences in brain functioning between those experienced in meditation and those who are not. This type of confirmation leads psychologists and other researchers to believe that the brain is capable of changing itself and ultimately how we function with consistent practice and effort.

Hemispheres

Lastly, I mention the two brain hemispheres. These spheres are connected by a brain cord called the corpus callosum. Thanks to pioneering research by Roger Sperry and others, much has been learned about brain functioning by studying people whose corpus callosum has been severed, usually surgically. This is originally where the left brain/right brain theory evolved. What I find interesting about this is the disproportionate number of left-handed people that I notice in the software development field (aka right brainers). There are times when I'll be in attendance at a software project meeting with five people and four of us are lefties. While it's been difficult to determine precise numbers of left-handed versus right-handed people in software engineering, I'm convinced that it's at least slightly more prevalent than society at large.

A quick primer on left-brain/right-brain is in order here. As you probably already know, the two brain hemispheres control the opposite sides of the body. The right brain controls movement of the left side, including vision and vice versa.

The left brain hemisphere handles most of the language duties such as reading, writing and speaking. Oddly enough, this is the case for nearly all right-handers but only about 62% of left-handers (Hellige, 1990). The left side is also responsible for most mathematical and analytical processing. So if this is the case, why are there so many left-handers in software engineering? It may be because lefties use more of their right brain and this hemisphere is thought to be responsible for spatial processing and general creativity. This may be supportive in developing complex algorithms. Interestingly, the right brain also appears responsible for negative emotions, while positive emotions are processed by the left brain. However, with all of this said, whether you are left-handed or right-handed may not make all that much difference in the end. This is because the two brain hemispheres are always exchanging information via the corpus callosum, even though one hemisphere may be dominant. Even so, it is still a fascinating topic that will hopefully be researched further.

Hormonal Activity

There are three hormones in particular that play an important part in our brain functioning and overall well-being. One is oxytocin and the others are cortisol and dopamine. These hormones appear to have a critical involvement in social interactions and stress. Much has been learned recently about oxytocin. It provides feelings of well-being and security and is produced by the hypothalamus. During times of stress our adrenal glands release cortisol, which may help us fend off injuries in the short term, but if high levels of cortisol persist for too long it may cause several long term health problems due to decreased immune system performance and other issues. Oxytocin has the ability to operate as a cortisol mediator and the two seem to be related in their function. Dopamine is a feel good hormone that injects intense pleasure into activities and can be very rewarding. It may be associated with addictive behavior (Goleman, p202, 2006).

You should not be terribly surprised to learn that men and women react to increased levels of these hormones in somewhat different ways. This may provide some insight into certain unproductive programming patterns for men and women, which will be highlighted in future sections.

Flooding & Amygdala Hijackings

The amygdala, part of the limbic system, is an almond shaped group of nuclei that is chiefly involved in emotional arousal and memory encoding, among other tasks. This may partially explain why certain memories arouse strong emotions within us. In a reaction to anger our bodies go through a transformation sometimes referred to as **Flooding** or **Amygdala Hijackings**. We become flooded with cortisol and adrenaline, which raises our heart rate and blood pressure in preparation for possible action. The amygdala is now in control; it has effectively hijacked the rest of our brain, and we're now in the throes of the classic "fight or flight" response. This state is not at all conducive to logical thinking and this is when we become vulnerable to making statements or carrying out behaviors that we may lament for a long time. Our senses become heightened as we literally prepare ourselves for confrontation or to run like mad to escape the situation. It's our caveman brain taking over and it's not particularly well suited for modern organizational life. How we effectively manage these potent emotions can determine our corporate fate, as well as our broader life outcomes.

Male and Female Hormonal Differences

According to government statistics that will be detailed later, men comprise a large percentage of those employed within the software development field, especially in terms of programmers. As it turns out, there may be at least some neuroscience explanations behind this phenomenon. The neurotransmitter dopamine, known for its addictive and motivational behavior, is found more prevalently in men. If my theory regarding why programmers are driven to program holds water (explained later), then this dopamine knowledge may help explain why this is so, at least from a neuroscience perspective. As it turns out, the male Y chromosome causes more dopamine neurons to be created in the brain, which also happens to be why men experience a higher occurrence of Parkinson's disease, as it is related to dopamine disruptions. When you also consider the fact that women tend to excel in speech while men stand out when it comes to spatial reasoning, it becomes quite clear why men are perhaps more naturally attracted to a career in programming and why some women might not be so enthralled with this occupation.

It has been proven, beyond a reasonable doubt (at least for me, but researchers are still debating the issue), that women do indeed have an edge when it comes to speech and overall verbal processing skills (see side bar). So sitting behind a computer monitor a good part of your workday is probably not an especially attractive option for many women. That's likely why we typically find them in other software development roles that require more of this capability, such as Business Analyst and Quality Assurance roles. It is exceptionally important to be able to articulate and document requirements for successful software projects, and verbal and writing capabilities comprise the majority of this skill set. It's no wonder then that we tend to see more women as BAs in our industry. In fact, I have a difficult time recalling many male BAs that I have worked with over the years and I'm guessing that I've worked with dozens of them during that time. While this is not a scientific survey, finding reliable data on job classifications at this level of granularity within the software engineering field has been elusive to this point.

Future of Neuroscience

Where the field will ultimately go is unclear, but one point I'm convinced of is that our knowledge of brain functioning will explode within the next 10 years.

As scanning and other yet to be invented brain research techniques become less awkward, it will allow researchers to conduct more realistic and higher volumes of experiments. Our understanding of many areas of the brain will then improve dramatically. Just as in many other areas of research what we learn may not be what we want to know and some of it may be used for non-humanitarian intentions. In any case, the future of neuroscience will most likely be exhilarating.

The more research I've performed in this area the more I've become generally convinced that our brain physiology and biology has a tremendous effect on our behavior, more than I would have originally suspected. I would not be terribly surprised to see more and more behaviors attributed to physiological brain abnormalities in the future. A great case in point is that of Charles Whitman of the University of Texas. In 1966, the day after he murdered his wife and his mother, he climbed to the top of a tall tower on campus and randomly killed fourteen people and injured many others before being shot himself. Ironically, in a suicide note which was left behind, he asked that an autopsy be performed on him to determine if there was any "visible physical disorder" that may have caused him to carry out the killings he had planned. As it turned out, he was found to have a malignant brain tumor in the basal ganglia near the amygdala. As you'll recall, the amygdala helps with the regulation of emotional responses. Of course this does not necessarily mean that anyone with a similar brain tumor will resort to the same type of extreme behavior, but it certainly exemplifies the importance of brain physiology. In Whitman's case he suspected that something was wrong with him as he could not justify his aggressive impulses and thinking.

Another somewhat alarming trend neuroscientists are beginning to notice is the rapidly changing behavior of younger adults. Their patterns of incessant disruptions via text, chat and mobile web are altering their social skills and ultimately they believe, their brains. Where this will eventually lead is not certain at this time, but as adults who have grown up with constant multitasking and massive amounts of "mini communications" with little face-to-face contact, several ramifications are possible. First, they may have difficulty focusing on more complex tasks that require extensive periods of concentrated attention and just as importantly, their social skills may not fully develop, causing all types of unexpected long-term problems.

CHAPTER 2

Personality in Software Engineering

Our personality governs how we understand and react to the people and circumstances around us. Since many of the issues we regularly encounter will be colored by our personalities, a better understanding of how personality traits and tendencies impact our profession is a good starting point.

The field of Personality psychology is enormously vast and complex, so I will summarize the key history as it applies to our use within software engineering. My coverage of the field will only provide you with a flavor of the concepts and issues. Throughout the book, there will be discussions of how personality psychology impacts the software engineering field and how you can utilize it to your advantage. First, one quick warning; attempting to predict behavior can be a tricky (and risky) business and trying to put people into nice clean, rigid behavioral boxes may have unexpected consequences.

Analyzing people's personalities (yours and others) has been going on since the dawn of mankind and continues unabated to this day. In fact, you and I are analyzing personalities all the time, every day. You make judgments about people whom you've never met that you run into at the grocery store, the airport, sporting events, etc. However, before we dive into all the particulars, let's do a condensed review of where the field has evolved to at this point in time.

GATHERING PERSONALITY DATA

For starters, gathering good, reliable data on personalities is a bit problematic. A person's "true" personality can be difficult, if not downright impossible to define since we many times act differently in different situations (a very large debate amongst psychologists which we'll discuss shortly). Have you ever overheard your kids (or someone else's) talking about something when they didn't know that an adult was around? If so, you may have heard things that you might not normally hear and in tones you may not typically associate with those people. So defining a "true" personality is challenging, if one exists at all.

Another issue surrounding personality research is that collecting data is far from a perfect science. Here is a quick review of some of the various methods researchers use to collect personality data.

Types of Data

There are basically just a few techniques used to gather information about a person's personality: ask them about themselves, ask people who know them well, or gather more factual information such as test score results, career choices, hobbies, etc.

S Data – The most common type of personality data gathered is that which is self-reported. Generally this is because it's the easiest way to acquire information. Just ask people how they might respond to a situation or how they have already responded to certain situations or what they do or don't like. Most of us have responded to dozens of these types of questionnaires. The principal problem with S Data is that you must rely on the subject to respond honestly or perhaps in some cases they may not really know the best answer.

L Data – Life outcomes data is another possible type of information that could be collected and used to construct one's personality. Sort of a reverse engineering exercise is one way to think about L Data. However, L Data can be misleading because many outcomes in a person's life may be attributed to a variety of factors, such as luck, other unforeseen circumstances that may have occurred, or the influence of others.

I Data – This data comes from people who know the subject under study and is technically known as Informant Data. This data can be useful but it is also limited and may be somewhat biased depending upon the relationship the informant has with the subject.

B or O Data – This is Behavioral or Observer data that is either witnessed or collected in certain personality tests which are constructed in a particular manner. Observing someone's behavior is quite cumbersome and impractical for the most part, but can be partially accomplished in lab situations.

There are a few popular personality tests that collect B Data, but most collect S Data. One prominent B Data test is the Minnesota Multiphasic Personality Inventory (MMPI), which is considered the gold standard in personality testing. Another is the infamous Rorschach ink blot test. The Rorschach test is a good example of B Data because the person must essentially perform an act of interpretation, essentially a behavior of sorts. There is no right or wrong answer per se, but the psychologist is looking for how individuals respond to what they see in an inkblot. (These are referred to collectively as **Projective Tests** where the individual attempts to interpret something with no inherent meaning so the researcher can understand how he thinks).

B Data is the best type of data, however it's also the most expensive and impractical data to collect, therefore it's used sparingly. One downside to B Data is that the most you will end up collecting is a small sample that may not be representative of the larger population or accurate across all situations and times.

Using the Data

Once personality data is collected it can be used in a variety of ways in an attempt to construct one's "stable" or enduring personality qualities. However, since personality data is very limited, it may be inaccurate, incomplete and possibly misleading (Funder, 2007). It turns out that S Data is by far the most practical type of data to utilize and that's what you'll find behind most of the common personality tests. The other types of data are better suited for more specialized needs, such as counseling in cases where there are moderate to severe behavioral or thinking disorders. For these cases the extra time and expense required to collect the necessary personality data may be justified.

PERSONALITY-SITUATION DEBATE

As I mentioned in the beginning of the book, I'm drawing heavily upon the fields of Social Psychology and Personality Psychology (as well as other fields of psychology). These two fields are at odds to some degree because personality psychologists are trying to identify why people are different and that in fact people actually are different from one another. While the social psychologists, on the other hand, look at specific situations and determine how most people will generally respond, regardless of their personality. So you could say that, at an abstract level, social psychologists are situationalists and personality psychologists are individualists.

So just what exactly is the final resolution here? Well, like many outcomes in psychological research, it's probably a little of each. It appears, at this time anyway, that people will generally respond the same in certain unusual social situations, but that people do have somewhat distinct patterns of general behavior over time. This should not be a huge surprise to anyone based upon the complexity of the human brain. There is actually a formula for Personality (how convenient for us analytical types) that goes like this:

$$B = f(P \times S)$$

The formula reads as follows: Behavior is a function of Personality combined with Situation. This makes sense in that only certain personality traits will be revealed in certain situations. If you have a temper, a personality trait of sorts, it would usually only be exhibited if something triggers it, such as one of my bad golf shots.

OPTIMISM & PESSIMISM IN PROGRAMMING

Over the years, there has been some on and off debate about whether the best programmers are, or should be, pessimists. There is a substantial amount of research which supports the core concept that people who are more positive and optimistic generally outperform those who are more pessimistic and negative (see Seligman, 2002 for more on this entire topic). Seligman features one distinctive collection of professionals who exhibit more pessimistic traits but that are also decidedly successful as a group. Any guesses here? Well if you selected attorneys you were correct. Seligman goes on to say that the purpose of most lawyers is to anticipate the worst scenario for their clients so that they may better protect their clients from those perils. Therefore, this profession appears to attract a more pessimistic type of person, or possibly they become more pessimistic during the course of their career.

The same reasoning might well apply to programmers and more acutely to software designers and system architects. These specialized roles, to a certain degree, are intended to prevent disasters. Perseverating over all the potential circumstances that could go awry does perhaps require a negative approach in order to determine what disasters could happen. Astute developers are also attempting to build bulletproof algorithms and are generally ensuring that unintended negative consequences will not be the result of their labors. Anyone who has coded professionally for more than a few months (or days maybe) realizes how easy it is for unanticipated coding faults to surface. Therefore, over time, it's entirely feasible that coders might naturally gravitate towards a more pessimistic thinking style, especially if they've felt the embarrassing sting of flawed logic several times already. When one of your primary goals is not to appear obtuse in front of your peers and supervisors, a pessimistic approach certainly is an avenue one might pursue, whether consciously or unconsciously.

There are, naturally, those who believe that optimism is a crucial trait for developers to succeed. The research here seems to interpret optimism more as a means for continued persistence so that one does not get too down on themselves when coding algorithms and facing other obstacles that habitually arise.

Psychologist Julie Norem has studied students who employ both optimistic and pessimistic styles of thinking (1989, 2002). Both methods seem to produce reasonable motives to succeed. The optimists keep moving forward assuming that everything will ultimately come together while the pessimists are desperately attempting to account for all the possibilities that could go awry. Both types seemed to have approximately equal chances for success.

My interpretation of the data and studies in this domain lead me to believe that either method of thinking, whether pessimistic or optimistic, can suffice as long as the extremes on either end are avoided. Most technical professionals have probably already established their preferred style of optimism or pessimism well before they begin their careers, so any major adjustments are somewhat unlikely. However, Seligman also claims that optimism can be learned through specific training and that people are capable of developing more optimistic habits. See his book entitled *Learned Optimism* for more information.

My summary of the research indicates that in general pessimists have a mindset well positioned for preventing problems, while optimists appear ideally suited for solving current problems.

TRAIT THEORIES

Personality Trait Theory is a much debated and complex topic among psychologists of all types. For the purposes of this book, the assumption is that personality traits exist and that they are relatively enduring. Personality tests of all different varieties employ some type of trait model taxonomy. We will review several of the most popular models, including the Big Five and the Myers-Briggs. Many personality tests are now based upon, or have been subsequently adapted for, the Big Five model. There are many other models and corresponding personality tests on the market but that is beyond the scope of this book. Two older yet popular models not discussed in depth are the California Personality Inventory (CPI) and the Minnesota Multiphasic Personality Inventory (MMPI). To give you a feel for the complexity of this domain, the MMPI has traditionally been used for assessing people with psychological issues whereas the CPI is used for assessing normal individuals. Both have been used for pre-employment screening, a legal issue addressed at the end of this chapter.

Big Five

One of the major, or more likely THE major, personality trait model currently, is known as the Five Factor Model or FFM. It seems as though, at least for now, personality psychologists have honed in on this being the preferred and most comprehensive trait model. The key to the seemingly wide acceptance of this model as being practical is that there are some indications that FFM data can be used to predict job satisfaction and optimal career choices.

The five traits of the FFM have been "boiled down" so to speak, over decades of research, from a broad list of generic human traits that span generations and cultures. The five traits are Extraversion, Agreeableness, Conscientiousness, Openness, and Emotional Stability (sometimes labeled in the opposite vein as Neuroticism). These definitions come from Costa and McRae (1992) the early leading proponents of the theory.

The trait of Conscientiousness seems to be the trait most closely associated with job performance, with Extraversion also being relatively important for management and sales related positions as well as others. Jobs with higher stress levels show good correlation with Emotional Stability, such as police work. People in service oriented fields show good correlations with Agreeableness, as one might expect.

There has been a vast amount of research performed on the FFM and the personality research literature is dominated by discussions of the Big Five theory. It appears as though this model will govern the future research in personality for many years to come. Here are detailed adjectives, on both ends of the spectrum, of the five traits according to researcher Lewis R. Goldberg (1990):

Extraversion

Talkative, extraverted, assertive, forward, outspoken

Shy, quiet, introverted, bashful, inhibited

Agreeableness

Sympathetic, kind, warm, understanding, sincere

Harsh, cruel, unkind, unsympathetic

Conscientiousness

Organized, neat, orderly, practical, prompt, meticulous

Disorganized, disorderly, careless, sloppy, impractical

Openness

Creative, imaginative, intellectual

Uncreative, unimaginative, unintellectual

Emotional Stability

Calm, relaxed, stable

Moody, anxious, insecure

Myers-Briggs Type Indicator (MBTI)

The Myers-Briggs Type Indicator is probably the most popular personality inventory used in business settings today, partly because it has been packaged so tidily. There are 4 trait pair continuums and a fairly simple self administered test (usually performed on-line) that determines which one of the pairs you most closely resemble in terms of your thinking style. Therefore, every person gets a four letter (one letter for each scale pair) acronym and so consequently there are a total of 16 different personality types that one can be assigned. Once you then know your personality designation there are training programs that coach you in how to best work with the other 15 defined types of MBTI personalities. As mentioned earlier, you now need to know what your co-workers personality designations are as well. Most companies who embrace the MBTI will have an entire division, or perhaps the entire company, be tested rather than just certain individuals. It then becomes part of the vernacular and people talk in terms of personality types with one another – or at least this is what the MBTI practitioners hope will happen.

The MBTI test classifies people into personality types based on four bi-polar, continuum-based scales:

Extraversion-Introversion (E–I)

Shows a tendency for focusing awareness on, and capturing vitality from, the outside world of people and things (Extraversion) as compared to the inner world of thoughts and ideas (Introversion).

Sensing-INtuition (S–N)

Has an inclination for gathering data directly via the senses as facts, details, and examples (Sensing) versus indirectly as patterns, and possible outcomes – or what some refer to as a gut feel (INtuition).

Thinking-Feeling (T–F)

Demonstrates preferences for making decisions based upon logic and considered analysis (Thinking) compared with subjective, person-centered values (Feeling).

Judging-Perceiving (J–P)

Prefers to have events planned and ordered (Judging) compared with a more flexible style based more on staying open to alternatives than deciding (Perceiving).

(Adapted from Psychometric Success and numerous other Myers-Briggs sources).

There are several issues with the Myers-Briggs types. One problem is that since the paired traits are on a continuum, providing a slightly different answer on a question or two might cause you to flip from Extraverted to Introverted. This is the case for my test results. My classification is an ENTJ, but I'm just over the center line or neutral position on the E-I scale. Therefore I could easily test out as an INTJ on a subsequent test or when using another set of questions. Some

MBTI detractors claim that a significant percentage of people will re-test as a different type. The problem lies in the fact that you may be near the midpoint on more than one trait pair and now you could be potentially one of 4 or 8 different personality types.

Another drawback is that reliability and validity results from MBTI are highly suspect by many personality psychologists. If one could subsequently re-test as a different type it may mean that the test's reliability is low. Lastly, in my on-going research on personality psychology, I have reviewed several college level texts on the topic that either don't mention MBTI at all or reference it just briefly in passing. The researchers are certainly not as excited about it as the MBTI practitioners have become, and to a certain degree it has been oversold in my estimation. Personality psychology is exceptionally complex and any simple test that tries to package it up so tidy and neat is somewhat suspect.

With all that said, I do believe there is something to learn from the MBTI tests, especially if the test taker is answering as honestly as possible. For personality tests to be practical they must do some packaging. For example, if you score on the far end of the continuum for Extraversion, then you are most likely an extravert. But then again you may have already known that about yourself.

Some test takers will attempt to answer questions in a certain way so that their MBTI type will come out differently than it really is so that they can qualify for management or some other desirable position. These tests, in certain cases, can be fooled by perceptive people. This brings the issue of test validity into question.

MBTI Profiles for Software Staff

While there are not many MBTI studies with software subjects available, two studies will be highlighted here. In a study published in the *International Journal of Human-Computer Studies* led by Luiz Capretz, (2003) entitled, *Personality types in software engineering*, the key findings are summarized below:

Introverts:	57%
Sensing:	67%
Thinking:	81%
Judging:	58%

This particular study reveals that the Thinking dimension is far and away the dominant type found in software engineering roles. The author believes this is in part due to the large makeup of men in the industry, and hence his study, which was comprised of 80% men. The percentage of Introverts was lower than I would have expected. While it is somewhat higher than the number of introverts found in the general population, other studies may shed more light on this topic.

Another, though much smaller MBTI study (25 subjects), on software testers conducted by Cheryl Meyer at the University of Colorado at Colorado Springs found that 20% of all testers were ISTJs compared to 10% of the population at large. Interestingly, the ISTJ type is known as an Inspector. A perfect fit for software testers no doubt. However, that leaves 80% of software testers as something other than an ISTJ type, so it's unclear if this information is ultimately valuable.

Hogan Personality Inventory (HPI)

Developed by respected personality psychologist Robert Hogan, the HPI is primarily designed for business usage. Even though it can be used by anyone, Hogan had the business setting in mind when it was developed. The Hogan model is known for its strong validity as attested to by over 400 independent validity studies. Reliability is also high compared to other personality models. Reliability refers to the likelihood that one will display the same characteristics upon subsequent re-testing. It is based upon the Five Factor Model and it has seven core scales of personality inventory:

Adjustment

Ambition

Sociability

Interpersonal Sensitivity

Prudence

Inquisitiveness

Learning Approach

I would heartily recommend the HPI for organizations considering personality testing, as it is scientifically sound and yet also remarkably practical. The HPI is more geared for finding optimal fits for personnel within organizations and some companies will employ it for screening candidates for certain roles or positions.

Traps of Trait Theories

There are two major traps when trying to effectively utilize personality trait theories in an occupational environment. First, it's essential for everyone in the group to undertake the profile test. Second, the tests utilize self-reported or S Data, as described earlier.

In order to get the maximum benefit from these personality systems you need to know and understand your type and everyone else's personality type as well. That can be more than a little cumbersome at times. Of course in many instances you'll know roughly what personality type someone is and you really only need to focus on understanding the people you're having a difficult time with. Most trait theories are based upon a quadrant model. See figure 2.1 for a partial list of available trait theories. You usually will fit into one of four quadrants that will most closely match your primary personality tendencies or traits, and you may possibly have a secondary tendency quadrant assigned to you as well. So for example, you'll be designated as a Driver type personality with a secondary category of Amiable. In some systems you will have a clever name assigned for your two-quadrant set, such as our software testing "Inspector." Once you know that you're an Inspector, then you can find out how to best deal with all the other defined types and everything works just great. You can see from my slight sarcasm here that I'm not completely sold on these systems yet. However, I do think they have some utility in certain instances and even though it may be impractical to know what personality type everyone in your group is, it may allow you to deal more effectively with people in certain critical situations. Most departments in larger companies have people coming and going on a regular basis, so always knowing what everyone's profile is may not be plausible. Also, there are certain people who do not like being "labeled." Even the trait theorists understand that people don't always act the same. Many factors are involved in human behavior and being labeled an ENTJ obviously doesn't predict how someone will act in every situation. At best it predicts broader tendencies over extended time periods.

Table of Equivalents for the 4 Personality Types

Merrill-Reid	Driver	Expressive	Amiable	Analytical
D.E.S.A.	Dominant	Expressive	Solid	Analytical
Hippocrates Greek Terms (370 BC)	Choleric	Sanguine	Phlegmatic	Melancholy
The P's	Powerful	Popular	Peaceful	Perfect
The S's	Self-propelled	Spirited	Solid	Systematic
The A's	Administrative	Active	Amiable	Analytical
LEAD Test	Leader	Expressor	Dependable	Analyst
ARRAY (Jonathan Knaupp)	Production	Connection	Status Quo	Harmony
Geier	Dominance	Influencing	Competence	Steadiness
DiSC(r)	Dominance	Influencing of Others	Steadiness	Cautiousness/ Compliance
McCarthy/ 4MAT System	Common Sense	Dynamic	Innovative	Analytic

FIGURE 2.1

Adapted from 2H.com

Assuming you do decide to take the plunge, it's very important when taking these tests that you are completely honest when answering the questions (see Figure 2.2 for a sample set of questions). These tests can be fooled, though it may be harder than you think because they're looking for patterns, and if you're trying to be labeled as someone you're not, you may get "caught" and your test validity score will be low. If however, you are completely sincere while taking these profiling tests, you can gain some insight into your own behaviors and feelings and start playing out scenarios in your head prior to known upcoming difficult encounters. In the long run it doesn't really pay to try and "cheat" the personality tests because you'll constantly be given the wrong suggestions on how to deal with certain situational circumstances. It also requires some hard work to cheat on these inventory tests.

Sample Personality Questionnaire

Here are a number of characteristics that may or may not apply to you. For example, do you agree that you are someone who likes to spend time with others? Please write a number next to each statement to indicate the extent to which you agree or disagree with that statement.

Disagree Strongly	Disagree a Little	Neither Agree nor Disagree	Agree a Little	Agree Strongly
1	2	3	4	5

I see Myself as Someone Who...

____ Is talkative

____ Tends to find fault with others

____ Does a thorough job

____ Is depressed, blue

____ Is original, comes up with new ideas

____ Is reserved

____ Is helpful and unselfish with others

____ Can be somewhat careless

____ Tends to be lazy

____ Is emotionally stable, not easily upset

____ Is inventive

____ Has an assertive personality

____ Can be cold and aloof

____ Perseveres until the task is finished

____ Can be moody

____ Values artistic, aesthetic experiences

FIGURE 2.2

Adapted from The Big-Five Trait Taxonomy: History, Measurement, and Theoretical Perspectives Oliver P. John and Sanjay Srivastava (1999).

Legal Issues

Over the years there have been various legal issues raised with taking personality inventory tests if they are used as a means to screen applicants and limit employment to certain groups or types of people. Companies must be very careful that these tests do not limit the ability of certain broad groups (such as African Americans or women) to be considered for employment. As you could probably guess, if you live in the U.S., companies have been sued for not screening applicants and they have also been sued when they do screen applicants. However, for the most part, this issue seems to have been resolved and there have been fewer complaints in recent years.

One of the main issues in these pre-employment screenings is that of "Disparate Treatment" and "Disparate Impact." Disparate Treatment refers to the screening of one group of candidates but not another. For example, issuing tests to women but not testing men. Disparate Impact refers to the situation where many people from one particular group, say women, may be excluded from employment. The employer must then be able to demonstrate that the selection process is related to the job and is a valid business requirement.

PERSONALITY TRAITS

As a reminder, there are some researchers who are still reluctant to admit that people really possess meaningful personality traits, even though these believers are in the clear minority. By traits we refer to long-standing, stable characteristics that essentially define a person. This book assumes that people do indeed possess unique and relatively stable personality traits that one can expect to be revealed on a generally consistent basis. Those who resist the trait theory are your staunch social psychologists who believe people respond solely and uniquely to their situational circumstances, as mentioned earlier, regardless of any alleged enduring personality traits.

A review of the numerous personality models devised can be rather entertaining. There are dozens of clever adjectives describing the various distinct personality types. This type of nomenclature, while convenient and simple, may not be the most accurate approach. People will have varying combinations of traits, some stronger and more obvious than others and therefore any one person within a named category may be substantially different than others classified likewise. Here is a partial list of personality descriptors to be found, in no particular order:

Enthusiast	**Idealist**	**Scholar**	**Inventor**
Investigator	**Hedonist**	**Warrior**	**Traditionalist**
Enterprising	**Inspector**	**Reformer**	**Artisan**

Many personality trait inventory instruments that have been developed over the past several decades are considered reliable and valid. These include, among others, the Adjective Check List (ACL) and the Hogan Personality Inventory (HPI) as noted previously. Most are either based upon the Five Factor Model originally, or have been subsequently adapted to the FFM, as is the case with the ACL.

So, assuming that people actually have consistent, identifiable and reasonably measurable personality traits, what are the ramifications for software development? I would propose a general personality trait framework approach, as follows:

> Identify and understand those traits that are optimal for the assorted software development roles (see the Optimal Traits for Software Development section later in this chapter).

> Decide on a method for determining who possesses the desirable traits.

> Realize that many people attracted to the various roles will have the bulk of the desirable traits they require anyway.

> Understand the strengths and vulnerabilities of various personality traits, in general, so that you can be on the lookout for potential problems and conflicts (see Software Trait Vulnerabilities section forthcoming).

> Realize that being in the personality modification business is virtually fruitless, so finding best fits is a judicious alternative.

Drivers & Analytics

Social Styles is a program developed by a former employer of mine, Wilson Learning, to describe the general and persistent personality traits of all people. Two of these defined trait types are a Driver and an Analytic, probably the two that you will encounter most often within development. A Driver is a results and task oriented person while an Analytic is very detailed and logical. A Driver is a good candidate for a Project Manager, while most developers are probably Analytics. I would suspect that nearly all organizations would benefit a great deal more from adopting the *Social Styles* model versus the MBTI, as *Social Styles* is backed by extensive psychological research and has ties with many other practical corporate training programs.

Type A

Most everyone is familiar with this popular, yet generic, personality type, even though it really isn't a single trait but rather a collection of them. However, what most people probably don't realize is that this personality type was identified and defined by cardiologists and not psychologists. In the 1960s, cardiologists Meyer Friedman and Ray Rosenman noticed some similarities in the personality characteristics of their patients who had experienced heart attacks. This pattern of traits emerged after some time and includes hostility, hurriedness, aggressiveness, competitiveness and impatience. It turns out that researchers now have honed in on hostility as the primary culprit associated with increased incidences of coronary heart disease (Wright, 1988).

Optimal Traits for Software Development

There have been very few formal research studies conducted in this area that have used software development subjects exclusively. Therefore the results here only provide us a slight glimpse into what might be. Both of the featured studies are based upon the Five Factor Model.

The first study, from the Interdisciplinary Journal of Information, Knowledge, and Management (2007) studied 489 software professionals, in various roles, from Nigeria. Whether these results apply to software professionals from other Western and Asian countries is not certain. Interestingly, the researchers have created a sixth factor for software development personnel, referred to as Cognitive Ability. Some psychologists would probably not consider cognitive ability to be a personality trait per se; others view cognitive ability as a trait that is both measurable and relatively stable. However, there are distinct types of intelligence such as mathematical and verbal (and others) that you see differentiated in popular college admission tests such as the SAT and ACT.

The summarized results of the Nigerian study that pertain to us are depicted on the next page in Figure 2.3 using a Low, Medium, and High classification. The required levels of personality traits suggested by the team leaders in order to attain high performance is displayed for all six factors for three of the main software engineering positions; Business Analyst, Developer, and Tester.

The results here of note are those where personality trait levels are different for a single factor. These include Extraversion, Conscientiousness, and Openness. These will be discussed together with the next study shortly.

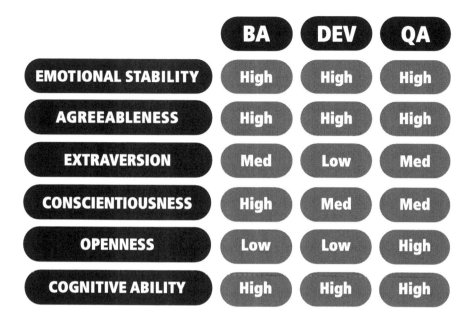

	BA	DEV	QA
EMOTIONAL STABILITY	High	High	High
AGREEABLENESS	High	High	High
EXTRAVERSION	Med	Low	Med
CONSCIENTIOUSNESS	High	Med	Med
OPENNESS	Low	Low	High
COGNITIVE ABILITY	High	High	High

FIGURE 2.3

Our second study, from The Communications of the Association for Information Systems (2002), is focused on identifying the personality characteristics of exceptional developers. The first notable finding of the study, at least for me, was that high college GPA scores did not correlate positively with exceptional performance on the job. This actually shouldn't surprise anyone as this has been known for decades, but it does provide some contradictory data for our previous study, which suggests that high cognitive ability is required for most software development roles. The likely and obvious explanation here may be that GPA is not a perfect indicator of cognitive ability. Other factors such as motivation, personality conflicts, extracurricular activities and numerous other reasons may account for GPA discrepancies.

The remaining results of this study indicate that the top developers were significantly more extraverted and conscientious than ordinary developers. This would mean that the majority of developers are introverted and slightly less conscientious, which also aligns with the Nigerian study outcomes.

So it appears, from the limited research studies, that we now have a more complete understanding of what constitutes an ideal developer. High levels of extraversion and conscientious are desirable traits. Medium or high levels of agreeableness along with medium levels of Openness (more on this soon) are ideal.

Software Trait Vulnerabilities

For most of the FFM trait factors, scoring on either extreme end of the scale is usually not particularly desirable. For example, if a developer were excessively extraverted (which is rare), he may become bored when working in isolation while developing complex code and may end up interrupting co-workers, besides disrupting his own efforts.

Here is list of possible vulnerabilities associated with extreme personality scores on the big five FFM personality factors – those either too high or too low:

Openness to Experience

High: Over designing solutions; becoming sidetracked while discovering benefits of new, unrelated technologies

Low: Closed to potential new, never before attempted solutions; general negativity

Emotional Stability

High: May become too apathetic; hard to get motivated to reach critical deadlines

Low: Not able to cope with scheduled delivery dates; constantly worried about completing work competently; distracting teammates with concerns

Agreeableness

High: May go along with the group too quickly and not provide other alternative options

Low: Short with others and closed to ideas not generated by him; stubborn and overly hard to convince

Extraversion

High: Distracting to self and others; tendency to try new technologies before their time

Low: May not seek input from others when necessary; overly confident; difficult to communicate and read

Conscientiousness

High: May never be completely satisfied with a solution; hard to please

Low: Hard to keep focused on the task at hand; may have a trying time finishing work completely and properly; may not be a good team player causing undo distractions

Identifying Team Traits

There are several measurement instruments, already mentioned, that organizations can use to determine personality traits of team members. Most of these can be conducted on-line, are reasonably priced, and can be completed relatively quickly in a straightforward manner. However, I'm not necessarily convinced that using these tools to screen applicants is a good idea. Teams generally work best when there is a mix of personality types. If everyone is highly agreeable, nothing may be accomplished. This becomes the art of management in determining how to best select teams that provide the appropriate mix of personalities and skill sets to be successful. Hogan claims that companies continually assign people to roles without any regard for their personality. Since software is primarily the result of teams, understanding personality is an integral component of any software organization. Lastly, since these instruments are not perfect and are self administered, screening candidates as a result of these tests is a delicate and complicated business. I think it's best to use them as one of several tools to increase your chances for improved development results.

PERSONALITY STABILITY

One vital question, that has almost become a philosophical one, is whether or not one's personality can or will change over time. I have this debate with others on occasion and my research indicates that some parts of personality seem to be locked at quite an early age, while other components may possibly be changed. However, it may be difficult at some point in one's life to convince others that you have actually changed. Altering one's reputation takes time, especially if you're middle aged or older. According to personality expert Robert Hogan and others, certain pieces of your personality puzzle are primarily determined at a very young age and that approximately fifty percent of your personality traits are inherited. One such trait is conscientiousness, which happens to be a key predictor of adult occupational performance. Hogan argues that this trait is formed during infancy and will be difficult if not impossible to change significantly as an adult.

This means that troublemakers on your development team may likely continue being troublemakers, especially if they're over age 30 or so. Changing personalities is difficult business at best and one would be wise to focus on behavior management or better yet, finding the optimal vocational fit for team outliers.

Personalities generally tend to stabilize over time. However, there are some tendencies that are worth noting. People do tend to become slightly more conscientiousness and agreeable as they age as well as less impulsive and more rigid in their ways (Larsen p. 151).

Hogan also claims that certain fundamental personality characteristics are genetic, such as temperament. Several other researchers also claim strong links to heritable personality traits. These are more heavily resistant to change and people will wrestle with these inherited traits their entire lives. Hogan also goes on to claim that understanding how one is perceived by others is an ability learned during childhood and is an indicator of team performance in adulthood. These are the social skills featured in Chapter 8, Analog Intelligence.

Generation Gap

While individual personalities may stabilize over time there is some data to suggest that personalities of different generations may show disparities. That is, as a society (at least in the U.S.) our personality traits appear to be changing possibly as a result of our culture. A recent generational personality study by Twenge and Campbell (2008) finds that "Generation Me (sometimes called Gen Y or Millennials) demonstrates higher self-esteem, narcissism, anxiety, and depression; lower need for social approval; more external locus of control; and women with more agentic traits." **Locus of Control** refers to how people generally view their circumstances – are they in control or are external factors in control? People with an external locus of control may give up easier or use outside events as an excuse for not trying hard or succeeding. Agentic traits are those such as assertiveness and brashness as compared to communal traits typically associated with women such as being likeable and trustworthy (Reid, et. al., 2009).

What this indicates is that for the younger people in the workforce their expectations of work and their relationships with co-workers may be different than middle aged or older employees. The impact on software engineering could be considerable. These potential Gen Y trait changes may cause people to change jobs more frequently, have more difficulty when working in teams, and in general require additional care and feeding. More research is needed to validate these findings and these trait changes are found across a broad population. As the popular saying goes, "Individual results may vary."

PERSONALITY PROFILE FOR DEVELOPERS

My review of the personality literature, along with my decades of software experience, has led me to develop a classic personality profile of your "archetypal" developer. While there really is no such thing as an average or typical developer, here are my results nonetheless:

- Highly analytical and logical thinkers

- Prideful in their work

- Slightly defensive and paranoid in nature

- Creative

- Introverted, but there are probably more extraverts then you might think

- Persistent when interested

- Aloof at times to non-technical associates and issues

- Somewhat egotistical

Of course not every developer will possess all of these attributes and some unusually small percentage may not possess any of these attributes. However, as a larger population, this is our makeup based upon my interpretation and research. Obviously I have worked with developers who are more outgoing, not especially creative and with little or no ego. In any one group the personality mix may be quite diverse, but on the whole this is what you should expect to find.

Having worked in software quality for nearly a decade, I have acquired a unique perspective on developers. Many of the QA consultants at SWAT Solutions inform me that when they report a code defect against a project the developer's initial reaction, in many instances, is that of disbelief. Comments such as "No way" or "That's impossible, show it to me" are quite common. However, in the vast majority of identified defects, it is indeed legitimate.

CHAPTER 3

Major Issues in Software Engineering

SOFTWARE ESTIMATION

This is where many of the specific planning problems seem to originate. Again, there are entire books written on this subject (the software icon, Steve McConnell of course). Many organizations do not take this early phase very seriously or at least seriously enough. There's this incredible rush and tendency to just jump right in and start designing or even start some coding on a prototype. Many estimates are very rough approximations and people in our industry seem to be overly optimistic in this regard. There's a dramatic lack of discipline and rigor when it comes to these pre-development chores. We may just provide lip service and go through the motions and do the absolute bare minimum in many instances.

Part of this predicament may be due to ordinary human guilt. If you're a good conscientious employee and want to provide some honest value to your employer, you certainly don't want to be wasting their time, right? So the tendency for many people is to start doing something that they believe is valuable to the organization, yet it's quite difficult for many technical people to plan because they're really just longing to start implementation. They weren't hired to be planners and they likely didn't have much training in planning methods. The rush to quickly get to the good stuff is what derails many software projects. Add to that the relentless pressures from sales or other groups in the enterprise and you've got a potential problem looming.

Fred Brooks in his old, yet classic, book *The Mythical Man-Month* claims that we (programmers) are the most optimistic people in the entire engineering field. Brooks' key suggestion is that we are optimistic in our estimates because our medium is tractable. That is, we can undo things quickly if necessary. He compares it to artists who work with intractable mediums, such as painters. A painter of course needs to plan ahead, for any mistakes made on the canvas is difficult, if not impossible, to undo. Programmers create from "pure thought" he goes on to say and because we have faulty thoughts at times, there are naturally bugs. This all leads to more calendar time to redesign the product, re-code, re-test, etc.

As McConnell states in his book *Software Estimation*, our industry has a problem of underestimation, not just poor estimation in general. If we had generally poor estimation results you'd expect them to be roughly split between overestimation and underestimation errors. Yet we consistently seem to underestimate software projects. We really want to deliver software on time and I truly believe that most developers are high in Conscientiousness (see the Personality chapter). So when you combine what we desire to do with what we're also pressured to do by the business side, it's understandable that we will attempt to convince ourselves that, "Yes, I think we can get that done in nine months if we just really focus and put our minds to it."

There is a little bit more to the estimation story however. There are several theories that assert that any work will expand to accommodate the schedule, regardless of the schedule's efficacy. Therefore, it's not too surprising that we err on underestimation versus overestimation. This is the real trick in estimation exercises and perhaps you're better to plan for the schedule going over from the outset, but knowing it may still possibly come out ahead in the end if high level planning included project underestimation. This sounds a bit recursive, but planning on bad planning is what some organizations have resorted to out of sheer desperation. That's a disheartening reflection on how serious this problem has become.

Psychology & Estimating

There are several other potential explanations for overly optimistic schedules from a psychological point of view. Let's discuss some of these and you can determine for yourself whether any of these concepts may possibly explain the estimating issues in your organization.

Anchoring

Anchoring is a common pitfall that all of us inevitably become victim to at some point in our professional lives. Sometimes people will use it intentionally, in attempt to influence or persuade you. Other times it may be used without someone actually knowing it. However, it's such a common technique that many people probably use it subconsciously to persuade others and don't even realize what they're doing.

How many times has a manager or business person come directly to you, the programmer, and said something along the lines of "Hey Dave, can we have that new feature we talked about yesterday in the cafeteria by the end of the week? Can't be that big of a deal, right? Especially for a senior programmer like yourself. You really seem to know that system inside and out." Well, as you've probably surmised, there are a whole lot of interesting dynamics happening within that dialogue. But let's just review the Anchoring. And by the way, this sort of discussion is quite common and occurs in some variety or another nearly every day in most development organizations.

When someone asks you if you are able to complete a task by some preferred deadline that they have in mind, they're setting an anchor or baseline for you. Dave may have been thinking it might take a month or more to implement that new feature. Now, because of the Anchoring influence, he's probably re-thinking his estimate and he's almost guaranteed to reduce his estimate, or at least reconsider it, because of this Anchoring effect. Dave perhaps begins thinking; "Maybe I really could get that wiziwig feature done by the end of the week. I pretty much know the algorithm I'm going to use and I really do know the entire system like the back of my hand." Dave doesn't want to disappoint his stakeholders and appear technically challenged or inferior in any way. These are strong feelings for developers and it is difficult for us to resist the lingering effects of anchoring conversations. Technical people, above all else, want to appear wholly competent.

The key is to recognize Anchoring when it occurs and because you'll now be on the lookout, you'll likely find it happens quite frequently. It would also be especially useful to know if it's being used on purpose. One obvious counter method that you can employ is to re-anchor the person who sets the anchor originally. This is basically giving them a taste of their own medicine. In our example, Dave could say that he was thinking more along the lines of the new wiziwig feature taking perhaps as long as two full months, if completed properly of course. After all, you do want it implemented correctly, right? Now the one-month estimate that Dave originally had in mind might not look so out of line to the various stakeholders. However, we programmers have a really hard time doing this because we believe it makes us look irrational, uneducated, or just plain slow and stupid. Most programmers I know think that they're pretty darn smart and of course I can get that feature done by the end of the week. Why couldn't I? I'm betting that most developers would just agree to a shorter time frame and pay the price later. Or worse, they might actually think they can get it done by the end of the week, because after all, I'm a really sharp programmer and the company must really want this new feature if they're asking me to implement it.

Not all Anchoring is a horrible thing and it's definitely not always done on purpose. There are times when the developer's estimate is significantly higher or lower than the business owner's estimate. This may help determine the appropriate level of the feature set and also ensures that our scheduling and understanding of the scope and intent of the project is aligned properly.

When Anchors are out of bounds, this should initiate a discussion to aid in general planning. This may be the natural result of the typical disconnect between technical and non-technical people. This is referred to in psychological terms as the **False Consensus Effect**. For our purposes, this effect is defined as the divergent levels of understanding between those who understand programming constructs and concepts and those who do not. Programmers and other software staff have a hard time understanding how non-technical people envision software development. Once you fully comprehend what software development is and isn't, it's nearly impossible to think the same way as before you knew anything about the subject. The genie is out of the bottle and there's no putting it back. This is the cause of countless issues between technical and non-technical personnel. These types of problems even exist within development staffs. There are many BAs and PMs who have never coded themselves so it becomes complicated when dealing with developers whose mindset is quite diverse.

Studies have shown that people may be unduly influenced by a variety of anchor types. Extreme anchors, on one end of the spectrum or the other, still may generate anchoring effects. Something as simple as someone dropping by your desk to tell you that it hasn't rained in 22 days, may also serve as an anchor, as unbelievable as this may sound. The number 22 has now been anchored in your mind and you may have an unconscious tendency to use this number in some way, even though it is essentially meaningless. While the psychological mechanisms for anchoring are unclear, there is a theory that people become distracted by the anchor value itself (the number 22 in this example) and then attempt to make adjustments independent of the anchor, but typically neglect to adjust enough to be effective. Regardless of the cause, anchoring can be a very powerful and persuasive technique that will entrap many software professionals of all types, even when we're aware of the anchoring.

Overconfidence

Most people it turns out, not just us programmer types, are irrationally overconfident. Numerous studies have been conducted in this vein and when many studies return the same overall results, a new term is coined and sometimes it even becomes part of the societal vernacular. Research in this arena shows that people typically have more confidence in their own judgments than is actually warranted by the situation. The **Overconfidence Barrier**, as it is called, has been found in a number of other professions such as medicine, law, security, engineering, and especially finance in regards to securities trading. This doesn't mean that everyone is subject to this condition at all times, but rather, it's a tendency over time for most people in many situations. This effect can be mitigated to at least some degree by presenting factual data and discussing what has happened in similar situations previously, but even this works infrequently.

This is likely what Fred Brooks was referring to when he claims that the second system someone designs is the most dangerous. The first successful system has created a false sense of confidence and now he believes he's infallible. This is also referred to as knowing just enough to be dangerous.

According to Norwegian researchers Jørgensen & Moløkken (2004), there is about a 60% chance that a software developer will complete the task he estimates within the minimum and maximum ranges, which he himself estimates as "almost certain." In a similar astonishing report, Lichtenstein and Fischhoff (1977) found that higher levels of intelligence, expertise and experience have little or no effect on reducing overly optimistic estimates. These reports essentially suggest that only conversant outsiders, with nothing at stake in the project whatsoever, are perhaps the only legitimate liberators of rosy software forecasts. However, by the time they themselves get up to speed on the project, they may well be tainted goods too.

Therefore, it's inevitable that overconfidence is a leading contributor to a number of poor decisions in our field and unfortunately for us, men are more likely to demonstrate overconfidence than women (Hallinan, 2009). This only serves to compound the problem as men are much more predominant in our industry.

PLANNING PROBLEMS

Many of our most challenging problems start right here, with the dreaded task of project planning. Most organizations I'm familiar with have excellent intentions here. In fact, almost all projects I have been even marginally involved with start out with adequate and organized planning. It's just that life and reality eventually get in the way and shortcuts ensue. There are budgets to watch and marketing schedules to meet. Key people on the project quit or get recruited to plug a hole in the dike in some other department. You've seen the bumper stickers, Stuff Happens. The real issue is that most technical workers want to focus on the actual technical efforts and everything else is just what they need to do to be game eligible, to use a sports analogy.

There are really two major issues in play here; procrastination at the start of a project or what Steve McConnell refers to as the "fuzzy front-end" and pseudo-procrastination of a sort, that is jumping in too early before all the proper planning and organizing is complete because the clock is ticking and the deadline looms.

In terms of procrastination, it appears to be a rather ubiquitous trait. Research shows that most people, or at least the vast majority of college students, will procrastinate at times. Professor Dan Ariely of Duke University has found in his research studies involving his college students that while most have issues with procrastination, those who will admit to their procrastinating tendencies have a much better chance of using precommitment practices to improve their situation (*Predictably Irrational*). The techniques that worked best in his student studies involved someone with a higher authority (in this case the professor, but in our case perhaps a PM or a CIO) dictating schedules that are somewhat equally spaced out in time. This is one example of a pre-commitment practice.

Allowing people to select their own schedules was not as effective in reducing procrastination. Sound familiar? This is commensurate with what we will discuss shortly involving fallacies of our own planning. However, as we will discuss later, this goes against some of the motivational research that suggests that people will live up to their own goals better than those dictated by others.

As far as what I refer to as pseudo-procrastination, when you jump in and start coding without doing the real planning required, it's effectively just another form of procrastination based upon rationalizations. Rather than engage in the preparation work that needs to be completed now, you jump in to carry out the activities that you prefer, rationalizing that the schedule is getting out of control and we really need to get moving on something. Really what is happening is that you're skipping an entire step of the process in an effort to avoid the tasks you detest. With all this said, there are issues in spending so much time planning that projects start too late. This tends to happen on longer projects when the date seems so far out in the future that we really don't need to worry about it right now. This is a great argument for using an iterative type of development methodology where dates are more accurate and impactful.

Planning Fallacy

Roger Buehler, a Canadian psychologist, has conducted some very helpful research for our industry in his valuable experiments in this arena. Essentially, Buehler has found that people will underestimate their own tasks, but are reasonably good at predicting estimation times for other people's tasks. In addition, he found that people will generally find excuses (or what is referred to as external factors) to explain past results in similar situations. I'm quite certain that there are bells going off in your head that can be heard down the hall as you read this and think about software project planning. Most software professionals who are not involved in a particular software project can smell out the bad planning quickly and precisely, but yet they can't spot the obvious planning mistakes in their own project. Unfortunately, I notice this type of behavior on an unrelentingly regular basis. In fact it's now come to the point of a tragic comedy and was essentially the driving motivation behind the Agile movement in our industry. More on that subject later.

This poor planning on our own tasks is called the Planning Fallacy and to some degree is similar to the **Overconfidence Barrier** discussed earlier. A key for using this research in software development is that most of Buehler's test subjects did not consider their past experiences when planning for future activity of a similar nature. We've all turned in estimates that have been overly optimistic and we probably even knew so in the far reaches of our minds, but for some unknown reason we think it will somehow be different this time. We're now reasonably sure that those delays that happened quite regularly in the past will probably not surface again. It turns out that people have a difficult time actually planning for misfortune. It just looks bad to assume things will go wrong for competent people. How do you justify to the boss and other stakeholders that you're planning to fail a little here and there? As it turns out in Buehler's experiments, people who actually did review their past experiences ended up focusing on just those times that justified their optimistic thinking and NOT those times where things went awry. According to a report by Buehler, Griffin and Ross, "attention to and awareness of the past is not enough to make the past relevant to the future."

Another key finding here is that subjects in these experiments always predicted they would beat the deadlines. Does that sound familiar? Brooks must be right after all; we are an optimistic lot and not just us software professionals.

So, it appears as though we need some outsiders to help us when providing software estimates for the management team. Management themselves, if they have any experience in our field, will challenge software estimates or pad them by themselves rather than try to shrink them to a bare minimum (planning for bad planning). Of course we know now that padding an estimate may not be such a good idea either – remember the Anchoring concept that we just discussed? Management has now just been anchored and padding a little bit here and there may not be enough to entirely repair the problem. It's been my experience over the years that just padding estimates by some small percentage, say 15% or 20%, does not really work out often enough to use it as a good guideline or rule of thumb. Sometimes 20% may be well and good and other times it may need to be doubled or tripled, especially on smaller projects. Once you've become anchored it becomes really challenging to start thinking about doubling or tripling your estimates and this can be a major trap in software development. One technique that might be considered is for management to pad estimates in their own planning, but not for the development team. This way when the project arrives in typically late fashion, there really is some padding on both the calendar and financial aspects of the project to account for reality. It is doubtful this would happen however, because it would likely only work the first time. Thereafter everyone will come to expect the extra project time and budget dollars and will adjust their plans accordingly.

Other research on this topic suggests that there may possibly be some benefits with selecting aggressive schedules. These include increased motivation, the chance to be a hero for the company, and that some predictions are known to be self-fulfilling. That is, people will work to whatever the estimate states. However, I would counter that in our industry, unless there's a lot of loafing going on and the features are locked down tight, it will be hard to meet an aggressive schedule unless there's a lot of overtime involved. These points bring up other issues that will be described later; Social Loafing and Feature Creep.

Another major issue in regard to the Planning Fallacy in our industry is the issue of parties working together on a fixed bid basis. When you combine the notorious track record of software development, documented previously, with the effects of the Planning Fallacy, you expose yourself to considerable risks. The obvious risk is shortchanging yourself and the other is potential alienation of the customer. As an employee of SWAT, a software quality consulting firm, my experience has been that software development and fixed bids are challenging propositions at best. Even though in theory you can "manage" them by carefully crafting and executing Change Control addendums to the statement of work, it sometimes results in one party or the other being left feeling disenchanted. Another downside is that a fair amount of overhead cycles can be spent in managing and negotiating the necessary change controls and creating the original Statement of Work. It is highly likely during a software project of any significance that changes will occur throughout the life of the project, many times in several domains. If expectations are not defined and managed extremely carefully up front, before any work actually begins, there will almost assuredly be subsequent issues. In the end there sometimes tends to become a lot of "he said – she said" games along with the associated finger pointing if everything is not entirely and distinctly defined beforehand. One useful idea for fixed bids is to agree on some kind of common denominator. It might be the number of web pages created, testable requirements or some other clearly measurable entity that can be used to control runaway projects.

One last thought on the Planning Fallacy – creating estimates that are too generous, that is with too much padding built in, is not a good thing either. Managers want estimates to be as accurate as possible and there's the issue of crying wolf. People realize this and they know that management can do the simple math and multiply X days by 8 hours by Y dollars/hour yielding some astronomical figure that will surely be rejected. Many times these same managers end up paying much more than that initial "astronomical" figure when it's all said and done anyway.

General Planning Issues

Planning can be a mysterious process. Sometimes it's very autocratic and groups just gather to nod their heads to whomever has the most positional power within the group. Other times it's very democratic and too much compromising occurs and it takes far too long to complete. The last case is where the planning is done by a single person, a small company perhaps, and all kinds of problems may crop up here too. For more information on this topic see the section on Decision Making in Chapter 9.

Contingency Planning

For reasons already mentioned there seems to be a disproportionately large percentage of software development teams that do not actually plan for things that may eventually go wrong. Since I can't remember a single project I have known (both ones I've personally been involved with and others that I'm familiar with as a consultant or buyer) that has not run into at least some problems, this really baffles me. You can be almost guaranteed that on any project of significant size there will be a few unplanned builds, some added features and probably several modified features as well. So knowing what we know, why isn't there a more reasonable effort spent on contingency planning for software development projects? You'll find some exceptionally detailed contingency plans for IT computer operations groups, especially in large companies whose business depends on these systems running smoothly and properly. These plans can be quite detailed and also expensive to implement. Since we effectively know that some type of serious issues may arise, we should practice software project risk planning at some nominal level and while this does take place in some organizations, I've found that it's usually not adequate and too many organizations turn their backs on this issue. This is frequently a time and budget constraint.

My first thoughts on software contingency planning take me back to the Overconfidence Barrier and the Planning Fallacy discussed earlier in this chapter. However, management teams clearly need to assume ownership on this issue and demand that at least some form of contingency plans be put in place. These plans do not need to be at the same level of those that the Operations teams are implementing, but at least some core fundamentals should be in place. A little could go a long way here and I think it's an area where some realistic benefits can be scored for software organizations at a reasonable price point.

One practical and effective method employed by many organizations in this vein is to label all software features according to their Technical Complexity (TC) combined with their associated Business Benefit (BB). By ranking all features using this method, organizations can relatively quickly prioritize those feature sets that may be postponed until future releases. Simply rank each feature's TC and BB using a High, Medium, or Low grading system. Any feature high in TC or low in BB should immediately be suspect candidates for development but even more so when the two conditions coexist on a particular feature. This effort does require close collaboration with technical and business teams and should be directed by a qualified project manager or a higher-level manager of some sort. It also serves as a great team building exercise early in a project's lifecycle, something that we'll later learn is critically important for effective teamwork.

Over Planning & Perfection Paralysis

On the other extreme, over planning is occasionally found in certain susceptible areas of our work. Attempting to account for all the possible states in a large system can be daunting and most often is not necessary. Certain industries must absolutely consider virtually all states that could occur in order to avoid catastrophe, including loss of life and significant financial losses. Building systems for the NASA space shuttle come to mind. Most other systems development would be better off designing around unpredictable states to the best extent possible.

Our analytical personal nature, while generally required to effectively perform our job duties, can often work against us. Designing "perfect" systems is nearly impossible and certainly not practical in most instances. Many groups insist on spending vast amounts of effort and time designing a system up front, with limited knowledge that accounts for all possibilities. While accounting for the most obvious conditions is common sense, back tracking a bit later to perform some redesign is usually a more efficient methodology. Becoming paralyzed by perfection is a condition to be cognizant of in our industry and can cost unnecessary time and money. The software business is plagued by exceptions and I'm not referring to code faults. In some extreme cases, nearly 80% of development centers on the handling of errors and special cases. It's important that these conditions be designed out of the system, if feasible.

Doing What We Like

Most developers would probably admit that they really don't care to participate in much project planning in the first place. After all, they're programmers and that's what they prefer to do. For most tasks that we don't enjoy, we may try to do the absolute bare minimum that we believe we can get away with. Do just enough of the icky stuff, so that it appears as though a reasonable attempt was made, and then jump into what we really enjoy. This is human nature to take the path of least resistance, at least for those tasks we don't prefer. We may begin to rationalize with statements like "well that's about the most we could do anyway, based upon the sparse requirements from the business team." When you hear comments with this type of theme or tone, you may want to take a step back and examine the bigger picture. Are they (or you) making excuses and trying to rationalize their (your) behavior? If so, you may need to play to your team's strengths.

Knowing your individual player's strengths and tendencies can help substantially in this area. There are some developers who may never be able to plan effectively. So maybe they can partake in some other activity while the planning effort is taking place. They might be able to do some research into some technically challenging parts of the forthcoming project. Perhaps they can review the plans of others. Many times those that can't or won't work on an activity are great at critiquing the work of others that are capable or willing. This seems to be particularly true in software development. Perhaps it has something to do with the personality traits inherent in many technical people.

A few words on the strengths of individuals are needed about now. There's been a debate raging for decades over whether you can develop certain individual strengths or not. Certainly one can teach technical skills, otherwise programming would not have grown into such a large discipline. However, fighting personal trait characteristics and tendencies appears to be a losing battle. A developer, who won't carry out satisfactory planning work, may never be capable of performing planning work at an acceptable level. If that's truly the case, then spending the time trying to change some undesirable or missing characteristics of one of your team members may be a futile exercise and a waste of everyone's time. Not only do you waste time, you may actually alienate the person in question, not to mention your own frustration. Differentiating between the ability and the motivation to perform a particular duty may help you determine the best approach to working with these teammates.

Self-Discipline

Many business people and psychologists alike attribute much of people's failures to a lack of self-discipline. Studies by Seligman (2005), Baumeister (1994) and others provide conclusive evidence that self-discipline plays a more imperative role in success than intelligence and other factors. The distinguished software researcher Watts Humphrey dedicated a significant portion of his career helping developers and organizations improve programmer discipline. His Personal Software Process (PSP) was created and designed to foster a practice of discipline and ultimately enhanced software quality. Most people start out with good intentions, but are not able to sustain their momentum and desires. One method used to increase goal commitments is called **Mental Contrasting and Implementation Intentions** (MCII).

To use this system, one must first imagine the set of reasons one may be inhibited from attaining a specific goal. Once this has been defined, they must then create three implementation intentions to remove the obstacles blocking them from their goals. One intention is to overcome the named obstacle, the second intention is to prevent the obstacle if possible and the third one is a way of identifying a good opportunity to proactively take charge of achieving their goal.

An example might be a developer who wants to improve his personal interactions with the business team. To overcome this obstacle he may choose to schedule a check-in or catch-up meeting with one of the business team members when there is no specific agenda or issue to resolve. This is merely a chance to show that he cares and wants to lend a hand. A method to prevent the obstacle may be to better prepare himself prior to meetings; perhaps by using some visioning techniques to rehearse how he might respond to various requests or assertions that might come up. An opportunity for him to act might arise when one of the business people is in a jam and could use his help on an estimate or an emergency problem work-around of some sort.

Another method psychologists promote for improving one's self-discipline is the **Standards, Monitoring and Strength** model. Before one can improve there must be some defined and agreed upon standards of performance to attain. Perhaps it's the average defect count in one's code over a defined period of time or specific meeting participation goals. Whatever it is, there must be something to measure oneself against in order to properly assess progress toward the goal. Once standards have been satisfactorily defined, then monitoring the progress against those standards must occur on a regular basis to determine if additional or different behavioral changes are required to effectively meet the standard. Self-discipline is an extremely critical trait for successful developers. Developers who procrastinate on algorithm design may eventually pay the price many times over in code maintenance throughout the life of the product. Creating what are referred to as elegant solutions can be a worthwhile pursuit in many coding situations, especially if maintenance or additional features will subsequently be handled by others.

Laziness and Human Nature

This topic can be somewhat academic, but I would like to provide a few thoughts about laziness and some glimpses into human nature nonetheless. Generally we speak about laziness as an attribute or trait someone possesses as a permanent part of their general makeup. The declaration "John is a lazy person" attempts to describe John in general terms, which means laziness is part and parcel of who he is and what he represents. Many psychologists believe that laziness is more likely attributed to other factors such as intrinsic motivation, possibly one's level of aptitude, and how one's life history and experiences have molded that person. Laziness can be a potentially misunderstood concept when taken out of the larger context of one's individual circumstances.

When developers are not getting their components done on time are they lazy? Maybe they've just spent night and day learning a new technique or technology, which has caused them to miss their deadline. Is that being lazy? It may be irresponsible perhaps and maybe not particularly judicious either, but not necessarily lazy. Psychologist Leon Seltzer lists several reasons why someone may appear to be lazy and I will highlight a few that I consider to be pertinent to our subject: lacking a sense of self-efficacy, fear of failure, and lack of interest.

Self-Efficacy refers to knowing or believing that we can accomplish a task if we actually put our mind to it. If someone is not sure they can carry out the assignment they may be hesitant to undertake it and therefore be viewed as lazy or as a procrastinator. Good management can mitigate much of this issue. Knowing who to assign to projects of a certain level of difficulty or encouraging their efforts is all that may be necessary to get over the hump. More related techniques and concepts are featured in the Motivation section.

Fear of failure sometimes emerges when people are not sure what might result if they can't pull off the assignment, even if their self-efficacy is intact. Much of this may be due to the environment or culture that prevails in the company. If things are very competitive and hostile someone may be reluctant to dive into cutting edge projects for fear of reprisal later.

Lastly, developers sometimes could care less about the tangible outcome of the project. They're just not that interested. Occasionally you never witness or experience the outcome or end deliverable of your project. I had once worked on code for the Navy Trident submarine project many years ago and yet I had never even seen one of the subs, nor had I known anything tangible about it. It's more difficult to get inspired to develop code where the outcome is vague. Developers and other technical people would usually rather focus on techniques and technology – something that they can really sink their teeth into and get excited about because they can see immediate results and develop a reusable skill. See the discussion on delayed gratification in the Why Programmers Program section in Chapter 4 for more insight on this issue.

This is also why programmers seek the "holy grail," technical short cuts or silver bullets. They can then afford to spend more time finding more such short cuts, something that offers a tangible value, not to mention the prospective bragging rights.

Spending time learning new features and techniques may eventually pay off, but often times it doesn't come about when it's needed. You may then be forced to play catch-up to get the actual coding done according to the schedule. This type of behavior may essentially be a veiled form of procrastination or what was referred to earlier as pseudo-procrastination. The programmers will claim they are working, and to an extent they are, however this type of conduct must be managed very carefully. Putting timelines and functional constraints on research activities is a good practice to consider.

No Regulatory Body

In some project management circles certain people, half jokingly, talk about issuing government permits before someone could build software, analogous to local housing permits issued in the United States. At SWAT Solutions we spend quite some time working with certain clients who in effect do need a permit. These are companies who work within regulated environments such as those monitored by the Federal Food and Drug Administration (FDA). Companies who build medical devices or develop pharmaceuticals fall into this category. Those companies who are regulated by the FDA must provide evidence that their software has been built according to the usage requirements and that it has also been validated to perform as such. These companies must develop and adopt a Quality System that governs the creation and maintenance of this critical software. I've always felt that many non-regulated companies could benefit by adopting a modified version of these practices as well. It's so difficult and almost beyond human nature to force ourselves to be "regulated" when we're actually not; especially in the era of web apps that are so easily updated.

Software governance bodies can essentially perform the same role. However, these require extensive time commitments from many individuals and disciplines, but once established can create a culture that fosters improved software quality and a more consistent delivery mechanism.

PROJECT EXTREMES

Ironically, there are two polar extremes that confound our industry; one is those projects that are completely abandoned and the other is those runaway projects that never seem to end. Thus, Project Abandonment and Project Escalation will be discussed in greater detail so that we might have some glimpses into the driving forces lurking beneath.

Project Escalation

While it's essentially impossible to determine the exact frequency of this problem, myself, along with many others, suspect that it's a substantial issue in software development. Professor Mark Keil is an expert in this domain and has compiled some self-reported data. How many people accurately report embarrassing and negative data is unclear, but that which has been reported is not encouraging. Keil's research data show that somewhere between 30 – 40% of all software projects escalate to some level.

Definition

Project escalation is said to occur "when there is a presence of negative project status information that fails to be processed appropriately, resulting in continuation of what appears to be a failing course of action" (Keil, 2000). The key is having visibility to negative project metrics on a timely basis. There is an incentive to hide or positively spin bad news once it's manifested. Of course all data is collected after the fact and how far project data reporting lags behind project activities is critical in creating effectual corrective action plans.

Potential Causes

Two of the prime candidate psychological sources appear to be **Prospect Theory** and the **Completion Effect**. These are both explained in greater detail in the Decision Making section, but here's a quick overview. Prospect theory is concerned with how people perceive their prospects for a particular situation. When the prospect is viewed or framed as a loss, people may consider more risky responses, hence a possible tendency for project escalation behaviors. The completion effect is centered on people's desires to finish what they've started, especially as they approach the goal state. Other psychological mechanisms may come into the picture here too. These include **Sunk Costs** and the associated cognitive dissonance it creates, also described later in more detail.

It has not yet been determined if the **Gambler's Fallacy** factors into escalation decisions or not. In effect, the gambler's fallacy is a belief that one's luck or outcomes will change only because people believe that eventually their fortunes must improve. Casino gamblers sometimes expect the dice to change based on previous rolls. But regrettably, the dice have no memory and unless there's some corrupt behavior going on, the odds are the same for every toss. I have personally witnessed developers who think in this manner and believe that eventually their algorithms will fall into place and the previous schedule losses will easily be made up later. They essentially believe that things will get better on their own because "they're due." This is in contrast to those optimistic developers who are relying upon their hard work and dedication and therefore confident that it will indeed pay off with a successful outcome. In defense of those developers who believe that their luck will improve, the process of elimination may help in honing in on the correct algorithm – as long as they persist in making reasonable attempts.

Another potential cause of escalation may be at least partially explained using the **Approach-Avoidance Conflict** theory developed by Dollard and Miller, (1950). While there are several corollaries to this theory, the one that might apply to project escalation would be the following: The tendency to avoid a negative goal increases the closer one is to the goal. When someone is aborting a software project it is almost certainly perceived as a negative goal and therefore the closer one becomes to the goal the more they will likely resist abandoning, or significantly modifying, the project.

One final possible reason behind escalation tendencies may be as simple as the tendency people have to avoid decisions, also referred to by Social Psychologists as the **Omission Bias**. This claims that people will just continue on with whatever course of action that does not require a change (Baumeister, Bushman). You can think of it basically as psychological inertia. It takes effort to make a change and there will likely be unknown consequences for any changes that are implemented, perhaps even making the situation somehow worse.

Ramifications

There are several possible ramifications of project escalation. Most are negative in nature, however, there are many lessons embedded within these projects. You would hope that these egregious instances would instigate major changes in how development organizations monitor and track large development efforts. It's not entirely clear that this is the case. For some elusive, imitable reason we have yet to be able to escape this morbid trap. Perhaps organizations are learning one at a time or perhaps just certain groups within organizations are learning, but as an industry it appears we haven't learned all of our lessons quite yet. One way to possibly control these projects is by implementing an iterative or Agile development methodology. These projects are more apt to stay under control.

Potential Remedies

I would argue that most technical people would have an extremely difficult time dropping a challenging software project when they can "see the end." This of course depends upon a number of factors, most significantly, how far away project completion really is. Since our estimations are known to be rather faulty in the first place, this may be hard to accurately judge. We've all been part of (or have heard of) projects that sit at 90% completion for weeks, months, and in some extreme cases, years. In fact "90% completion" has become somewhat of a renowned punch line in our industry.

When one closely reviews the potential underlying psychological causes that may come into play with escalating projects, it's quite obvious that outsiders must be involved in some manner in order to remediate the situation successfully. The people involved have become very attached to the project and abandoning it on their own, or even considering it, might well be virtually impossible. However, outsiders will need to be peripherally involved throughout the project; otherwise it may take them too long to make an informed decision. Conversely, if these same outsiders are too involved in the project then they may suffer the same psychological fate as the rest.

Project Abandonment

Abandoned software projects obviously pose serious threats to our industry. There is no definitive data on the number or types of software project abandonment. This is frequently the case when there is bad news involved. The little reliable data that I could discover show that perhaps around 30% of projects are abandoned either totally or partially. This is an astounding number to comprehend, even if it isn't completely accurate.

In one review of abandoned projects (Ewusi-Mensah, 2003) it was found that most were abandoned prior to the coding stage. Also, interestingly enough, the majority of these same projects were considered to be of low or medium risk and low or medium complexity in nature. This leads one to believe that planning and other non-technical related problems are the root causes of many of these failures. In the following sections other reasons will be highlighted that may provide further insight into the reasons why projects may be abandoned altogether.

"RETRACTABLE" MEDIUM

While Brooks mentions a tractable medium, I view this just slightly differently. I think of it as a retractable medium now. With the advent of web applications now dominating the development space, these applications are viewed as retractable – that is, we can take back what we published and replace it with something better or different, in a matter of minutes in many cases. In Brooks' day this was not necessarily the case. New releases had to be built and somehow distributed and installed on company's or people's systems. Now you just need to push out some new web functionality and voila, you've just updated your application.

However, because our medium is retractable, and developers understand that more than anyone, coders may be easily enticed to resort to short-cuts with sincere intentions of "coming back to it later." They now have a crutch to lean on which is dangerous for developers. This crutch is hard to ignore and it may promote further procrastination behavior. Many times, as has been recently highlighted here, schedules become compromised and suspect or inferior code is never updated. And while developers may indeed come back to it later, it will be too late in some percentage of the cases. This may now lead to additional subsequent issues including problematic code maintenance and an end product which is now more prone to defects. Code maintained, even just a few days after it has been written, is much more suspect to logic errors because the developer may have forgotten why they implemented some feature a certain way. They will instantly recall the logic though when the production defect report arrives. Unfortunately, I can personally attest to that.

ABSTRACT ACTIVITY

Business owners and most business people, by and large, have a difficult time understanding software development and the underlying issues that cause it to go haywire. Why? Mainly because most business people, and many others involved in software development, have never written code. Someone who has never programmed before couldn't possibly understand all the issues involved in creating good, solid code. Nor could they completely understand how bugs are introduced into software algorithms, much less the more obscure algorithms that are deeply buried in the bowels of larger systems.

I suppose it's plausible that you might be able to explain "hard coding" to someone if you had an example that they were familiar with and how it had caused a problem they could relate to. The misuse of data types or variable names might also be comprehensible. Other more complex issues would be nearly impossible to completely explain. When a builder is putting up a new home for you, it's fairly easy to relate with many of the situations that can go awry. You'd understand if the joists were too short or the wrong wiring was installed, even though you might not be able to see the actual wires. With software, it's an entirely different story. It's both abstract and complex, which is a vicious combination, and that's just for relatively straightforward application software. When it comes to programming device drivers or other system type software, it's especially difficult for non-technical people to grasp many of the key concepts required.

Unmanageable Feature Sets

This leads us directly to the next problem on our list. When it's hard to grasp the nature of the work, it becomes really quite effortless to ask for extended or altogether new feature sets. The business team, once they see a working prototype, may likely have "aha" moments and make requests for other related features not previously conceptualized. Adding another bathroom to the house is tangible and you can visualize this in your mind's eye as a reasonably arduous and material addition. More plumbing is required, wiring, fixtures, etc. You can rather easily determine the scope of the effort in relation to the rest of your home and you wouldn't be shocked if your builder said that it would add another $40,000 dollars and three weeks to your estimate.

But extra software features don't seem to work this way. A new feature may require several database changes, which now may require some new stored procedures and linkages to other database fields. Entirely new modules may need to be created and interdependencies with other existing modules must be accommodated. Then there's the extra documentation, test cases, testing, and updating the design that is required (at least in theory). The business teams aren't thinking about all of these duties and extra work. They're now entranced by what could potentially be a great system or application and they have a tendency to get carried away when they get on a roll.

A related problem (perhaps one more frustrating for developers, BAs, and testers) is material changes to existing features. Once, in my role as CTO for a small company, our team developed an application we were convinced was exactly what the business team requested. In fact we sat through many weekly meetings reviewing and discussing just these details. I can vividly recall how proud we all were as we prepared for our final walkthrough, fully expecting the appreciative stamp of approval. It was then, just before the time to launch the service, we found out that some of the major user flows were not what they expected. What they thought were just minor changes ended up becoming significant refactoring efforts. This put the project at significant risk since there were client commitments that could not be reversed (codes printed on consumer packages). Such are the perils of working in an abstract field.

UNREALISTIC EXPECTATIONS

All of this naturally leads to expectations that are just not feasible and yet somehow we are still mystified at our unrelentingly poor track record. Clearly, moving the needle in the proper direction will take more than just technical breakthroughs. Yet that is our inclination, as technical people, to persist in applying more and ever better technologies in our continual effort to find that elusive "silver bullet." These dreaded "silver bullets" may be the ultimate curse of our industry. To compound this problem, much of the modern world has become programmed to believe that new technologies are the only conduit to an enhanced existence. There has been a proliferation of new gadgets over the past decade. Can you imagine living without a television or, more recently, without a mobile or smart phone? This means that today's business and management people may be just as likely to believe that more and better technology is the ultimate answer as well and they may also be in dire pursuit of silver bullets. It's rapidly becoming part of the global culture.

PART II
Psychological Factors in Software Engineering

CHAPTER 4

Rewards, Goals & Inhibitors

WHY PROGRAMMERS PROGRAM

My core theory on this fascinating topic is that programmers and many other people, especially men for reasons soon to be discussed, like to engage in activities with variable reward mechanisms. Hunting, fishing, golf, and gambling all are common everyday examples of activities with variable rewards and I'm sure that you can imagine others. That is, you never know when that big fish will bite or even if it will actually bite at all. But this is exactly what makes it exciting to participate in these events in the first place. If you knew that you'd catch a trophy fish on every cast, then what's really the point? If you birdied every hole in golf it wouldn't be much of a challenge and it would soon lose its grasp on you.

So let's take a quick review of the scientific research that supports this theory of variable rewards for programmers. There are four basic types of reward schedules defined by psychologists (mainly behavioral psychologists); fixed and variable ratio and fixed and variable interval. The key is that one set is based upon activity (the ratio ones) and the other is based upon time (the interval ones).

Fixed and Variable Rewards

Fixed-ratio schedules would be where the subject receives a reward every n^{th} time he performed a specific activity. The value of n could range from one to almost any number within reason. If you caught a fish every fifth cast for example, this would be a fixed-ratio reward. More likely however, it might involve some piecemeal rate compensation in a factory where a worker receives so much compensation for every five widgets assembled. This is a strong motivator of human behavior for as long as the individual can hold out. This reward mechanism is used quite frequently in work settings where good data can be easily tracked, such as manufacturing.

A variable-ratio schedule is where rewards come periodically with no exact pattern to them, although they usually have some typical average. Nabbing birdies (a birdie is one stroke under par for a particular golf hole) on holes 5, 11, and 14 (out of 18 holes for you non-golfers) would be a variable ratio reward. You would not know what holes you might make birdie on, but you may know that on a typical day on a typical golf course you notch around three birdies. Variable-ratio reward systems can lead to exceptionally high rates of response and usually keep people interested over the long term in the associated activity.

Fixed-interval rewards are those where rewards occur in a certain period of time; if you caught a fish every 15 minutes for example. This reward scheme generates low interest, especially just after the reward has occurred. Think about your annual bonus.

Variable-interval rewards are more exciting because one never knows exactly when a reward will happen, but they must know within some range. For example, you probably wouldn't have many people fishing if you went eight hours between catching fish (unless perhaps you're fishing for very large game fish, such as Marlin – variable rewards are relative to the activity). At some point people will lose interest in unrewarded activities and of course this will vary based upon the particular circumstances and the person involved. Variable-interval rewards can be very addicting and will keep people highly engaged in activities, in some cases for a lifetime. The gaming industry knows well the lessons of variable rewards and how much it can take control of one's focus, especially in certain vulnerable individuals.

One of the key areas of the human brain called the Ventral Tegmental Area (VTA), located in the mid brain, is responsible for manufacturing dopamine, which as you'll recall is a complex functioning hormone released when people feel good. It's a feeling that people intensely cherish and the VTA region of the brain has been found to be more active in men. What better way to elicit a quick dose of dopamine than to find out that one of your code snippets works just as you expected? Whether or not this means that men are more likely to release dopamine as a result of incremental programming achievements is not yet clear, but it's potentially another indicator to explain why men are somewhat more attracted to careers in programming than women.

Delayed / Instant Gratification

One more related topic here before we continue. When you combine variable rewards with relatively quick gratification (perhaps not instant) you have a formula for strongly addictive or sought out behavior. So while a programmer is entranced in their daily work they receive periodic "rewards" whenever their unit tests or even partial unit tests succeed. When they are working on a complex algorithm they can obtain variable rewards even when very small code segments begin to function properly.

These small fragmented rewards can be played out rather quickly, depending upon the type of programming being done. On your typical web app development project, you can quickly fire up a browser pointing to your development environment and promptly see if your code in question works properly or not. This type of scenario can literally play out hundreds of times within a single day. This is why developers sometimes lose complete track of time and are not punctual for meetings (or at least you hope that's why they're late). I firmly believe that this is a major reason why many people choose a career in programming. It's difficult for me to think of too many other professions that have a combination of both variable rewards and quick gratification, although I'm sure there are others.

In many job functions the results of your work will not be known for months or even several years. Once you become accustomed to this near instant gratification, having to wait months to see real-world results can be a rather difficult adjustment. These near instantaneous results are really many miniature rewards, accompanied by a small shot of dopamine, that occur throughout each workday. It's no wonder that we like this type of work; our self-esteem is constantly being fostered all day long. This may be another indication as to why developers would rather not spend as much time on planning and design activities. These upfront duties aren't typically providing the frequency of rewards that programming creates, and besides, programming can be done in private with no one disrupting you, a situation many developers prefer. The variable reward portion of this equation comes from the fact that not every code change or addition will work the first time or even subsequent times for that matter. Sometimes the code works just fine and other times there are problems that may take days to remediate. Not knowing whether a certain chunk of code will work is what keeps us going. The thrill that occurs when it works just like it was designed to can be particularly addicting. I've known developers who have labored on for 20 hours and even longer, without significant rest breaks, in order to track down and solve a problem or fix a logic error. Most likely, there were several mini breakthroughs, or rewards, here and there that kept them going until they finished.

Studies on gratification teach us that men are less prone to delay their gratification than women, at least in the U.S. (Funder, pg 190). That is, in general, males prefer not to wait as long for their rewards. This, if even remotely true, may partially explain why there are substantially more male programmers than female programmers in the United States. Refer to the chapter on Culture and Gender for a more detailed breakdown of women in software engineering. My own experience reflects approximately the same results. I have worked with a limited number of female programmers over the years and even fewer female hardware engineers and network administrators.

WHY PEOPLE DO AND DON'T WORK (AKA MOTIVATION)

Rewards

As it so happens, I was an interested spectator on a great lesson in human motivation several years ago while working for a light manufacturing company. The company decided to launch a program to provide recognition to certain high performers in the warehouse, in the hopes that everyone's performance would improve and therefore the company as a whole. The way the program was conceived was that every month some hardworking and deserving employee would be designated as the "Employee of the Month" (there's actually a movie with this title that plays out similarly). Their name would be printed in an extremely large font on a huge banner hung high in a frequented part of the warehouse. In addition, their name would be added to a running banner of all the month's winners over the years. If I recall correctly, there was a nominal bonus distributed to the lucky employee as well.

However, after a few months, some unintentional and unwanted behavior began to emerge. Employees who were not selected as monthly winners became jealous and offended. At first it was somewhat civil, but several months into the program certain employees were now becoming quite vocal and agitated about how they had been snubbed and that they had certainly performed better than so and so and was therefore much more deserving of that month's acknowledgement. Soon after the casual grumbling it became such a mess that it was now a downright de-motivating situation for many employees. The thinking went along the lines of this; "well if they don't think I'm better than Jim, I'll never get that award, so I might just as well give up now." As you may have already surmised, the program was soon cancelled and I do not recall another taking its place.

This concept will be elaborated upon later in this section; however the key point is that the warehouse workers had become focused on the wrong goal. The goal was an external item and the motivation to work hard did not come from within the person, but rather as a response to the reward program. This is a common theme for motivation within the workplace and there will be much more discussion in this vein forthcoming. The warehouse motivational program just discussed is quite common throughout the American workforce. At first glance it appears to be logical. Reward the desired behavior in the workplace and people will repeat it. Well as it turns out, this logic is actually somewhat flawed and it may be closer to the other way around.

Behavioral psychologists have been promoting this type of reward program for decades. It's based upon studies with animals such as rats and pigeons. Reward them with a pellet of their favorite choice and you can reinforce many incredible types of simple behavior. The risk here is two-fold. One is that you may inadvertently reward the wrong behavior, thereby reinforcing something that either provides no value, or in some cases, make things worse. A classic experimental example is that of a lab pigeon that happens to be turning around when a pellet is randomly dispensed in his cage, which now begins spinning around at a furious pace, assuming incorrectly that the pellet was a result of the turning behavior. Of course, people are much more complex than animals and what works with a pigeon may not necessarily work with your lead developer. Let's hope not at least.

The other more serious case is where external rewards come into play with real thinking people. A classic experiment was performed many years ago by Edward L. Deci, a noted social psychologist. This experiment, and many other supporting ones over the years since, revealed that once people were externally rewarded for doing something they naturally enjoyed, their desire for that activity would begin to diminish. The thought process is considered to be along the lines of: "well I must not like it that much if I do it for money (or other comparable rewards)." It was found that elementary age students who were paid to read a certain number of books would at first work harder to read the books in exchange for the money. However, follow-up studies determined that their desire for reading had now dropped below that of their pre-reward program levels. The net result was that external rewards improved short-term performance, but actually degraded long-term performance. What someone once did for just the intrinsic joy and satisfaction it garnered was no longer satisfying for them. And that's the basic problem with reward systems; once the rewards stop the preferred behavior may well stop too. Year-end bonuses fall into this category. Once companies start dishing them out, year after year, they become expected and they begin to lose their perceived value for the employees and hence the company.

Psychologists have a name for this scenario (of course you knew that was coming by now) where one loses interest in an activity after being paid for it. It's called the **Overjustification Effect**. What was once a rewarding diversion in its own right is now considered to be work and therefore not nearly as enticing. Obviously this is an obstacle that the business world cannot do a great deal to overcome. People are not going to take up programming or project management on a full time basis just because it's fulfilling for them. They need to earn a living. However there are other ways to help resolve this dilemma.

Deci and Ryan represented this external reward system more broadly to signify outside control of our actions. So instead of performing some activity because we inherently wanted to, we are now being controlled by an outside force in terms of said activity. This continuum of control must be balanced where the individual feels in charge of where they find themselves on the range of outside influence versus self-control.

William McKnight, the visionary founder of one of Minnesota's most famous companies, 3M, has a quote that I've referred to many times. I've actually modeled my style of management around his philosophy. Many believe that McKnight's greatest contribution was as a business philosopher, since he created a corporate culture that encouraged employee initiative and innovation.

So here's McKnight's basic rule of management that was laid out way back in 1948:

"As our business grows, it becomes increasingly necessary to delegate responsibility and to encourage men and women to exercise their initiative. This requires considerable tolerance. Those men and women, to whom we delegate authority and responsibility, if they are good people, are going to want to do their jobs in their own way.

"Mistakes will be made. But if a person is essentially right, the mistakes he or she makes are not as serious in the long run as the mistakes management will make if it undertakes to tell those in authority exactly how they must do their jobs.

"Management that is destructively critical when mistakes are made kills initiative. And it's essential that we have many people with initiative if we are to continue to grow."

To this day 3M maintains its policy of allowing employees a percentage of time to tinker and explore new ideas. Many of their most famous inventions came as a result of this policy and they continue that tradition even in times when business ideas such as these are routinely mocked by other companies. They realize that autonomy is a key motivator and they keep control to a minimum.

Management should ideally be focused on what tasks need to be done and not rigidly define how they must be done. This is where technical people need to exert some control of their own and management becomes a sounding board and cheerleader. Management certainly needs to guide and monitor what is going on so that business objectives are met, but exerting too much control over "how" something gets done can be severely disabling for technical people. The exception here may be in teaching one a new technique of how to do something more efficiently, something nearly all technical people crave. However, it's unlikely that managers are the ones who are the experts in how something technical should be implemented.

I once worked for a highly intuitive and successful manager who was technically competent, genuine, and engaging, a rare combination of attributes in our technical world. He taught me many valuable lessons, but one I distinctly remember, was to keep customers focused on requirements and not solutions. Well now I realize why this makes so much sense. People want control of what they consider to be their domain of knowledge and expertise. Having someone tell them how to design a solution, while they may actually be correct, is not the best way to intrinsically engage a technical resource. This is especially true when it comes to working with men.

John Gray, in his now famous book *Men are from Mars and Women are from Venus* points out how men like to "solve" women's problems (and men's problems too) whereas women just want their emotions to be understood. Leading people to their own conclusions will almost always yield higher rates of job satisfaction. While this is not universally true, it is a good rule of thumb. There are certain categories of people who are more risk averse and these types of employees may well appreciate clear and distinct directions from superiors, so as not to be held too accountable when unexpected outcomes occur. So it appears that people have an innate need to be in control of their work and not have their work be in control of them, at least to a certain degree. There needs to be some challenges to keep people interested and focused, but extreme challenges on a regular basis will begin to create dangerously high levels of stress, which is described in more detail later.

The real key here becomes personal choice, but of course we can't have everyone doing just what they please. That is why good managers and leaders focus on the "What" and let the competent people they've assumedly employed focus on the "How." In software development the How can be critically important, as certain high profile incidents have clearly demonstrated.

Intrinsic Motivation & Rewards

There have been many studies in this vein beyond those conducted by Deci and Ryan just reviewed. Cameron et. al. (2001) performed a meta-analysis (see Chapter 1 for a review) on several studies on the effects that rewards may have on different types of performance. Their results are somewhat different from those of Deci and Ryan as subsequent research has reviewed the effect of additional performance parameters. These parameters include more specific instances of performance contingencies such as rewards offered for surpassing a specific score or exceeding the work of others. The results of this meta-analysis show that providing rewards for exceeding others has a positive effect on free-choice intrinsic motivation rather than a negative one, as Deci might not have predicted. Additionally, in studies of self-reported task interest, rewards offered for surpassing a specific score and exceeding others showed positive effects. Cameron's group also found that for those tasks of high-interest, verbal rewards were found to improve both free-choice and task interest, meaning that the boss' approval still holds some weight whether a monetary reward is involved or not.

The bottom line, at this point in time anyway, is that rewarding performance and success provides positive effects compared to rewarding for simply doing in and of itself. So it pays to be especially careful when constructing reward mechanisms.

Goals

So if we work on the assumption that a feeling of autonomy is good for development teams, then we need to consider other ramifications. Software project goals, such as feature/schedule estimates, are better defined by the group than dictated from above, at least in terms of personal commitment anyway. Development teams will strive harder to achieve the goals they set for themselves rather than those coming from the business units or upper management (however, while they may work harder to achieve their own goals, they may also set them too low – this will be discussed later). The trick comes in how this mutual goal setting is executed by both parties. Defining the broader issues facing the company will usually help the team set goals that are realistic for their development needs as well as for the company. Even though we technical people don't always make the most astute business decisions, we do know that what is good for the company may ultimately benefit us too. This is why walk-around-management is helpful. People can rally around the larger mission and stretch themselves to achieve what's necessary to succeed when they understand the linkages and their personal involvement, as heard directly from their supervisor. Technical staffs need to be reminded on a regular basis about the larger corporate mission, since we have a tendency to dive deep into technical details and may easily lose sight of the broader picture and the ultimate business outcomes.

There are many other psychological impacts in regard to goals. Researchers Locke and Latham (1990) and others report that contributors who were convinced to attain specific goals performed better than those who were just asked to do their best. While people will vehemently exclaim that they cannot achieve any more when specific goals are established, because after all they are already doing their level best, the research just doesn't support these assertions. Furthermore, when people are asked to set their own goals they inevitably set them too low. Of course with certain tasks, such as programming, setting goals may have adverse and unforeseen consequences. Coding can be done in a myriad number of ways. Just requiring that modules are completed on time is not enough. Hard coding and not handling special cases and error conditions properly may actually cause additional rework further downstream and end up being counterproductive in the long run. This is yet another reason to have experienced development managers in place and another rationale for utilizing code reviews on a more periodic basis.

Motivation in Software Engineering

Motivating a computer programmer is somewhat like motivating an eleven-year-old male gamer. There's absolutely no problem getting the kid to play X-box for nearly 18 hours a day while he's desperately trying to set his personal high score or beat another kid six time zones away. But the trick is how do you get him to play the games you want him to play, when you want him to play them? This is the basic problem when you have an abstract and challenging activity that you're trying to conquer. You might become so entranced in the "game" that you may then lose sight of the overall objective. Programming really does become a game of sorts for some developers and it is very easy for them to lose focus of the bigger picture. That is why developers may lose complete track of time and miss appointments or that important code review that's been scheduled for weeks. They begin tinkering with a new algorithm that uses some new technology, AJAX perhaps. Soon they're deep in the weeds discovering all the pitfalls and advantages of AJAX. They're off searching the web looking for code snippets, reading forum threads to find answers and suddenly they're out of bounds on their project and conquering AJAX has now temporarily become their top priority.

Therefore, motivation of programmers is more a matter of focus than of actual motivation. Developers want to learn more "tricks" and find those hidden passageways so that they may have bragging rights in front of their fellow programmers. Many people in the software development profession are naturally motivated. So one way to achieve your goals and keep programmers suitably motivated is to promise them that there really will be time available for some exploring of new techniques, as long as the larger goals and schedule objectives are met. Allowing developers time to explore and experiment is a tremendous motivational technique. After all, this has worked successfully at 3M for decades. But, here's the best part, it probably won't cost you any calendar time, and if your programmer is a salaried employee (and you're not paying them by the hour) it won't cost you any more money against your budget either.

That's because time will get lost when the developer is immersed in learning a new technique and if you're at all lucky your project may actually benefit from the learning at some future point and perhaps even on the current project. I've seen some extreme cases where entire breakthroughs have resulted from this approach enabling projects to achieve results that were not previously planned or predicted. The project now has taken on a whole new perspective with exciting novel possibilities that were not even an option previously. After all, this is why we're all in the business, right?

Researchers have identified two broad types of achievement goals; performance goals and learning goals. Learning goals focus on the attainment of new skills while performance goals are focused on mastery of a particular ability. It has been discovered that learning goals may be better suited for acquiring new skills than performance goals, especially when there are set backs or negative feedback on performance goals. This research fits right in line with what many of us have suspected all along; that developers love to learn and when new tasks are framed as learning opportunities, they tend to flourish (Moskowitz & Grant, 2009).

Hawthorne Studies

Back in the 1920s, a group of researchers from the National Academy of Sciences began studying workers of the Hawthorne telephone equipment plant of Western Electric in Chicago, Illinois. Later on, researchers from Harvard Business School also worked with employees of this same plant. These studies were designed initially to understand what effects certain environmental conditions might have on worker productivity. The results surprised the researchers; this is what tends to happen in studies that ultimately become famous. It didn't seem to matter what conditions the scientists altered. No matter what they did, productivity improved. The first study was to observe the effects of changing illumination levels on productivity. Increased lighting did indeed improve productivity. However, a short time later, when lighting levels were reduced back to their original intensity, productivity surprisingly improved again. Not all environmental changes produced increased output and the resultant effect, now known as the **Hawthorne Effect**, is not terribly long lasting. Increased productivity can be observed for several days or somewhat longer. These experiments initially confounded scientists of all types. Eventually the ultimate learning here was that it was the attention and feelings of importance garnered by the workers that improved the worker's production and not the actual physical work conditions.

So what is the lesson here? For me it means that even though we work in an industry dominated by introverted and analytical males, they still need to sustain feelings of importance and be genuinely included in all related activities. Just because some of us are typically not as social as other people, we still require and desire feedback on our work and to know how we fit into the bigger puzzle. Feeling important is one of the most significant of all human needs according to the soft skills legend Dale Carnegie. This is basically true for everyone. Never underestimate the power of inclusion and exclusion, perhaps the most powerful force known to humankind.

While it may be easy to assume that because someone does not initiate many conversations with you, that they prefer not to interact with you, this is usually not the case. Introverts are thinking many thoughts; it's just that many of them never see the verbal light of day. The Hawthorne Studies reveal that the Walk Around Management technique featured earlier really can be effective in demonstrating to employees that you care and that by extension they are important to the organization. This is why it's also imperative to spend the most time with the most important people on your team.

Respect

Many Industrial/Organization psychologists believe that most workers really just yearn for respect. One would think that highly educated professionals would crave it even more so. My experience with developers and other related technical staff unscientifically confirms this hypothesis. Providing reasonable delivery schedules and resisting the management enticement to micromanage in excess are basic privileges that convey professional dignity and respect. Perhaps nothing de-motivates one more than lack of respect for basic worker considerations.

Organizations have what is termed a **Psychological Contract** with their employees. It is unwritten in form, regardless of the actual written agreement if one exists, and is typically an unspoken contract as well. This agreement basically specifies a set of expectations that workers and employers have for each other and it is unique for each employee. Generally these psychological contracts stipulate that in return for respect from the employer, the employee will be loyal to the company (Statt, 2004).

The potential problem with these unwritten psychological contracts is that they may be interpreted differently by virtually everyone. As mentioned in the

Generation Gap section, younger employees, who scored higher as a group on narcissism than older employees, may expect that they are entitled to additional overall compensation and benefits. This may subsequently lead to more serious problems such as employee turnover or low morale. Managers need to be cautious in how they deal with these delicate issues and not just with Gen Y employees. It's very easy to make off-hand remarks about potential rewards for project successes and while the manager may quickly forget these conversations, the employee will absolutely not. And I highly suspect that this holds especially true for analytical people.

Köhler Effect

The **Köhler Effect**, named after researcher Otto Köhler back in the 1920s, occurs when a less capable person working on conjunctive or cooperative tasks increases their efforts in the presence of more capable performers. If work partners are either too much better or about the same at the task the effect appears to be mitigated. The theory here is that workers do not want to be responsible for the poor results of the group and the other thought is that they will not care to be designated as the weaker developer or whatever the task may be. Not surprisingly, these same studies reveal that men appear to strive harder when paired with women on the same task. While these tasks were generally physical in nature there is some evidence that the Köhler effect applies to cognitive tasks as well.

The key here is to pair people together that are reasonably comparable in their skills in order to realize the benefit from this effect. Too much skill discrepancy and people may lose the motivation to keep up.

PERSISTENCE

Attribution Style and Task Persistence

Attribution style refers to how one views their connection and responsibility with situational outcomes. That is, do they think that outcomes are a result of their internal capabilities and corresponding actions or a result of circumstances outside of their control. This may seem somewhat academic but it appears to be a factor in task persistence, something clearly vital in software engineering. The theory differentiates between ability and effort and people who believe that they succeed primarily due to their own innate ability may not perform as well as those who believe that their effort was instrumental to their success. This would suggest that managers should focus on supporting vigorous task effort rather than convincing someone they have the innate intelligence and talent to succeed. The underlying logic is that if someone fails on a task initially, they may feel that it's outside their scope of capability and therefore why should they bother continuing with something they just aren't capable of solving anyway. However, someone who believes that the effort that they exert has more to do with successful task completion may have an improved chance of triumph. There is a limited amount of research that supports this claim (Rozek, 2006) showing that participants with internal attribution styles do persist longer than participants with external attribution styles, at least on certain types of cognitive tasks.

My own personal experience in the domain of task persistence provides further evidence that this is the case, although it may be rare. I've witnessed software professionals that had somehow become convinced that they didn't have the capability to complete their project deliverables. They thought it was hopelessly beyond their competency level and felt they had exhausted all of their options. Once software professionals cross this cognitive divide their output may plummet noticeably. Rather than begin working even harder to overcome the obstructions they may start looking for political ways out of the predicament. Asking to work on other projects or even challenging the project requirements are common outcomes.

Persistence and Goal Visibility

Research has shown that people will lose interest in completing tasks for several different reasons. One major cause is lack of goal progress visibility. If someone has no real idea of how close they are to completion of a complex task, their performance tends to diminish (Moskowitz p. 282). In development this can occur when modules are not properly divided. Modules that are too large and wieldy may be more difficult to monitor in terms of completion status. Sometimes there may be no realistic choice in the matter, but when possible smaller more compact modules will allow developers to have more of a laser focus on the efforts required for task completion. Another issue for developers is that in certain problem situations the solution is essentially an all or none proposition. In these cases you really don't know when the breakthrough will come, until suddenly, there it is right in front of you. This represents what is frustrating, but also rewarding about our undertaking as was highlighted earlier in the variable reward discussion.

A second reason people lose concentration on goals is related to what is referred to as expectancy. If people believe that they have the capability to accomplish a task, they will have a better chance of persisting than if they are uncertain in their abilities to succeed. Even if the rewards are high, if people are not convinced they will succeed, they may have diminished motives to proceed. A third and related factor for staying on task is its perceived importance or value. This probably will have a less significant role for developers than people performing other types of tasks, in my experience. A developer's concept of value is typically more related to conquering and delivering a functional working module. They are unlikely to be seriously influenced by the business value of the actual module as it probably holds less interest for them. It may help if they're convinced that the module is absolutely necessary, but then if it wasn't necessary they realize they probably wouldn't be coding it in the first place. Developers however will almost certainly be sensitive to continually being assigned to code the mundane or boring modules.

Task Interruption

This is a topic that surfaces now and again in the software development sphere. It usually comes up when debating private offices versus cubes for developers and other technical staff that are required to get in the "zone" in order to work effectively. It seems quite obvious to me that this battle has already been fought (and lost) long ago. I see very few developers working from private offices, even small windowless ones, even though there is substantial research showing the benefit of quiet work areas for programmers. Technical people, the savvy problem solvers that we are, have responded mostly by adopting headphones to reduce open office noise levels.

Here is a brief synopsis of the research on task interruption. It appears as though it is now generally accepted by most psychologists that task interruptions on more complex cognitive tasks inhibits performance and this seems rather intuitive as well. An interruption on simpler tasks has a smaller negative impact and on very simple tasks may actually improve performance slightly. There is some data to support the notion of optimal interruption times, which is basically between task steps (planning, execution, and evaluation). For personnel who work exclusively on computers, basically all software related workers, there are additional task interruptions that might potentially reduce productivity. These are primarily instant messaging, web assistants and email. Users who do not deactivate these applications may be bombarded with hundreds of messages and interruptions per day and this is clearly not conducive to elevated productivity.

How bad is the problem? Developers spend an average of 11 minutes on one task before being interrupted to deal with another, according to Gloria Mark of the University of California at Irvine's Department of Informatics, who has spent years examining developers' work environments. Amazingly, it then takes them an additional 25 minutes to return to the original task. This type of data, even if it's only close to being accurate, is astonishing. How you can accomplish anything of significance in this type of environment is beyond my comprehension and certainly provides a case for more privacy for developers.

One of the principal arguments against providing private offices for software developers is that it will inhibit project collaboration. And while I agree with this to a certain point, I think it's mainly an excuse for saving office related expenses. Other reasons are political in nature. If you are required to provide private work areas for developers, who's next? Suddenly everyone in the company will be expecting a private office. The only corporate environment where I was able to attain private offices for my development staff was in a startup web based services company. Perhaps being a small organization and a part owner of the company was the difference.

If you run into the roadblocks mentioned here, your best alternative is to find a quiet, out of the way location in your facility and request the higher cube walls that help reduce the ambient noise. See the Reducing Resistance section in Chapter 7 for some ideas on how to best request these features.

CHAPTER 5

stress

Software development has become a routinely stressful activity in some organizations and in most organizations there are occasional periods of significantly high stress levels. The consequences of stress are extremely expensive and disruptive and some psychologists believe that stress has additive effects as well. By some estimates it's costing the U.S. and Europe over 120 billion dollars a year. That's a mind-numbing figure that should be a call to action for HR personnel and management worldwide. When you combine the costs of corporate stress with that of software failures in the U.S. (over $50 billion) it becomes a staggering number that just beckons for some meaningful answers.

Are the software failures the cause of the stress or is stress the cause of software failures? While it may seem more probable that stress is the cause of the software failures, the situation is obviously much more complex. Our legacy of recurrent software failures puts more pressure on development groups to deliver on time, thereby causing more stress regarding future projects from the outset. Our industry has garnered such an atrocious reputation for delivering behind schedule with unacceptable defect counts AND, in many cases, abridged feature sets. This has now become a major hurdle and focus for any large-scale project. From a stress standpoint, we're starting out in the hole even before the first line of code is written.

However, if you research the events in people's lives that are commonly agreed upon by psychologists to cause major levels of stress, software development is not usually very prominent on the list. Items such as divorce, loss of a family member, and unemployment typically top the stress level charts. However, with the track record just described, there must certainly be an abnormally high level of stress involved in software engineering. When projects are continually changing, adapting, and attempting to recover there will doubtless be many stressful moments along the way. Developers are being asked to accomplish appreciably more for less, especially as I write this book in 2011 when companies are under enormous pressures to reduce costs and optimize revenues. Those developers living in the U.S. and other Western countries must also be concerned about losing their jobs to offshore outsourcing firms, hence the magnified pressure to continually do more for less, with heightened worries to stay on schedule besides.

Our industry is not particularly well setup for efficiency. When product feature sets are in constant flux and build dates change on a regular basis, it's nearly impossible to be efficient. Inefficiency isn't the real culprit though. More realistically it's chaos and the unpredictable nature of one's work environment that becomes a primary stressor for many in our rapidly changing field.

Another major issue regarding stressful conditions in software engineering is that many technical professionals tend to avoid discussing topics of this nature. For many software professionals, being in touch with their feelings is not always foremost on their list. This may, at unexpected times, lead to explosive or other disruptive behavior but in numerous cases stressed out technical staff just quietly leave their employers and hope it will be less hectic somewhere else. Even if the new company isn't ultimately any better, at least you can wipe the slate clean, start over and enjoy your honeymoon period for a short time.

TYPES OF STRESS

Psychologists, and scientists in general, prefer to classify their findings, and stress is no different. Here are the "official" types of stress that psychologists and other health professionals commonly refer to.

Acute

This is what most people think of when they hear the term stress. Acute stress may be a result of the daily pressures and burdens of work or other hectic life events. Symptoms range from headaches and stomach aches to feelings of general agitation.

Episodic

This is technically known as episodic acute stress and is associated with recurrent episodes of acute stress. This may result from overly demanding jobs where there are continual high levels of stress.

This type of stress is more severe and may contribute to serious longer term health issues such as stroke, high blood pressure and depression.

Traumatic

This type of stress is usually associated with an extremely disturbing life event. This may be military combat or witnessing a mass murder such as some of the recent and infamous school shootings in America. People suffering from traumatic stress may be significantly impaired for long periods or in some cases, the rest of their lives.

Chronic

This is just what you might think. Stress on a regular basis day after day. This type of stress may quickly weaken immune systems and cause a variety of serious illnesses.

Most types of stress found in software engineering are likely to be Acute or in some cases Episodic. Those with Chronic stress often find alternative positions or new companies at which to ply their trade. In some cases those exhibiting Chronic stress will leave the industry altogether.

CAUSES OF STRESS

Before diving into the specific causes of stress it should be noted that there is a diverse response to the various stressors in the workplace. How a person perceives events is central to the amount of stress someone feels, along with their coping skills. What may be routinely stressful for one person may not cause any level of stress in someone else. Additionally, the exact same event that was stressful one day may not be stressful the next.

Lack of Control

When employees have little or no control of their work environment, they can become stressed. Most developers have very minimal control of what they are asked and expected to accomplish. They have requirements defined for them, many times without their input and often times these requirements are vague and incomplete. They will almost certainly have a timetable introduced by the Project Manager, again sometimes without any input, and then there are the changes that undoubtedly occur as the project comes into focus and the business people begin to see what they really have on their hands.

Responsibility

The amount of responsibility one has may contribute to stress. Being held accountable for the success of a large complex project may add a great deal of stress on top of the already existing day-to-day project stressors. Software professionals understand all of the possibilities that can go wrong and they realize they work in a risky profession. Those in positions of project responsibility have a great weight to bear, as they recognize the perils they may face.

Overload

Finishing tasks completely and on time can be challenging for many developers. There are times when we become stuck on a particularly devilish module or algorithm and it can be difficult to estimate how long it may take to finish. How long does it take an artist to finish a painting? There are few hard deadlines associated with a painting because it may be tricky to plan for inspiration. It comes when it's ready. That's how many complex algorithms are solved by software developers and it's not something that's easily predictable. You may have several remarkable inspirations in a single day and then none for a week or more. It's also quite certain that you are less likely to be inspired when under pressure to perform quickly. This is one reason why developers resort to short cuts, usually with the intention of returning later to rectify any poor coding techniques that were implemented. They may feel guilty about that approach too, possibly causing just as much stress as doing the job right the first time.

Ironically, technology itself contributes to the problem in significant ways. Smart phones and anywhere internet connections via WIFI or cellular connections can coerce us to being always "on" and available. The number of people in the United States who claim to be overworked has risen dramatically in recent years.

Dealing with Groups

This cause of stress is not one defined by most psychologists, but is quite real for some people in software development. As highlighted in the Personality chapter, our signature and prevailing personality trait is one of introversion for a great many of us, particularly developers. We generally prefer to work alone and enjoy getting in the zone, many times with headphones on, to shut out neighboring distractions and to avoid contact with others. When we are asked to solve a problem by group consensus we may become uncomfortable and when asked to give a public talk, even to a small group, we may actually launch into a full-blown anxiety attack. Dealing with the business side of the industry is annoying to some software professionals and therefore may contribute to stress levels.

STRESS RELIEF

These various types of stressors can be alleviated in numerous ways. Managers can coach employees on how to be more effective and provide a confident and caring atmosphere; and employees themselves can use relaxation techniques (including social support and other outlets) and visioning to help get them through difficult encounters.

Before we discuss the various techniques to reduce the effects of stressors, let's examine some factors that influence stress levels in individuals. The primary determinant in how someone will respond to a stressor is their personality. In the Personality chapter we defined the Type A personality. Briefly, it's someone who is most always in a hurry, exhibits competitive behavior, and has hostile tendencies. There are multiple traits then that constitute the Type A individual.

It just so happens that Type A people respond more negatively to stressors in their environments and often times the result can be increased hostility. Type B people however, usually react more calmly to stressors and display fewer out-bursts of hostile conduct. There are tradeoffs here of course. Type A people will typically accomplish more in a given period than a comparable Type B person. That is after all, the basic definition of a Type A personality. However, staffing your project with all Type A personalities could jeopardize your project and using all Type B personnel may put you perennially behind schedule. This is important when defining your development teams, especially if you expect the project to become intense due to the nature and importance of the mission. A mix of Type A and Type B personalities can be an effective strategy for staffing software projects. Usually this would be the case regardless of your desires, since it would be rare to have all members on your staff of a single type. However, for smaller projects you may want to keep this idea in the back of your mind.

Visioning

Several years ago I was required to make a presentation to the majority of employees at a mid-sized company at a prominent annual event. Even though I had delivered many casual talks and formal speeches in the past to large groups, this felt different to me because it was all the leaders of the company and my talk was regarding strategy, a topic I was less comfortable with, being new to that industry. I had somehow managed to get myself so worked up over this situation that I came to the point where I felt I could barely speak a word. Fortunately for me, the talk was delayed until the next day because other speakers went on excessively long. That night, while at home, I utilized a visioning technique and also had time to put things into their proper perspective. The visioning helped immensely as I was able to picture myself confidently before the group delivering my message and handling tricky questions with ease and grace (well mostly anyway). It also allowed me to predict some possible questions and rehearse my likely responses.

This took a while however. Putting the talk into perspective by realizing that my career probably wasn't in the balance helped me calm down. The next day I performed admirably during my talk and things didn't feel so terrible afterwards. There's another lesson here: when things seem bad, they're probably not as bad as you might think. On the other hand, when things seem to be going smoothly, they may not be as good as you believe either. This type of approach may help get you through the inevitable ups and downs of a lengthy career.

It turns out that there are numerous examples of known links between thinking about something (envisioning) and actually performing that same activity (Restak pg. 58). It so happens that neuroscientists have discovered, via brain scans, that the same areas of the brain (the anterior cingulate) are activated in either case, offering at least some scientific proof that rehearsing via visualization is a practical and viable technique. For example Rhesus monkeys, while watching a fellow monkey eat something, activates the same brain area as if he were actually eating himself. These are referred to by neuroscientists as mirror neurons because they are mirroring actual behavior.

Social Outlets

Having something important in your life that you enjoy doing outside the workplace is one of the best means for reducing stress. Ideally this will involve interactions with others that may provide support and listening. One of the best ways to reduce stress is to just talk about it with someone you trust. They may not even be required to say much, but just knowing that you have an outlet is important.

Some developers become easily obsessed and sidetracked with solving a software problem and will find themselves working long hours, even when they're not actually coding. They keep working the algorithm out in their minds until they think they have it just right and then they race for the nearest machine to see if indeed they are. Having the ability to code almost anywhere at any time is probably contributing to stress levels in our business, since people then don't get the required recuperation and social support they need from their outlets.

However, I've also witnessed developers I've worked with who slogged through several days of near round-the-clock development. When they finally emerged victorious, although physically exhausted, they were elated and thrilled with their experience. Rather than causing stress, they seemed to be on a high having succeeded in their quest. Of course had they failed, who knows what might have happened. So stress is definitely dependent upon how one interprets and manages potential stressors in their life.

Supportive Managers

Managers can have a considerable impact on how a team member feels regarding a high-pressure project. Supporting people during these times is crucial and it's best done with a frequent amount of small doses. Checking in with them daily and keeping them abreast of the bigger picture and how they contribute helps teams look beyond the stressful nature of the project and towards the final outcome. Also, letting them know that this will actually end at some point may be reassuring. Another way managers can help is by simply asking what they can do to relieve some of the perceived pressure. Maybe taking care of some of their other duties, even personal ones can be helpful. Listening is also good, but be careful to not encourage team members to engage in rants. These will typically not help. While at one time the Behaviorist Psychologists thought that catharsis was healing and therapeutic, it turns out that this is usually not the case. When people become enraged they must eventually validate their actions and in order to do so it usually means coming to the conclusion that their outburst was justified by the situation. The thought process goes something like this: since I'm a good corporate citizen and a loyal, hardworking employee I wouldn't act like this without having a good reason. Therefore, they must provide the reason and the reason may be that they're in a lousy company or working on a terrible project. This may leave them actually feeling worse about the project or whatever precipitated their emotional eruption originally.

Proper Job Selection

There are many types of positions within a software organization and some people struggle finding the right type of work for themselves at first. Some graduate from college or technical school with a programming degree or certificate only to find that they really don't enjoy programming in a professional setting. They may end up in QA or working as a database administrator for example. It can be difficult during training to determine what your calling really is because there's more to it than just the actual technical workings. The teamwork and flow of the job can be vastly different than completing an assignment for a class. I have yet to meet a project manager that knew while they were attending school that they would ultimately become a PM. The same is true for most quality assurance professionals that I am acquainted with and I've worked with hundreds of QA professionals. Once people get in the IT department, they can experiment and learn where their strengths really lie and then pursue them with the help of their manager or possibly another manager. I once recruited a woman from a call center to become a junior DBA because of her aptitude and proactive nature. As far as I know she is still in this field today after nearly 15 years.

Finding the right path, the one that provides challenges and regular successes, can sometimes take years or in extreme cases even decades. If you struggle and don't feel as though you're on the proper career path, it will inevitably produce stress and you will need to seek out professional help. I've had many technical staff come to me asking where I thought they would best fit in the organization and once they find that ideal match their productivity and spirits soar and it is very fulfilling for all parties. For some unknown reason, most people outside of our profession don't seem to know about all of the different roles that exist within a development group. BA, QA, DBA, PM, Tech Writer and Release Manager are all important roles that can provide rewarding careers in software without writing a single line of code. Once someone finds the right position, the stress levels will drop and productivity and happiness will flourish. Many technical organizations actually prefer to have staff undertake different roles over time for numerous reasons. One is to find that potential diamond in the rough and another is to provide backup roles for departmental emergencies. But perhaps the best reason to do so is because people who have seen development from all sides will become indispensable assets for any development team. A former QA person who later becomes a BA knows how important it is to create properly documented testable requirements for example. Many project managers started out as developers or BAs so that they better understand the multiple facets of the business.

Seligman, in his revolutionary book, *Authentic Happiness*, describes the concept of signature strengths. Determining your signature strengths, and finding a vocation that utilizes them every day, is the key to fulfillment in both your professional life and in your life overall. Seligman's web site www.authentichappiness.org has a number of free on-line instruments that enable you to determine your level of happiness and your signature strengths. I have a firsthand view of this exact situation being in the consulting business. A consultant could have one assignment where they struggle mightily and other engagements, only a few months later, where they have clear sailing and deliver superior results. A large percentage of their success will depend upon the precise nature of their duties and the unique mix of personalities involved on the project team.

STRESS AND PERFORMANCE

Negative Impacts

While there is evidence that some moderate levels of stress can contribute to increased performance, there happens to be an inverted U shaped graph, depicted below in Figure 5.1, which shows how increasing stress levels eventually causes a precipitous drop in performance. This happens once stress reaches a certain tipping point that can vary widely for different people. The term to define those people who can withstand higher, sustained levels of stress is **Hardiness**. Hardy people have learned how to cope with stress and in some cases even embrace it. This may be because they have a strong locus of control and believe that they can positively influence outcomes. Hardy people may also view acutely stressful situations as personal challenges and therefore are better equipped to cope with the circumstances.

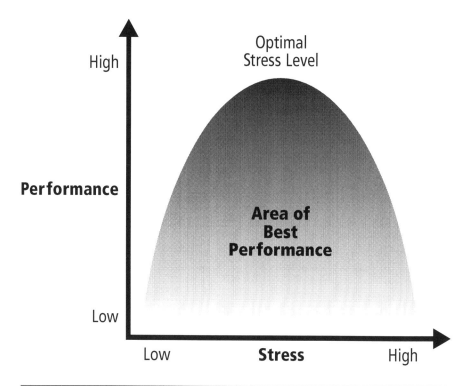

FIGURE 5.1

Additionally, stress increases the probability that someone will rely on heuristics, or cognitive short cuts, for decision making rather than considering a more exhaustive set of alternatives (Kavanagh, 2005). However, there are instances where employing heuristics can actually result in equally attractive solutions while also saving time. Group decision-making under stressful conditions may result in lower status members conceding to higher status members, thereby reducing the overall effectiveness of the entire group by considering fewer alternative solution options.

Over the past several decades, researchers have found that college students in the United States are scoring more and more on the external locus of control. This concept was introduced in the Generation Gap section earlier. This means they perceive that circumstances in their lives are essentially outside of their control. This is an alarming trend and it would be interesting to know if this is occurring in other countries as well. Improved mental health and psychological well-being is associated with one having perceived control in how they experience positive or negative effects. If you sense that you have little or no control over the affairs in your life you may experience elevated levels of stress. However, it is possible for people to have an internal locus of control in some areas of their life while experiencing an external of locus of control in areas where they have less skill or experience.

Benefits

While it may seem somewhat illogical to think there are benefits to stress, there do appear to be at least a few. Many of these benefits seem to materialize later, however, after the stressor has been relieved. The lions' share of the benefits seems to be a result of Cognitive Dissonance. Studies on hazing for contingency of group acceptance (think fraternities here) show that people who have been hazed feel much more strongly attached to the group or organization of which they are now a member. The logic behind their thinking goes something like this: "I must really value this organization to have put myself through that ordeal." Many rational people would not normally subject themselves to the hazing that occurs on college campuses as part of a fraternity or sorority rush. Therefore they need to reduce the dissonance in their actions by convincing themselves that the group really is worth the membership benefits.

I've been involved in many difficult and challenging projects where I have formed a strong bond with the other team members because of what we collectively experienced. Lastly, it appears that some moderate levels of stress keep projects moving forward. Completely stress free projects (if that's even possible) could languish and may likely be late and over budget. Finding that moderate level of pressure is the key to optimal development.

CHAPTER 6

Cognitive Malware

UNDERSTANDING COGNITIVE DISSONANCE

Considered one of the biggest "discoveries" in the entire field of psychology, Cognitive Dissonance, the basis for confirmation bias and self-justification, has possibly spawned more psychological studies than any other single concept over the last 50 years. In my mind, cognitive dissonance explains a large portion of human behavior and is one of the cornerstones of human psychology. Therefore, a more detailed review of this phenomenon will be explored along with its potential significance within software development, which I believe is profound and yet at times a bit subtle.

First off, let's define the basic concept, just for review since you're probably already familiar with the term from your Psychology 101 course. Originally coined by social psychologist Leon Festinger in 1957, cognitive dissonance is the state of holding two contradictory beliefs, or cognitions, in one's mind at the same time. For example, I'm a health conscious person and I love to eat most any type of dessert. These two ideas don't really go together. They create dissonance within my mind. Something has to give. So in my mind I need to justify that eating lots of desserts maybe isn't that bad, after all there aren't any trans fats in most of these products. They're vitamin fortified and you do need some carbohydrates and glucose to keep functioning. The other alternative is to convince myself that I do many other things as part of my health consciousness, such as diligently taking the stairs at work. Either way something has to give when two contradictory thoughts are held in someone's mind at the same time. Of course, the final and ultimate alternative is to change one's behavior, but that is usually considerably more complicated as it likely involves changing long-standing and dominant personal habits and associated lifestyles.

The basic thought process proceeds as follows: "How could I, being a reasonable and intelligent person, eat lots of candies and other deserts knowing that it is detrimental to my health?" The "reasonable and intelligent" factor contradicts causing harm to one's health. Most reasonable and intelligent people will not purposely inflict harm on themselves. And of course we all think of ourselves as "reasonable and intelligent," especially, I might add, us technical people. Typically, if someone doesn't believe that they are reasonable and intelligent then they may have other psychological problems. I have met very few people in our profession who do not think of themselves as highly talented, at least in terms of their primary job duties.

So now that we've reviewed the basic premise, here are the ramifications. People will do almost anything to reduce dissonance, once it's "declared" to be there. It's an exceptionally uncomfortable feeling; this constant idea that one is doing something inconsistent with who they identify themselves to be. In essence, as long as dissonance is present we are in conflict with ourselves and must eventually resolve it in some way. This is the crux of the issue for us humans and it's one of the basic ways we separate ourselves from animals.

Reducing Dissonance

As a predominantly logical and analytical group, we realize that there are really only three fundamental ways to reduce dissonance: we can change our behavior to align with the belief originally causing the dissonance (e.g. quit eating too many desserts); or we can alter one of the dissonant cognitions (my grandfather ate large quantities of desserts for 70 years and lived until he was 92, therefore desserts can't be that bad); or lastly we can create new consonant cognitions (desserts help me keep my stress levels down and that's a much healthier alternative for me). Are any of these beginning to sound familiar?

People may employ one or more of these methods to help reduce their poor self-image, but many times it will be the last two methods that are chosen. It's somewhat more rare, and much more difficult, for people to change their behavior, especially for the long term. Just look at the increased incidence of poor health in the United States while at the same time we have much more health care information available to us and access to more and better therapies. While many people do change their behavior (at least temporarily anyway), the problems occur when the last two strategies are invoked to reduce dissonance.

Cognitive Dissonance – Looking under the hood

Hordes of studies have been conducted on Cognitive Dissonance since Festinger first introduced the topic in 1957. Studies of this magnitude generate a surplus of academic attention and many psychologists were quick to point out possible flaws in the theory. What the ensuing research essentially determined was that it's the inconsistent behavior that triggers dissonance, but only under certain circumstances.

Generally, the decisions that lead to inconsistency must be made by us and not forced upon us by a superior or someone with higher positional power. After all, if we believe that we really had no choice in a behavior or decision then little or no dissonance will be created within us. The behavior in question must also lead to some type of aversive result. If everything turns out okay, then what's the problem? And lastly, at least for our purposes, the poor or unexpected results must not have been anticipated. If we had no way of knowing that our actions could have caused a problem, it is doubtful that any dissonance is generated within us. These caveats are important to note and they will be significant later, especially in regard to **Sunk Costs** on escalating software projects. The Sunk Cost Effect is where people are compelled to expend more resources in order to justify the resources exhausted on previous efforts. It's also known as, "throwing good money after bad."

The Varied Ways of Confirmation Bias

Confirmation Bias is a rather simple concept on the surface, but perhaps nothing is a more powerful determinant of human behavior. I believe it is both pervasive and detrimental in the software development field. Its definition is easily understood. People tend to confirm what they already believe, which is essentially a means used to keep dissonance in check. Thinking that you've strongly supported some particular technology or solutions camp over the course of many years, which may not always be the optimal choice, will almost assuredly cause some level of dissonance.

Raymond Nickerson (1998), in his extraordinary landmark paper, provides excellent support for the concept and the assorted ways it exposes itself. Once a person has laid claim to a position on some topic, subsequent behavior is primarily to justify that position rather than seek out other more suitable positions on said topic. According to Nickerson, and he provides ample evidence, people will focus their attention on their favored hypothesis, give preferential treatment to evidence only supporting their favored position, and they will overweight positive evidence and underweight any negative data relative to their stance. Basically people will find what they are looking for regardless of the facts. We conveniently ignore dissonant data and dwell on the consonant.

In a U.S. based political study it was found that people who are Democrats will side with positions if they know it was supported by the Democratic Party, even though it was a traditional Republican Party stance. Before all of you Republicans get too arrogant, the study applies when the parties are reversed as well. It's exceptionally taxing to avoid confirming our strongly held biases.

The consequences for software development are significant here. We have our own version of Democrats and Republicans in our field. Microsoft versus Java is an obvious and noteworthy example and there are many others as well. We become entrenched, and waste excessive amounts of time, bantering about the benefits and pitfalls of certain technologies because we have taken a strong posture and don't want to admit we may be wrong periodically regarding our preferred flavor of technology.

Another interesting concern of note is that confirmation bias is an equal opportunity bias. That is, if someone is biased in your favor you achieve only good things in their eyes, regardless of your actual behavior. However, the opposite also holds true. Once you find yourself in someone's (say your supervisor's) bad graces, it can become extremely difficult to invalidate and escape this situation. That is, no matter what you accomplish, however wonderful and successful, it may be viewed in a negative light because of the prevailing bias against you. If you should find yourself in this exasperating position, especially with your supervisor, it must be addressed immediately. You must confront your supervisor and discuss, very specifically, his expectations of your performance. You might also have exhaustive examples prepared of what you consider to be your achievements and how they compare to others in the group. This may be an uncomfortable conversation to initiate with your supervisor, but things will almost certainly not improve without some type of intervention on your part.

COGNITIVE DISSONANCE IN SOFTWARE DEVELOPMENT

Software developers are prone to basically two major classes of errors; the first being algorithmic in nature and the other involving the misinterpretation of

THE POWER OF COGNITIVE DISSONANCE

Over the centuries many cults and sects have predicted the end of the world by various means. While these groups' forecasts have obviously been erroneous, it's far more fascinating to note the subsequent behavior of the group members. Several decades ago Festinger and two of his colleagues managed to infiltrate just such a group. This Chicago based faction believed that the world was going to come to an end, via massive flooding, on a predetermined date that they happened to be privy to (December 21 – winter solstice in Chicago).

Fortunately, those group members who believed in the teachings of the "Guardian," via "automatic writings," would survive the ensuing catastrophe. The believers were to be whisked away to safety by a spacecraft of some type, presumably to another planet. One notable behavior (among others) was identified by Festinger's team. That is, the group members were so completely devoted to this mission that they made grave and irrevocable changes in their personal lives such as quitting good jobs and abandoning their families. Some members were even threatened with legal actions from neighbors and family members. The essential point here is that there was such a complete commitment to the beliefs of the group by many of the members that would be hard to later refute.

Of course, no spaceship arrived and there was no flooding. The group was absolutely devastated and was yearning for answers. They had come too far, had made too many commitments and burned too many bridges to be wrong. Eventually the group leader received more messages from the Guardian exclaiming that because of their devout beliefs, the flooding was spared and therefore no emergency space craft was necessary.

What happened next was intriguing. The group members took to the streets and told anyone who would listen of the good fortune of the world being spared from certain disaster. The group leader made calls to newspapers and wire services declaring the good news.

Festinger and his team had predicted these results based upon the principles of cognitive dissonance. They realized that because the members had so completely committed themselves to this cause, they somehow just had to be right. Admitting they were wrong would have meant psychological suicide. Therefore, changing their cognitions to align with their irrefutable actions was the only sensible recourse. (Adapted from Tavris & Aronson, 2007; Cialdini, 2007; and others.)

requirements. They make plenty of other routine errors of course, like everyone else, such as poor priority setting, procrastination and such but in terms of core fundamental errors that's about it. It's much easier to deal with the latter errors than the former because it doesn't hurt as much, that is, it doesn't generate as much cognitive dissonance. There's really only one person to fault for an error in programming logic, but the requirements issues can be spread about the group. The BA didn't properly or fully describe the feature set or use the proper terminology, etc. The DBA told me to implement it that way because it would be easier for him. However, when the programmer causes a major flaw in logic it could easily facilitate some measure of dissonance within the developers mind. "How could I, being such a solid coder as I am, program such a fundamental logic flaw as that?" – is the thinking that may preoccupy the programmer's thoughts. This dissonance must now be reduced using one of the methods outlined earlier. It will likely go something like this: "Well I really didn't have time to fully implement the code the way I wanted to"; or perhaps an alternative tact may be taken such as: "I was planning to come back and revise that code later after everything else was in place." These are all weak attempts to reduce dissonance and many times the developer will truly believe this to be the case.

Code Reviews

The astute reader will perhaps see a way to capitalize on this situation. Code reviews, used by some organizations, although far too few, are really employing the power of cognitive dissonance. To a large degree these reviews work automatically. When programmers know in advance that they have an upcoming code review scheduled, they will work extremely diligently to prevent any dissonance. In this case they're changing their behavior rather than their thoughts, but there are times when they employ the tactics mentioned earlier, such as "I was planning to revise that code section later when all the logic was completely flushed out." You might get more of this type of response if you don't provide sufficient lead-time for reviews. Programmers do require ample time to make the suitable code changes so it's important when using code reviews to plan them well in advance or you will end up with altered cognitions instead of improved code. It's also imperative to make sure that enough of their peers are in attendance and when I refer to peers I mean coders they consider equal or superior (if there is such a thing!) After that, just get out of the way and let cognitive dissonance do the work for you (well it's not quite that simple). I've been involved in many code reviews where several of the attendees did not really follow the algorithms completely, but the developer, in walking the others through their code, resolves many of his issues during the process. He will not know when or if a programming colleague is not following his logic flow during the review so he must remain on his toes. For as straightforward as code reviews are, they provide a potent mechanism for improving software quality and reigning in runaway schedules. However, it is essential that these reviews are moderated by a staff person with positional power so that they don't become a "my coding techniques are better than yours" session. If this happens the meeting may soon lose its primary focus and possibly become contentious and counterproductive.

More evidence in support of code reviews was found in a study by Mitroff (1974). He found that professionals spent the majority of their time confirming rather than attempting to falsify their own hypotheses. This is what we discovered earlier with confirmation bias. However, when it came to other professionals, they were more than willing to attempt to falsify their hypotheses. So it appears that people will confirm their own work but attempt to falsify the work of others, a perfect recipe for implementing code reviews for everyone.

Author Joseph Hallinan, in his book *Why We Make Mistakes*, claims that as something becomes more familiar to us, we tend to notice the details less and not more, as you might expect. So, developers that have been slaving over their code for days or weeks may not always see the obvious defects, yet another potential advantage of code reviews.

It turns out that there's a preponderance of scientific evidence in support of implementing code reviews. However, with many organizations now using some variant of Agile development, most software professionals think that code reviews are passé. I would argue that in an Agile era code reviews are even more relevant because Agile methodologies tend to promote development speed over process, to some extent anyway. Some developers prefer Agile approaches because they think of it as coding without documentation, causing great heartache for QA and BA professionals who rely heavily on documentation for their efforts. Organizations who consider implementing Agile type methodologies would be wise to clearly define expectations for all parties at the outset of the project.

Developers and Testers

Another area where cognitive dissonance comes into play is when developers are required to test their own code. Not unit testing, but rather system testing in a small application where one developer may have developed the bulk of the code.

The foremost cognitive tripwire is the strong urge the developer has for NOT discovering any defects. After all, he knows that he likely introduced them in the first place and this may generate some amount of dissonance. Some developers in this situation will then only develop test cases they expect to pass, since they understand how the programming logic works. I can't count the number of times I've heard this famous line from developers (including myself); "Why would anyone ever do that?" We're referring to why a user would attempt to use the system in a particular way we never intended. Developers as testers may also find themselves performing less negative testing. Negative testing hits the special cases category pretty hard and many developers prefer to focus primarily on the "happy path." After all, why would someone ever do that?

Developers who do test their own code also know that they will almost assuredly be required to remediate the modules causing the problems. This is one more reason to only test the oft-travelled happy path.

Know-It-Alls and Cognitive Dissonance

The amount or severity of cognitive dissonance may also play a role in its manifestation of behavioral changes. It's theorized that people who consider themselves experts in some discipline have a noticeably more difficult time admitting that they've made a mistake or even in some cases having just performed a task at a nominal level. It reminds me of the old saying, "I remember making a mistake one time, I thought I was wrong." Therefore, if you have a standout technical person on staff it will almost certainly be harder for them to admit to design, coding or other technical discrepancies. Being the source of a serious flaw creates plenty of dissonance within acclaimed experts' minds and hence the dissonance reducing behaviors that characteristically follow. The typical self-justifying responses from top end technical people are usually along the lines of: "Well if I had known what you really meant by that requirement" or "of course it wasn't going to work once we made those last minute design changes."

According to Tavris and Aronson (2007), when experts turn out to be wrong, their professional identities are threatened and therefore the more confident and famous they are, the less likely they will admit to wrong doings. So there can undoubtedly be drawbacks to consulting with those who deem themselves experts.

This is also what is referred to as our psychological immune system, much like our bodies physical immune system. We need to protect ourselves from becoming mentally "diseased" or emotionally injured and so we merrily justify our behaviors so that we don't become overtaken by despair and come to realize that we're an absolute failure. We may well misfire many times a day, some more serious than others, so there is inherent value in having our psychological immune systems prepared to keep our self-esteem at a steady functioning level.

Self-Esteem and Expert Risks

Studies have shown that experts, at least those with high self-esteem (an expert by the way isn't always what I refer to as a Know It All – Know It Alls have an air of superiority about them whereas experts may or may not have this attitude) are more likely to make the riskiest decisions, at least in cases where the stakes are not too high (see Sunk Costs below for more information). Low self-esteem people may be reserved when posed with making a potentially risky decision so as not to damage their self-esteem any further. Of course experts may well have the ability to make sound decisions in risky situations; the problem comes when someone has high self-esteem but is not technically capable of making the decision at hand. Some studies have shown that people with high self-esteem are more than ten times likely to make the riskiest decision available when compared to low self esteem people. These results have been found in studies involving relatively minor decisions in a laboratory setting, so it's not exactly clear how they might extrapolate to software related decisions.

Commitment and Dissonance

There was a rather famous cognitive dissonance experiment conducted decades ago by Knox and Inkster (1968) where they surveyed horse racing bettors just prior to placing their bets and then again just afterwards. The bettors expressed much more confidence in their bets just after they placed them compared to before. Just to be clear, racetracks will not let you change your bet once it is completed. You can make another bet, but you can't reverse or cancel bets once they have been made. People are much more confident in their decisions once they know they can't change their decision. After all, the thinking goes, I wouldn't make such a ridiculous bet as horse number 5 winning race number 2 would I? Once the bet is made, in order to justify your behavior, horse number 5 is doubtless looking like a sure thing.

This now circles us back to Fred Brooks' retractable medium discussion we had earlier. In the software domain many people feel that you can change your mind. That you indeed can reverse and undo prior commitments because, after all, it's just software. And while this may be technically true, even though there may be serious cost and schedule ramifications down the road, this creates a somewhat unusual and unique situation for software professionals. If we are more confident in decisions that we cannot change and we believe that we can actually change our software decisions, does that mean we are not always confident in our original software related decisions in the first place? Do we make different decisions originally going into it knowing that we can always change or undo them later? I think this may actually be the case, at least in some circumstances. We know, way back in the crevices of our mind, that we can always change something that's not quite right if we absolutely must. We never really need to commit, especially when it comes to web based applications that are quite malleable and can therefore be frequently updated and uploaded into instant production. I see this pattern with many web agencies, companies that design and build web sites and web based applications for their clients. Having worked at SWAT Solutions for many years, a software quality assurance consulting boutique, I see a lot of this type of behavior.

This retractable medium concept may not always be such a problem then, at least psychologically. We don't need to cling to our software related decisions to save face with ourselves and others. We don't need to rationalize and justify our choices that we made previously because we can't undo them. Perhaps it even liberates us to make better decisions later, when they become more obvious, because we haven't had to convince ourselves that we were right in the first place because we were firmly locked into a permanent solution.

Effort Justification, Sunk Costs and Completion Effect

Two common manifestations of cognitive dissonance observed in technical projects are **Effort Justification** and the related **Sunk Costs Effect**. Both are coupled with people's tendencies to forge ahead on projects where they have experienced anguish or distress due to the project OR where they have exerted a tremendous amount and have a lot of "skin in the game." People are striving for consistency in their actions, at least those actions that other people have witnessed. Therefore, technical people attempt to justify their Herculean efforts on technical projects so that they don't appear foolish, and in some cultures, wasteful.

Other ways in which these effects are evident in society at large are fraternity and sorority initiation rituals. These long established factions have survived for a reason; they know that hazing their new troops will ultimately increase their loyalty and commitment to the group and thus the group's longevity and success. Gang membership has similar, albeit more severe, entrance requirements where some members must perform severe acts of violence to be accepted as members "in good standing." Once you've gone to extreme measures to be part of a group or an idea, it will be awfully hard to convince yourself it wasn't worth the effort. We constantly strive to justify our behaviors so that we appear consistent to ourselves and others.

There are studies that have been conducted specifically within the software development domain that suggest that in some cases doomed projects continue for reasons other than what effort justification or sunk costs might explain. It is referred to as the **Completion Effect** where some people, and therefore organizations, are compelled to "finish what they started" especially as they near the anticipated conclusion of a large project. This problem is most likely exacerbated by the inclination of software projects to be labeled at 90% or higher completion for a great deal longer than deserved. No one in our industry wants to be associated with an abandoned project because we feel as though we wasted our time and worse yet, we might appear incompetent. Management especially doesn't want to abandon a project, because they're held responsible for the decision.

In my first professional programming engagement, as a new college graduate, several of my projects within the first three years were cancelled outright. It left me feeling a bit empty. Yes, I was paid for my efforts the same as if they were completed, but I certainly did not feel fulfilled and had a desire to justify my work by convincing myself that I was learning new technologies and programming techniques. Research has also shown that uncompleted tasks will be remembered much more than those tasks that were finished (Moon, 2001). This is certainly the case for me as the projects I mentioned above took place long ago, yet I can still vividly remember the circumstances surrounding them. In fact, I can actually remember exactly where I was sitting when I received the cancellation news from my supervisor for one particular project. I have participated in many completed projects and these don't stand out like those that have been abruptly cancelled.

Further studies show some support that a vicious concoction of sunk cost effects combined with completion effect pressures may exacerbate the tendency to escalate projects. This means that those projects which are out of control have a strong inclination to remain that way. They've been launched into orbit so to speak, never to return. Once you're seemingly very close to finishing a large, expensive project it's that much tougher to completely abandon it. This is where senior management must be capable of visualizing the bigger picture and making appropriate decisions, some that may be hard for even themselves to defend.

To me the common denominator for all the project extension structures featured here is to justify ones actions as being reasonable and consistent. People try to protect themselves from looking foolish and this is particularly true when it comes to technical professionals whose reputations are on the line. Not being able to finish a project could be interpreted as a sign of technical incompetence to others. I would suggest that this is one of the most feared situations for nearly all technical people. See the discussion in Chapter 3 for more information on Project Escalation and Abandonment.

One final thought on project completion; when a protracted project begins to wind down, some technical professionals may become reckless and resort to various short cuts in an effort to finish. Getting through the project may now take precedence over getting it right and standards may be lowered. Developers may become distracted thinking more about the upcoming project than the current one. This is a time ripe for mundane errors to creep into your project – the ones that make you shake your head when they're discovered.

Dissonance and Overconfidence

There is a wide body of literature on overconfidence in the archives of psychology. Most of the research concludes that in many cases people are unjustified in their confidence in a variety of task types. Blanton et al (2000) claim, that at least in some cases, our overconfidence is a result of cognitive dissonance reduction. We have a strong desire to view ourselves as competent individuals, leading us to have overconfidence in ourselves. Further research in this field by Moore and Healy (2008) has attempted to decompose overconfidence into more distinct components; overestimation, overplacement, and overprecision.

Overestimation refers to one's capacity to overstate their ability to perform a certain task. Overplacement is when people perceive themselves to be better than others. This is also referred to as the **Better-Than-Average Effect**. It turns out that just about everyone believes that they're better than average and this includes those people not living in Lake Wobegon (read Garrison Keillor if you don't get the connection) and most assuredly programmers, architects and a host of other technical professionals. That is why the majority of you reading this book will suppose that most of the examples and research contained within do not actually apply to you, but surely there will be someone out there that will benefit from this information. This type of thinking appears to be universal and undoubtedly constrains countless of us from achieving our inherent potential.

Overprecision is an unwarranted confidence regarding the accuracy of one's beliefs. To summarize the key findings of Moore and Healy for our concerns, people will on average, overestimate their performance on tasks of a more difficult nature while underestimating their performance on easier tasks. For software projects, overestimating performance is not where we want to be. Overestimating one's performance means underestimating the time and effort required for the task. This lends support to our planning problems that were previously highlighted in Chapter 3.

Earlier we discussed the concept of Anchoring in software estimation. When you think about whom it is in most organizations that provides your estimates, or makes project escalation decisions, you'll probably realize that it's the smartest and most experienced staff members who are the ones chiefly involved. As it so happens, it's usually precisely these people who are guilty of displaying the most overconfidence and if they also happen to be male (which is likely) the effect may be even more pronounced. These are also the people who are least likely to admit to mistakes. When you mix all of these psychological ingredients together, you may end up with a recipe for trouble.

CHAPTER 7

Influence, Persuasion & Social Pressure

As a group I think you'd have to agree that quite a few of us engaged in the software profession are not especially influential and persuasive by nature. That's a pretty broad statement of course, and some refinement and further clarification is warranted. There are many notable exceptions including some very suave CIOs, domineering project managers and others who are naturally more outgoing. But by and large, these seem to be the exceptions within our space rather than the norm, and this deficiency may be the root cause of some of our troubles.

Why this is the case is largely due to the personality of people drawn to our industry as discussed in detail in the Personality section. When one speaks rarely or infrequently and prefers not to socialize much, it becomes quite difficult to be persuasive or influential. Another major cause is that this is not a skill most of us practice or for that matter are required to exercise on a regular basis. Lastly, some of us may not have been exposed to these types of proficiencies while growing up. If one's parents did not possess or exhibit these skills regularly then the learning opportunities while we were developing were just not there for the absorption. We also know that roughly 50% of our personality traits are inherited, so perhaps we came this way from the factory.

However, regardless of our skills and proficiencies in terms of influence or persuasion, we need to understand how we may be taken advantage of or susceptible to providing or performing something that others may cherish. This may not always be premeditated behavior; it may just happen when people are distressed. Regardless, when we are confronted with situations we inherently perceive as unfair, we at times lack the requisite social skills to remedy the issue while at the same time not ruffling too many feathers. Like a schoolboy who is being bullied we may sometimes respond by just taking it, by removing ourselves from the circumstances altogether or worse yet exploding at the other party. Usually, in a business setting, the former is more likely to be the case than the latter. When the crisis is over we then feel disappointed that we weren't able to speak up for ourselves effectively. The words just didn't come to us quickly enough and we probably had a dazed look upon our face as we tried to comprehend what was really happening. Then suddenly the others are gone and we just agreed to add some complicated new feature set that may well necessitate overtime to deliver. So let's now take a look at some of the specific techniques that we occasionally become victim to and how to react to them more appropriately.

THE POWER OF OTHERS

Software groups seem to be exceptionally susceptible to what others think of their development knowledge and prowess. On the whole, we don't like to appear as lacking in our development skills and overall comprehension of the latest coding techniques or processes. Bragging rights are a big deal for software professionals. When you feel this way you're liable to be influenced by others and have a tendency to succumb to conformity. I've often wondered how developers would have responded to the classic Asch experiments done in the 1950s (see sidebar in Chapter 11, Teams). On the one hand we pride ourselves in being technically accurate and correct and on the other we don't want to look like numbskulls in front of our peers.

Types of Social Influence

There are two generic forms of social influence identified by Social Psychologists; Normative and Informational. Normative influence is when people conform to be accepted under the norms of society or a particular subgroup. Non-conforming behaviors can, in rare and extreme cases, lead to death as was the case with Dietrich Bonhoffer, a religious resister during the Nazi control of Germany. Informational influence on the other hand is when people look to others to pick up cues, or information, about what is happening around them. This has also been coined **Social Proof** by Robert Cialdini, a social psychologist with considerable expertise in persuasion. That is, we look at how other people are reacting to an ambiguous situation in order to determine how we ourselves should respond. By looking at how others are responding we have social proof in determining what we believe is actually happening.

As development people go, I see many occasions when they will use Social Proof to determine how they ought to best respond when outside their particular domain of expertise, say in a business or marketing meeting of some kind. An example would be when a person on the business side, let's say a sales person, makes an offhand comment. The technical people may be unsure how to respond initially. Is it a joke or a serious statement? Not being sure, they check how others are responding so they know if they should muster up a chuckle or take the comment seriously. But beyond just checking to see how others respond, we typically will look to see how other people similar to us in the meeting are responding, in case we happen to be the butt of the joke.

Techniques of Influence

As a prelude to this topic I would advise that business people are not the enemy. At times, we can be our own worst enemy and I highly doubt that business people are continually scheming against us. It's doubtful that they're research-ing obscure and effective ways to control and influence software profession-als in their spare time. Rather, these are normal techniques they have possibly acquired unconsciously over the years and many may have been a part of their social upbringing. The business team has their objectives and they will attempt to find the most expeditious means to accomplish them, just like any other group.

Reducing Resistance

A common method for getting what one wants is to accomplish it in incre-mental steps rather than all at once. This is also referred to as the **Foot-in-the-Door Technique**. Once you've appealed for a relatively minor task or favor from someone it becomes much easier for them to ask for subsequent larger favors or tasks. Cognitive dissonance compels us to be consistent and once we've done someone a favor, why wouldn't we do it again? After all, they must have been deserving of my favor or I would not have obliged.

A related technique is to request a large favor that is fully expected to be refused, only to be followed by the intended smaller request later. By contrast the second request appears much more reasonable than the first request. Whether this is actually used intentionally or not, I do notice this type of behavior more frequently than the Foot-in-the-Door method.

Ingratiation

In my experience, technical people are susceptible to this method of influence. Many a business conversation with technical people will begin with a line similar to: "You're a smart and reasonable person ..." Because we pride ourselves on our technical acumen and intelligence our brains provide us a squirt of dopamine when we hear these endearing words. This puts us in a good frame of mind and we become more receptive to their requests, because after all: "they're right, I'm smart and reasonable and therefore I'll listen." I'm moderately sure that most technical people don't fall prey to this one, but those with larger egos who also happen to have an established relationship with the potential influencer may be vulnerable, especially when this happens in front of others. The victim may unconsciously be attempting to live up to the attributes of the influencer and now feels more compelled to demonstrate his reasonableness and intelligence. Many of us relish the opportunity to espouse our vast technical knowledge and by doing so we sometimes make unintended commitments that we then feel compelled to uphold.

Liking

Someone is much more likely to cooperate and collaborate with you if they have a particular fondness for you. Not in an intimate or sexual way (although this can be a problem that crops up in the workplace that will not be addressed here). In many software development environments there is natural competitiveness between the business areas and the development teams. This varies tremendously by company and more companies ought to be spending significantly larger efforts to get these teams working together rather than against each other. While a certain competitive level between these groups may actually allow them to professionally challenge each other and improve overall development efforts and quality, for many companies it has devolved into dysfunction. Over time members of these groups may have forgotten why they "hate the enemy," the culture has been established and it becomes a classic rivalry.

Most of us will likely admit that we software developers are not very approachable at times. We may become defensive when challenged, our interpersonal skills may not be as smooth as our business counterparts, and we aren't particularly verbose. We may well be thinking very actively while people are talking with us but our thoughts may not get expressed properly, if at all. This may be slightly more prevalent among male developers.

One principal method for increasing liking and influence is just spending time together. Numerous studies have shown that spending face time with others will naturally increase liking and cooperation. I've often encouraged my technical reports to spend time with the business and sales teams. When people don't spend enough time with each other they will naturally create suspicions and distrust of the others over time. They establish the creation of the "us vs. them" condition. They might hear some negative remark from a third party or read a forwarded email out of context. Nearly every time I've requested people to meet (or do it for myself) it generates positive results. They realize that the other person is basically good and wellintentioned and they can begin to better understand their issues and concerns. Doing this outside the confines of resolving a particular problem is even better. Go to lunch together or a sporting event and really get to know the other person, independent of the business environment and before a problem arises. Corporate softball teams, golf leagues and other similar activities can facilitate the creation of positive bonds and relationships that may bear fruit in the work environment. It can also act as a social outlet for stress relief. The problem with many of these activities is that they're segregated. The business people have their functions and the software developers have their own. Lately, it appears that many corporate organized activities have disappeared altogether because companies are under budget duress and strict timelines. Some activities are organized by volunteer employee clubs outside of normal work hours and these are great ways to get to know other employees beyond just the technical ones you already know.

Most developers will avoid, rather than spend extra time with, the business people. One potential cure here is to spend some of your free time with those that present you with the most difficulty. Doing so within a group will ease things for us, yet still reap benefits. Avoiding the person entirely will usually make matters worse.

WINNING OTHERS OVER

Physical Traits

Research shows that we generally prefer people who appear to be similar to ourselves. This usually begins with physical attributes and much of this interpretation happens automatically within our minds. So right out of the shoot we have a deviation with our business partners – they will typically be dressed in suits or at worst in business casual attire and we will most likely be wearing jeans and tennis shoes or sandals. It's these subtle differences that can establish the dreaded us versus them mentality. Perhaps dressing business casual for certain meetings will earn some respect from the business team. While this approach is unlikely to yield significant long-term results, the most reliable approach is always to be genuine and try to find other interests you have in common with people you need to work with regularly.

Little things like smiling and remembering people's names are basic fundamentals recommended by professionals for successfully engaging with others. Many of these types of techniques work subconsciously and people have a harder time resisting interactions with someone who approaches them with a smile and greets them by their name.

Ben Franklin Effect

Another way to win over someone who just doesn't seem to cooperate or collaborate with you is to entice them to provide you a small favor of some sort. This is referred to as the **Ben Franklin Effect**.

> "I did not... aim at gaining his favour by paying any servile respect to him but, after some time, took this other method. Having heard that he had in his library a certain very scarce and curious book I wrote a note to him expressing my desire of perusing that book and requesting he would do me the favour of lending it to me for a few days. He sent it immediately and I returned it in about a week with another note expressing strongly my sense of the favour. When we next met in the House he spoke to me (which he had never done before), and with great civility; and he ever after manifested a readiness to serve me on all occasions, so that we became great friends and our friendship continued to his death. This is another instance of the truth of an old maxim I had learned, which says, "He that has once done you a kindness will be more ready to do you another than he whom you yourself have obliged."

— Ben Franklin

This technique has its roots in Cognitive Dissonance in that the other person must now justify to themselves why they performed a favor on your behalf. Evidently it's because they like you, because they wouldn't just go around providing favors for people they don't prefer. Obviously this can be a manipulative approach and I suggest that you use these types of techniques as last ditch efforts only. As Dale Carnegie mentions repeatedly, insincere tactics to win people to your side will usually be sensed by others and will therefore only end up backfiring.

Reciprocation

One of the best ways to convince someone to do something for you is to provide something for them first. People feel obliged to repay or reciprocate when someone has done something beneficial for them or provided them with something they desire or need. This "something" could be a simple compliment or perhaps a design specification that includes a prominent feature they requested. We live in a tit-for-tat society and this is especially apparent in the business world. To a large degree, at least in the U.S., people "expect" payback for something they provide for someone in the course of business. The Dale Carnegie warnings apply here as well and insincere flattery will get you nowhere. However, that doesn't mean that you can't find something sincere to offer someone, whether it be a compliment or otherwise.

IMPACTS OF SOCIAL INFLUENCE

Social Facilitation

This phenomenon was first observed in animals many decades ago where the lowly ant could be found working significantly harder when accompanied by a fellow ant compared to working alone. This same effect was noticed by psychologist Norman Triplett in bicyclists. Racing cyclists would record much faster times when racing against a fellow cyclist of approximately equal ability. Scores of studies since then have boiled the issue down to this; people will typically increase their performance when others are watching or evaluating them on "dominant responses" and on more difficult or less rehearsed tasks performance will typically suffer. Dominant responses are defined as those tasks where we excel and have a habit of regularly performing. The psychological impact of social facilitation is thought to be based upon arousal, however if we become too focused on the evaluators it may work against us. You can guess how this might work when technical people are out of their comfort zones in business or planning meetings. This type of arousal may inhibit their performance, similar to speaking in front of a large group.

Agile Programming and Facilitation

Now that you have an understanding of the power of Social Facilitation you may begin to appreciate the brilliance of Agile development. Working with a co-worker, side by side, increases ones arousal, at least initially. I would suspect that mixing up programming pairs would help keep arousal levels elevated and therefore Social Facilitation working on one's behalf. Pairing males with females may also increase male programming performance, at least according to the Köhler Effect mentioned previously. However, pairing people who have large gaps in capabilities may not be especially effective, unless it's for training purposes.

Social Loafing

The opposite effect of Social Facilitation is that of Social Loafing, which was first identified as far back as the 1890s. This occurs when someone's individual effort is masked by the group's at large effort. It's likely that this effect has a relatively minor impact on software developers because it is usually manifested in purely collective efforts, such as tug of war contests. Studies show that it's slightly more prevalent in males from Western cultures, and I also assume that it's more likely in people with low conscientiousness. So be aware when your team is involved in general group activities that no one is using the group to mask their sub-par efforts.

Why the phenomenon of loafing within a group is more prevalent in Western societies and less so in Collectivist cultures, such as those found in many Asian countries, is not perfectly clear. The most logical answer is that collectivist cultures depend more on every team member and also know them better, thus making it more difficult to hide one's efforts. See Chapter 13 for more information.

Talking and Influence

Studies have shown that just someone speaking frequently, in and of itself, can have a strong influence on both groups and individuals. The person doing the talking may or may not have expert knowledge, but talking often and with confidence has a lot to do with one's perception of being a leader. So who does the most talking when it comes to business and development people in a meeting together? In my experience it's usually the business people who are more comfortable speaking in group settings and typically they are more outgoing and extraverted by nature. They interact on a regular basis with customers and vendors and their jobs are more focused on communications.

Based upon this understanding it might behoove us to become more adept at public speaking and to prepare our arguments and data beforehand. Where business people really outshine developers is their ability to quickly think on their feet during heated debates. Most developers, being more analytical in nature, need time to process and evaluate all the possible outcomes. Therefore, preparing and planning well in advance of these types of meetings is very prudent. I'm not necessarily suggesting that all developers enroll in a public speaking course, but those developers that are able to become more comfortable speaking in front of groups or within stressful meetings will become much more valuable team members and will have more career options at their disposal.

To adequately prepare for critical meetings in an attempt to anticipate arguments and potential rebuttals from the business side, consider the tactic of role playing. While most technical people will roll their eyes at the thought, it's a good way to analyze the situation so that you can have canned retorts for some of the probable responses. However, I've also found that technical people rarely foresee all the arguments that may come from the business side because they're not in tune with the market, other business aspects and impacts of software development. Even so, it's still a sound idea to rehearse beforehand so that you're more comfortable addressing the unknowns when the actual meeting occurs.

Influence in software development is rarely about technical details, which we usually prefer to focus on, but has to do with our social skills, emotional control, and building a plausible business case for our ideas.

Best Defense is Good Offense

One of the most successful methods I have discovered for working in cooperation with the business side is the exercise of the project trade-off triangle (shown here). It resounds effectively with business people because it demonstrates your grasp of the larger picture and because of its visual nature it is also straightforward to comprehend.

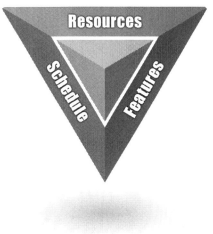

The real beauty of the trade-off triangle is that it presents options and demonstrates flexibility on your part. The way you present it is to consent to let them have control of any two of the three sides of the triangle. As a fair and noble partner, you only need one side and it can be the one of their choosing. How much more flexible and cooperative could you be?

Briefly, the way it works is that you bestow business the choice of determining two of the primary elements in any software project; scope (features), resources, and schedule. If they choose scope and schedule, then you will determine the budget. If they then subsequently decide that they'd rather control the budget then you will have control of either the schedule or the feature set. This forces the hand of business, but yet in a reasonable and professional fashion. Judicious business people realize that it's unreasonable for them to dictate all major facets of a project and I've found that most people will adopt this model as a way of conducting on-going business with software organizations. It works because it provides high-level options, is disarming, and is relatively simple to understand.

In most software projects, the resources and schedule generally have less flexibility, so it really comes down to determining the feature sets that can be developed within the constraints of the resources and schedule. Another adaptation of the trade-off triangle, from programming guru Bruce J. Mack, is to determine which components of the triangle may be adjusted and those that are fixed. For example in some small organizations the resources may be permanent but the feature set may have room for minor alterations.

This is a great model to use at the outset of a project, with all key stakeholders involved, so that commitments to a preferred strategy are made early on. Once people publicly commit to a course of action, it becomes more difficult for them to renege. This harkens back to our discussion of cognitive dissonance and the need people have to be consistent in their behaviors.

CHAPTER 8

Analog Intelligence

BUILDING A BALANCED SOFTWARE PROFESSIONAL

The use of the phrase *Analog Intelligence* encompasses what researchers refer to as Social and/or Emotional Intelligence. While we as software professionals work in a digital world, our ultimate long-term success is still partially determined by how we leverage our analog skills. Those who have known me for a long time recognize a favorite saying of mine; "In the land of the blind, the one eyed man is king." This is somewhat the situation (tongue in cheek) when it comes to us technical professionals and our social skills. Attaining some reasonable level of social and interpersonal skills will go a long way towards improving our organizational futures. Most software professionals prefer to focus on new technologies and techniques in an effort to bolster their careers. While this is to be expected, and indeed encouraged, most of us would probably benefit just as much, and possibly more, by enhancing our social and interpersonal skills. Expecting organizations to grant us expanded and more desirable roles with mediocre interpersonal skills is not especially realistic. A balanced software professional is much more valuable to an organization. These balanced professionals will be called upon to fulfill increasingly challenging roles and will ultimately have their choice of projects and positions within the company. Their compensation and status will also rise commensurately.

Defining Social Intelligence

As humans, we are actually hard wired to respond to people's faces. In fact, there is a particular region of the brain, called the fusiform gyrus, which activates

My own experience in this arena bears mentioning. Some years ago my supervisor requested a meeting with me to discuss my confrontational and aggressive approaches of selling my technical ideas to various superiors in the company. My approach was one marked by impatience and my frustrations were all too evident if someone even remotely disagreed with my proposals. I was falling victim to the classic mistake of associating my identity with my technical proposals. I was also forcing people to make either/or decisions with too little time for their own analysis.

My supervisor suggested that I first make some amends, which I did, and then spend additional time understanding my internal customers better. When technical people become too engrossed in their solutions and plans, while neglecting the people side of the business, it may all end up being for naught anyway. Forging ahead with many technical initiatives involves change for many stakeholders. Most people will resist change, at least initially, so forcing ideas upon someone must be done tactfully. This is just one example of why aspiring to become a balanced technical professional is a practical ambition for one's career.

when people view images of human faces. Numerous fMRI studies have confirmed this to be the case. It has been largely determined that autistic people make little use of this area – at least while viewing faces. Many of the informational cues available to be discovered while talking face-to-face with someone come from processing the emotions elicited around the eyes. There are nearly two hundred muscles controlling these finely detailed emotions. For those who cannot or choose not to make reasonable eye contact during a discussion, much of the true meaning of a conversation may be missed. Of course communication in a non face-to-face mode will have much of the potential hidden meanings lost altogether, a real problem for virtual teams.

This field is one of the emerging areas in psychology, particularly Industrial-Organizational or I/O psychology. It has to do with one's social skills, especially detecting and interpreting non-verbal cues from other people that you interact with on a regular basis. It also includes how to get along with your co-workers and clients in stressful or high-pressure situations and properly deciphering the social situation at hand. Social awareness is a large part of the social intelligence equation. Again, think about your prototypical programmer here. He may spend much of his average workweek behind a monitor, in isolation from others. Eventually your brain may begin adapting to your environment, possibly to the point that one begins feeling uncomfortable in certain business (or other) social settings. This cycle of behavior may have the capability of further drawing one into isolation and magnifying already fragile social skills.

A classic example of social intelligence, or a blatant lack thereof, happened to me many years ago while working at ETA Systems, a now defunct supercomputer company. I was making a detailed and complex software capabilities presentation to a large entourage from an Asian country. Many times the Ministry of Technology would come from these countries to the U.S. on a civic mission to select the best supercomputer for their nation. They would usually travel with a group of dignitaries and security personnel and these presentations could be rather tricky, since foreign protocol was somewhat different from one country to the next. During the portion of one of my more technological talks on parallel processing, one of my colleagues from ETA, who was part of the dog and pony show that day, challenged some of my assertions and claimed them to be preposterous. As you can imagine, this put me in a very precarious and untenable position. Being seriously challenged by someone from your own company, in front of a viable customer prospect, is not something I was prepared to encounter that day. I think I finally said that perhaps we should discuss this further at a more convenient time and moved on with the remainder of my presentation.

Unfortunately, this sort of social behavior is somewhat typical of many technical people. My colleague was so engrossed with the technical details of my presentation that he completely neglected the social context. I'm not sure of the reaction of the entourage, as I was focused on making a clean escape from my predicament. Luckily, being technical people themselves, they perhaps were engaged by my colleague's remarks. My lasting memory of this event is watching my enraged supervisor storm down the hall to his office, having completely come apart at what could have been a disastrous meeting. My fellow employee never did apologize about the incident, probably not thinking it was any sort of big deal in the first place. In fact, he may have thought he was helping me out and was awaiting my accolades and further discussions. This is the essence of Social Intelligence, or lack thereof, and it must be understood and embraced by technical professionals hoping to advance their careers.

Of course, Social Intelligence goes far beyond recognizing and interpreting social cues from others. It is better understanding ways to cleverly disarm a challenger in a social duel and perhaps even unwittingly converting him to a long term ally in the process. These are tools that may escape your average technical person who is, in too many instances, unreceptive to social cues and the social situation at hand.

Back in the 1980s and earlier it was quite common for top technical people to slide into management roles when they reached the top of their salary scales. That was your ticket to making some respectable money and not stagnating at the peak corporate pay level. However, most firms provided little or no management training for neophyte managers and many first time technical managers that rose up through the ranks ended up eventually deserting their positions. They became miserable and were largely ineffective. Corporations finally wised up and realized that they were much better off to pay good technical people higher wages so they would continue performing their technical duties and recruit managers from other pools of talent. These technical people were relieved to go back to their previous roles where they thrived and had fulfilling work. Management roles had taxed their social skills to the maximum and they were not accustomed to dealing with uneasy social situations on a recurring basis. On the positive side however, these frustrated managers did come to appreciate management duties and had a much better understanding of the issues they routinely faced. Poking fun at the managers was now a little less frequent and much less harsh having finally understood what they actually endured on a regular basis. Deciding to go the management route is a critical decision point for most technical people. Once you start down this path your technical skills begin to diminish and some of your technical peers may also begin resenting you. The more time you spend in management, the harder it becomes to go back to being technical once again.

Improving Your Social Intelligence

So what can we do to increase our social awareness and function? Are we to muddle along and withdraw even further into our world of bits and bytes? Of course the answer is no, but the techniques for improving your social intelligence are not necessarily straightforward, nor simple either. Much of it originates from your basic wiring, which as we are learning can come from your upbringing and environment, or worse yet, your genetics. Once you are fully wired it then becomes significantly more challenging to re-wire your brain pathways. The good news is that the human brain is the most advanced entity on the planet and as far as we know the entire universe. The bad news is that there are certain limits in what we all can reasonably expect to achieve, so attempting to optimize our capabilities is a more realistic approach.

The human brain operates on two levels in what is referred to by some research-ers as the low road and the high road. The low road is quick and reflexive in nature while the high road needs to actually "think" things through to add more specific meaning and context to events. It turns out that our low road can process many social cues, particularly facial ones, which the high road may not have the time to fully decode. It so happens that some video training, of all things, may in fact help people improve the odds of properly decoding subtle facial cues. Dr. Paul Ekman is an expert on detecting discreet emotions from people's facial expressions. He has developed a system where trainees watch as someone reveals a split second emotional cue via their face. These emotional indicators are nearly impossible to conceal but also very difficult to identify by the untrained eye. His MicroExpression Training Tool, called F.A.C.E., provides a way to practice the detection of these subtle cues. These cues come primarily from the eyes, so it is obviously of the utmost importance for people to focus on this key area of the face in order to decipher any concealed messages someone may be signaling.

This is the whole point behind social intelligence – picking up on signals that might be unknown to the owner. You're typically better off to believe the subtle meaning versus what the person is actually verbalizing. These are the signs that seasoned sales professionals are able to pick up from their prospects in order to know if they really do intend to buy their product or service. As an example, some people may avoid direct eye contact when they are not being completely truthful or when discussing an uncomfortable topic.

There are basically two ways to deal with people who demonstrate poor social intelligence in the workplace; remove them from the potentially precarious situ-ations or provide them with some basic training in the fundamentals. Many times it is not necessary for purely technical people, those whose main job is development related, to be involved in high stress meetings or other settings where social intelligence may be a crucial factor. CIOs and other management team members who have more experience in these areas will usually take part in these activities and the heavy techies will be excluded, to everyone's delight. For those instances where technical people need to be involved in some sort of sum-mit or big client kick-off meeting, the best tactic is to stress the fundamentals beforehand. It's important to train staff when it's suitable for them to respond to issues in the first place and when they should defer to more senior or other players. That is, they need to clearly understand why they have been asked to participate and to only participate when absolutely necessary. Coaching people immediately following these sessions is important so that technical people can become more meaningful participants in these types of activities and grow into management or senior technical roles. One small offhand comment from a technical person could ruin months of planning by the sales team. "When in doubt, leave it out" is good advice to heed for most technical professionals involved in critical client meetings.

One of my most vivid career memories involved a large company gathering of hundreds of participants from virtually every state in the country. Before the big extravaganza we all attended a mandatory Due Diligence meeting to go over the specific roles of everyone participating in the event. One of the topics involved a slide I was coerced into using for a presentation I was making by a senior vice president (another lesson learned the hard way). It was a benchmark performance slide comparing a number of computers against each other in various aspects of their performance. However, one computer didn't fare so well on the tests and as a result the legend entry for this machine was removed from the slide, so that no one would know which machine it was. The VP told me that no one would notice and to just breeze right along with my discussion. Therefore I didn't bother to edit the slide since it was a graphic and I did not have the source file. Well as you probably have guessed by now, the VP forgot that many of the audience members were analytical technical people and many of them started to ask about the missing legend entry they detected while carefully scrutinizing the busy slide. As I was dancing around the issue up on the stage with microphone in hand, one of my junior colleagues, who did not attend the mandatory Due Diligence meeting, eagerly jumped up and proudly identified the missing computer on the slide. I was severely booed and nearly run out of the room and scolded afterwards by the coercing VP besides. Many lessons are embedded within this story and hopefully you can learn from them at my expense! Obviously my colleague who provided the missing link was unaware of the social situation and he was trying to contribute in the only way he knew how.

Some technical professionals become frustrated when dealing with business people. They have a hard time relating to people who talk in unfamiliar phrases and more abstract concepts such as business partnerships and alliances. The tendency is to react too quickly and blurt out responses that we may regret later or more likely, that our supervisor may later lament. Learning to pause, reflect and engage our prefrontal cortex by thinking about our feelings and the various ways in which our response might be interpreted, may help this process according to some brain research studies. Our inner brain is responsible for these feelings of anger and frustration and it's critical to engage the other more advanced parts of the brain to prevent those unwanted primal behaviors from taking control of ourselves. Just thinking about and identifying your specific feelings and plans may actually be enough to engage your prefrontal cortex and therefore alleviate your anger. Now the logical you is in charge and for technical people the logical element is where we truly shine.

Basic Communication Strategies for Technical People

As we already know, this is an area where we tend to struggle periodically due to our introverted tendencies. Therefore, having some readily available techniques to draw upon is a sensible idea.

Communicating Up

Most technical people I work with, except for perhaps Project Managers, have an irresistible craving to dive deep into esoteric technical minutia during conversations. This is the one province where our verbal skills appear to be superb, the area where we have the most comfort. However, even when talking to fellow programmers this may not always be the most desirable approach. Before a manager even has a chance to get a feel for the larger picture, many technical staff become submerged in numerous technical details that may be quite difficult to grasp without the proper context and background information. They are not living from day to day like the developers or DBAs in the midst of these details, and if they had to remember all these sticky details they wouldn't likely finish their primary job duties.

One of the drawbacks of working in an abstract field that sometimes requires intense concentration, to the point of losing oneself in a zone, is the tendency to forget how deeply involved one can become in their own world of algorithms. We don't realize that others likely have little or no idea of what we're discussing and probably don't need to know all the sundry details. This is especially true with technical management staff. Therefore, an effective strategy for discussing technical issues is to start with a summary and work toward more detail from there, and then only when requested to do so. Technical management staff will ask for more details, if indeed they actually require them, but many times a summary is all they will need to make a decision. Often times details will encumber a senior manager and it's important for some people to remain detached from all the particulars in order to make the optimal decision.

For discussions where an important or critical decision must be made there are some enhancements to the model just described. CTOs, CIOs, VPs, and Directors will generally prefer that you summarize the situation, provide two or three solution possibilities, and then select one of the solution options and explain why you think it's the best alternative. This model will save considerable time and frustration for many technical people and will likely impress your superiors besides.

Rambling on and on about some technical information that someone may not fully understand will typically not move the agenda forward. In most cases technical management staff do not live in that technically intricate world anymore and you may lose their attention by focusing on figures they cannot fully comprehend. Managers also have egos and may be concerned to let on that they don't completely understand the issues. They've forgotten what it's like to become immersed in some code to the point where you are dreaming about it at night. If however you do feel compelled to explain the particulars or you've been specifically asked for them, you should consider providing it in smaller chunks in order to ensure that your audience has time to properly digest it. Asking them their thoughts about certain topics or ideas along the way is a good way to do this rather than letting your listener just nod their head periodically. This forces the listener to be active. Active listening is difficult for many people, even more so when the topic is complicated and unfamiliar. Their minds may begin to wander onto the other issues they need to handle or maybe they're still processing thoughts from a previous meeting.

Another key point to remember is that many managers may do better if they can see a diagram of some sort. A flow chart perhaps or anything that allows them to better understand the context and permits them to operate at the higher level they are comfortable with. Some people actually perform much better when they can visualize something versus just hearing it alone. These are referred to as visual learners. It is estimated by some that approximately 40% of the population consider themselves to be visual learners. Other researchers are not convinced that visual learners exist, but I'm a firm believer in visual learning, being one myself.

Many visual learners know this about themselves and may very well request that they view something on paper or a white board. Visual learners can remember problems and issues much better if they can conjure up that image in their mind later. It helps provide a learning framework for them and they will likely have more questions for you once they review some type of diagram or chart. Even reading the words on paper will probably help them process the information more accurately and completely. Many years ago I realized that visual learning was best for me, as anyone who has seen the white board in my office can attest. Therefore it's important to me that documents, charts, and diagrams are available so I can fully understand the situation and convert it to my long term memory. Some psychologists think that there may be two separate tracks or coding for learning and memory, one that is visual and another that is audible. Visual learners have brains wired or better equipped for visual learning or perhaps their audible coding is not as well developed.

Communicating Down

Requesting Information

When communicating with subordinates it is critically important to be crystal clear in what you need. In order to accomplish that goal you may need to ask questions so that subordinates fully understand your needs and aren't racing around gathering up information that is futile. Asking them to quickly summarize their understanding of your request will only take a few minutes and may save precious time and frustration later.

This is basically the reverse of the situation described in the Communicating Up section earlier. Technical subordinates live in a world of narrow and deep, whereas managers live in a much broader and shallower world (no slam intended, this is where I live now!) Managers are usually required to have a fair amount of knowledge in many areas of the business and the important linkages between them. So when asking technical experts for information it helps to specify the general level of information you need or you may well get much more than you bargained for. Now you need to sift through the extra data and the technical expert has spent some unnecessary time in gathering it.

Providing Feedback

If you're communicating negative feedback to a technical person, extreme caution must be taken. It's important to remember that many employees have the most difficulties with the relationship they share with their immediate supervisor. Technical people are highly sensitive to criticism, so rehearsing and planning out your conversation with them in advance is advisable. The goal is to separate the problematic issues from the person and to proceed carefully and without blame, even if the blame is there. Asking questions rather than making accusations is important, as perhaps you don't have all the required information. A good way to open these conversations is to ask how the situation at hand may have been handled more effectively. Another option is to inquire about how they perceived the situation and let them come to their own conclusions, with your guidance. Lecturing technical people rarely yields desirable outcomes.

If you plan to discuss a sensitive concern with your subordinate and you're emotionally aroused, you would almost certainly be better served to reconsider and talk at a later time. This will almost always backfire, especially with a technical person, and end up causing more hard feelings and ill will than it's worth.

Communicating with Customers

This is a potentially dangerous area for technical staff. Throughout my career there have been numerous occasions when technical people have made promises to customers or prospects that should not have been made. You must be very clear when allowing technical staff to speak with clients as this is not what they normally do. Just like managers don't write code and hence have no idea of what they're doing, technical folks are typically weak in this arena because they have limited experience. If a technical person is required to conduct a conversation with a client that may be problematic, someone from the business team should seriously consider joining the call as a moderator.

SUGGESTED GUIDELINES FOR TECHNICAL PERSONNEL WHEN DEALING WITH CLIENTS OR PROSPECTS:

Do not discuss billing rates or pricing

This is nearly guaranteed to get you in trouble with your superiors. Besides not discussing pricing, committing to dates or hours of effort for completing feature sets is akin to quoting a price. Many developers and other technical staff become trapped by their customers and feel an urgent need to satisfy them somehow. Unfortunately, many clients know that talking directly to a technical employee may get them what they want. Agreeing to a schedule (or most anything) during the midst of a conversation is usually a costly idea. Determine the customers' requirements and then agree to reply back at a later date, after you've had time to analyze and review your options with your supervisor. Even hinting at possible solutions or timetables may be interpreted as a commitment by the customer and later, when circumstances change, they could feel they were intentionally deceived.

Cautiously commit on behalf of the organization

There is some differentiation among client discussions. When technical people are speaking with other technical people, on a peer-to-peer basis, the concern that problems will arise is minimized. Technical communication is best done on a peer-to-peer basis, where managers talk with other like managers and programmers talk with fellow programmers. This will normally help minimize any possible damage. However it is always best to follow up conversations in writing, usually an email with other key personnel copied, so that all parties are covered in case of a possible misinterpretation. It's always easy for someone to say "I thought I heard you say that the new reporting updates would be finished by this Friday" when in fact it was a week from Friday or whatever the case may be. Many times I have asked to review these emails before being sent to the client, so that any necessary edits can be prepared.

Communication Mediums

Email

The principal mode of nonverbal communication in most organizations is still email, but texting and instant messaging are increasing in usage, particularly among younger professionals. There are several drawbacks involved with nonverbal communication that users must be cognizant of so that meanings are not misinterpreted. In a fascinating study conducted by Kruger et. al. (2005) it was found that message senders were quite confident that they could effectively communicate various emotions using email, such as humor or sadness, to both friends and strangers. The two primary results of this experiment were that people overestimated their ability to communicate the desired emotion and amazingly, they did no better with their own friends than with complete strangers. In regard to gender in decoding nonverbal cues, women appear to be better equipped to detect nonverbal cues when people are telling the truth. Men, it turns out, may be better at detecting lies in nonverbal communication (Aronson, pg 100).

Face-to-Face

The advent of email and other technical means of communication were viewed as a godsend by most technical professionals, who are good with computers but not so keen with the one-on-one personal interactions. The tendency for us, unless encouraged to do otherwise, is to maximize these impersonal methods of communication. And while they can be tremendously efficient, in certain instances, they are also ineffective at times. Chuck Martin (CIO Magazine, 2007) suggests that electronic means of communicating can be used to circumvent decision making and goes on to advocate that whenever some type of give and take is required, there is no substitute for face-to-face communication. Countless times I'm copied on a string of back and forth emails from people whose offices are close to each other. In many cases, one conversation could save a dozen or more emails and probably provide more clarity on the topic as well.

Video Conferencing

This method for meetings can be received well, but one of the possible drawbacks is that the person on the other end may not be able to see all meeting participants clearly. Even so, this is still probably the next best thing to face-to-face communications if the video connections are of high quality. Some other issues include people who are self conscious about being on camera. Also, making eye contact may not always be straight-forward and it may appear as though people are avoiding eye contact. Lastly, if sufficient bandwidth is not available for the system the latency effect can be rather bothersome.

Phone/Audio Only

This mode is the least desirable of those discussed here, due to the lack of facial cues, and should be avoided if at all possible. I recommend using this communication method for specific tasks with small teams and not for large group meetings. Besides being difficult to detect hidden meanings in communications it can also be challenging to hear all participants in large groups, even with full duplex (Polycom) phones. I can personally attest that staying fully engaged in these sorts of meetings is challenging when you're the one on the phone.

INTERPERSONAL WORK RELATIONSHIPS

I'm reasonably convinced that for the majority of workers in the software development trade the most enjoyable and fulfilling part of their vocation is the small fragment that concerns the actual development of software. When someone knows exactly what they are supposed to build and they're off in a trance coding away, that is the real joy of the job for most of us. The same applies for any other software related work: defining requirements, doing the real duties of project management, designing the database, writing test cases, or whatever it might be.

Where some of us may struggle is when it comes to dealing with people and all of the other non-technical issues we are deluged with every day. Get us in front of a computer monitor or technical manual and we feel comfortable and do quite well. Dealing with each other and especially with business people, well that's where our game starts breaking down. It feels like we're getting outgunned at times. When it comes to handling the meetings and other business related tasks associated with our trade, let's face it, we're typically better equipped for error handling. There are however, ways to mitigate these predicaments. It starts with understanding our strengths and weaknesses. Then, time and effort must be applied to our weaknesses, rather than continually bolstering our strengths.

I remember years ago when Ross Perot, a former computer guy, was running for President of the United States. During a speech he made regarding the unbalanced U.S. trade relationship with certain countries, he said something to the effect that they're whooping the U.S. and that the U.S. should do something about it. I liken this to the situation that some software people find themselves in today. We may lose our advantage to the business units because we don't have the tools and resources to defend our positions and prepare ourselves to effectively present and defend our ideas and plans.

Of course, like many issues in the corporate world today, there is often little or no training on how to become effective teammates. People are lumped together and fingers are crossed. "Maybe it will work out fine this time" is the strategy for many companies. While some companies carry out skills training in this area, I'm betting that most do not.

Physiological Consequences

Studies have shown that relationships with co-workers and even short interactions, sometimes referred to as connections, may have a powerful effect on us from a physiological standpoint. The research has focused on three main areas of human health. These include cardiovascular, immune system, and neuroendocrine.

It has been determined that even somewhat fleeting positive encounters at work can lower heart rates and improve blood pressure. Our immune systems exhibit improved strength and resiliency. The nervous system and its associated hormone production mechanisms are all noticeably enhanced when we experience positive exchanges with others.

By and large, all of these physical systems are bolstered and become more efficient as a result of positive social interactions with peers and superiors in particular. The impact that a leader, affectionately known as the boss, can have on their subordinates is profound and lasting. These positive relationships can be the difference between an employee functioning at their utmost level and one who is frequently calling in sick or doing just enough work to squeak by. And while these underperforming employees can be dealt with, it is costly to organizations in endless ways. Superiors must put performance improvement plans in place, HR may become involved and if a replacement becomes necessary, then hiring and training are now in play. These all consume valuable time and money, the two most precious assets of any business entity. But beyond that, there is now the issue of team dynamics – integrating a new resource into the existing team. This alone may have several unintended negative consequences. The pecking order must now be re-established and new relationships created. These all consume precious human CPU cycles that could be put to better use.

Relationships

There are many types of interpersonal relationships in software development groups and they are complex and intertwined. No two organizations are the same because the people and corporate culture will vary tremendously. Working for a consulting firm, I have the luxury of observing and learning about many different companies and their cultures. The differences can be rather drastic even within the same geographic region. Highlighted below are some of the common organizational relationships that exist and the typical nature of these relationships in many companies which create software (or do anything for that matter).

One Up and One Down

These relationships, officially known as Supervisor-Subordinate relationships in the world of psychology and Human Resources, are typically the most crucial contacts within a company. Many experts in workplace relations consider the relationship a subordinate has with his supervisor as absolutely critical in their success and longevity with the company (Hogan, Terry Baker). Several employees leave their employer owing solely to the dislike of their boss. Climate Surveys, used to measure employee morale over the decades, show that high percentages of workers view their relationships with their boss as the worst and most stressful part of their job (Hogan).

Having a conflicted relationship with a supervisor is, in most cases, indefensible. This goes back to the lack of training and experience level of managers in technical organizations. Investing the time to build relationships and understanding employee needs and matching them with the greater needs of the group are fundamental management skills many technical people never develop or take the time to provide. Some technical people who rise through the ranks do not possess the necessary interpersonal skills to manage others effectively and upper management infrequently provides support for these types of soft skill activities. Organizations with HR departments should reach out to these people for specific advice and counseling.

However, in software development, the typical hierarchal management structure found in most organizations may not always entirely apply. Many software development professionals effectively have two or more supervisors. They usually have an official boss, the person who decided to hire them and provides them with their official performance evaluation and an unofficial boss, usually a project manager or maybe a lead developer. Often this makes sense because development staff may be engaged in more than one project at a time or may rotate between projects over the course of their tenure. This complicates the situation because development staff may reach out to their official boss when relations aren't going well with the PM. This might in turn compromise the effectiveness of the PM and cause interpersonal triangulation to occur.

This is also referred to as a **Conflict Triangle** and they are regularly found in abundance in virtually all organizations. These triangles are vastly unproductive and squander untold hours every day, at least in the United States, and I suspect in most other Western countries too. If left unchecked, these conflict triangles will normally persist, and possibly escalate, until one of the parties departs. If the triangled parties need to work together for an extended period, the issues will need to be resolved before too long. Resolution will generally only occur when there is direct communication between the two parties. This can be facilitated by the supervisor and many times just the threat of assembling everyone to discuss the issue will be enough impetus to get the two parties into some meaningful dialogue. I've found that gathering the parties together to moderate the discussion works well with technical staff who characteristically struggle with these types of matters. When a moderator is present, people will normally be on their best behavior and the moderator will be able to keep the meeting on task and get people to focus on their interests and feelings, not their positions.

Lastly, due to our general personality makeup, some technical supervisors may not make the necessary time and effort to build solid relationships with their subordinates. This is not an area where many of us feel comfortable, or perhaps we just don't consider it necessary in the first place. Regardless of the reason, it's important to foster these relationships, and technical supervisors should be encouraged to do so.

Peer-to-Peer

These are also referred to as co-worker relationships, and while they remain important to overall employee functioning, they are not as critical as relations with a direct supervisor. Researchers Kram & Isabella (1985) in their extensive study on mentoring alternatives, depict three levels of peer relationships: information, collegial and special peer relationships.

Information Peer interactions are primarily task based relationships where the connection between two people is based upon gathering the requisite job-related information to accomplish their normal duties. They interact minimally and little is shared between them beyond the scope of the job. **Collegial Peers** on the other hand are differentiated by closer and more personal relationships. These types of peers share their feelings with each other more often and have more of a trust with their co-workers. This is what you would consider a good work friend. **Special Peer** relationships are relatively rare and involve deeper levels of friendship that may likely go beyond the office environment. These co-workers feel comfortable discussing practically any topic and are very trusting in nature. They may also socialize frequently outside of the work environment.

The theory here is that individuals who have many and multiple types of peer relationships will have more mentoring and career advancement opportunities. While there is little if any data in our profession to rely upon, it's evident to me that these peer relationships are somewhat limited within software development. Multiple studies have shown that women are more likely to develop collegial and special peer relationships, and these are most likely to be with other women (Sias p.63). Since we have fewer women in our profession and given that many of us exhibit introverted tendencies, it's therefore less likely that we will forge all the required relationships to promote effective mentorship. This may help explain the frequent observance of "lone ranger" or "gunslinger" types of developers. They'd rather just do it on their own and not invest too much in organizational relationships. This effect may also be compounded by the use of Virtual Teams for development. It's especially difficult to build a meaningful relationship with someone from another culture who you only interact with occasionally via phone or Live Meeting, therefore mentoring and other benefits of team building are mitigated.

If you'd like to minimize employee turnover rates while also improving performance (and who wouldn't?), there is data to suggest that employees with best friends at work are much more likely to be engaged in their work and deliver higher productivity as well (DuBrin p. 117 & Sias p. 91). On the flip side however, workplace friendships can also be the origin for several problems. These include people talking too much about non-work related events (hence a decrease in productivity) or in some cases ganging up on others in the group.

Overview of Common Software Relationships

This section is not based upon any scientific research or studies. It has evolved solely from my experiences over the course of my career.

Developers & Project Managers (PMs)

PMs want things to be predictable and developers like to discover new techniques and work with new technologies. Developers don't like to be bothered with annoying things like proper error handling and they don't like to be hounded when it comes to dates for specific feature sets.

However, PMs must report status on a regular basis to various management groups and they need some control over the development effort in order to report the status accurately and deliver the project on time.

Depending upon the personalities, the relationship between these individuals and the situation of the specific project, there can easily be a confrontational relationship here. Some PMs have never developed code themselves and are therefore at a disadvantage when it comes to understanding developer needs. Most developers have never been a Project Manager either, so it's rather easy for these two groups to experience some dissension.

Developers & QA

Developers typically don't like working with all the details brought up by testers and some will attempt to conceal as many coding defects as possible so that they keep their reputation as solid developers intact. This is perhaps where the "defect becomes a feature" originated. Many times the issue can be contributed to a lack of clarity around requirements and this would be a good common ground for these two parties to focus on. QA people might be better off asking the developer how they interpreted the requirement in question. This is a much more disarming way to approach a developer rather than waving a defect report in their face. A small percentage of QA people may be jealous of developers and may actually enjoy flaunting the defects they uncover.

Developers many times assume that QA staff are just frustrated or failed developers. Since joining SWAT Solutions I now recognize that most QA personnel are Inspectors (see the Personality chapter for more information) and at some point they realized that they have a knack for working with details. If not for qualified QA personnel, developers would need to functionally test their own code and most developers I've known would dread the thought.

It may take some time for these groups to meld together, but once they do it can provide for very effective development.

BAs & PMs

PMs appreciate that BAs can distill and prioritize feature sets from broader business goals and objectives. BAs like that PMs will schedule it, prioritize and get it done. Generally these groups seem to get along the best of those featured here as long as both parties are competent.

PMs & Business Representatives

Business product line managers generally want as many features for as little cost as possible and as quickly as feasible. They may also have a tough time prioritizing feature sets when they realize they can't have it all. PMs sometimes feel like they can't really win, even if they deliver according to plan.

These relationships are crucial to delivering great software on schedule. It is imperative that these relationships are managed by a Governance Board or Steering Committee of some type. This will help facilitate the relationships between these two key players.

Software Relationship Notes

When one technical person views the other as incompetent, then the relationship will usually begin to deteriorate. This is generally true for all technical relationships I've found. This is a supporting argument for having teams made up of similar skill levels. Teams that are skewed with one highly accomplished member and several mid-level members may have difficulties. The mid-level members may have a hard time admitting they are inferior to the highly skilled member and the higher skilled party may scoff at working with rookies. In teams where there is one obvious technically superior member and several mid-level members, it may still take a while for the mid-level members to actually acknowledge the superiority of the other. This may result in a "period of challenging" that may not always be civil. Once this phase is over, relationships will begin to improve.

Teams with one highly skilled member where the remainder of the team is at an entry level may actually work reasonably well, as those entry level members probably agree and accept their inferior position. However, accomplishing anything of significance with a team of this composition is considerably more challenging. This type of team mix might be better suited for maintenance activities where developers and other team members can grow with limited risks to the business.

Cooperative

These types of relationships are where the parties have mutual respect for each other and will give and take based upon the merits of the supporting evidence at hand. This is the ideal state of an interpersonal working relationship. Each party will listen to the other and make a legitimate effort to understand each other's perspectives and make accommodations where reasonable. If one party cannot accommodate the other, then an attempt to compromise or satisfy the request in another manner occurs. Many times it is merely this attempt to satisfy that establishes this mutual respect. Sometimes those people who score high on Agreeableness will exhibit cooperative behavior but many times at the expense of their true feelings. These relationships may subsequently deteriorate if one party is taken advantage of too often.

Sometimes cooperative relationships happen overnight, if the personality mix is just right. But typically it takes some amount of time working together to build these types of relationships as people get to know the strengths and weaknesses of each other. Working on a successful project together tends to have that effect.

Conflict

Perhaps the most challenging of all the occupational issues that might arise is dealing with interpersonal conflict, regardless of the adversary. This may be particularly true for many technical professionals. Often times, it's how we cope with conflict that will ultimately determine our success and longevity within a company or team.

Types

Lewin (1948), a researcher interested in marital conflict, distinguishes between two basic types of interpersonal conflict: one is related to specific tasks and outcomes, and the other involves relationships between individuals. This is also defined as **Affective Conflict**.

Task Conflict may occur when the desired or expected outcomes between two people appear to be irreconcilable while affective conflict develops when feelings and emotions are not aligned. Research shows that task differences are the most favorable type of conflict, where low to moderate levels of task conflict may occasionally lead to improved performance. Task conflict may help those involved by clarifying how work should be done and by the process of jointly determining how to proceed. Affective conflict, since it is rooted in the inner brain, can hinder logical problem resolution, diminish vital communication between individuals, and ultimately damage relationships, sometimes permanently.

Technical Critiques

Conflicts between individuals may arise within software teams for a variety of reasons. A common occurrence is when senior staffers criticize the work of other teammates, especially if the victim is also a senior member of the team. This is essentially a form of task conflict.

Technical people, due to their analytical nature, have a reasonably strong tendency to be critical, especially when it pertains to technical work within their domain of expertise. Encouraging and training technical people to focus on their dissatisfaction as it relates to the facts regarding the item in question, instead of using blanket critiques, may help to soften the blow and make it less personal in nature. To avoid blame it's best for technical professionals to engage in describing issues rather than judging others and refraining from using "You" or "You always" types of accusations. Another effective technique to successfully handle this issue is to provide technical examples that have worked in the past. This provides a mentoring opportunity as opposed to a critique or what might be construed as a personal attack. The beneficial part of these types of conflicts is that technical people crave learning and anytime you can turn the event into a learning opportunity versus a critique session, everyone will be better served.

When an interaction or meeting starts out with a critical remark, the situation could likely escalate, especially when technical professionals are involved. Since nearly all conflict generates emotional arousal, this disrupts the thought process and now our inner brain has an opportunity to seize control and nothing of value is typically accomplished. These results can cause undue distractions for software development teams and many times must be officiated by a higher-level manager, thereby causing even further distraction.

Conflict may also occur when there is a dispute regarding the optimal technology to be employed on a project. Since this is usually considered a religious topic, it is best handled by a more senior person with positional power or by a designated group within the larger organization tasked with such decisions. In larger corporations this is usually less of an issue since there are defined corporate standards and licensing agreements in place for common technologies and tools.

Condescending Behavior

In a condescending relationship there is little or no respect by the condescending party toward the other. This typically causes the disrespected party to oblige in return and the relationship almost certainly withers and languishes. These types of relationships are common in our world. The prima donna developer quickly comes to mind. This individual appears to know everything and scoffs at alternative suggestions to his ways, usually in a belittling fashion. There are some simple methods that can be used to disarm these technical bullies. Challenging them in a stern manner is not one of them however, and many times this is our first inclination and reaction. One of the best ways to disarm these people is to ask them to enlighten you. "You seem to know an awful lot about this area, how did you pick all of this up?" is one general means of approaching the situation. You must be sincere however or many of these disarming techniques may well backfire on you instead. The long-term approach to dealing with these types of people is more complex. Building a trusted relationship or involving more senior management may take longer to yield constructive results. The "Hire Slow Fire Fast" model discussed in Chapter 10 may apply here too.

The Bad Apple

We all know of the bad apple and the associated poor taste. This is the person who is difficult to work with and may purposefully undermine the efforts of teams and individuals. Gottman (1994), a marriage counselor, claims that the ratio of interactions between two people must be in the range of 5:1 of good experiences to bad. At least this is the preferred case for couples. The focal point here is that there must be substantially more pleasant experiences than awful ones in order for people to get along effectively.

Felps, et al (2006), define the three attributes of the bad apple as; withholding of effort, being affectively negative, and violating important interpersonal norms. In our case we are more concerned with the latter two attributes as they are more subjective and therefore it becomes more difficult to illuminate this behavior for superiors to judge. Bad apples can have countless toxic effects on teams, especially when the team consists of those with identical positional power.

Plenty of the teams' collective energy and time may be duly wasted dealing with just one person. According to Felps, teams may suffer from withdrawal, reduced trust, behavioral outbursts, eroded motivation, defensiveness and several other related maladies. Ultimately, these bad apples cause reduced productivity and creativity and may create ill will and lowered confidence among teammates. Unfortunately, what sometimes results is that the best people leave the team, or the company altogether, and now the situation has deteriorated even further. In some extreme cases, the group may incorrectly blame the bad apple for project failure as he becomes the convenient scapegoat.

There are several ways to mitigate the negative impacts of the bad apple. Usually management intervention of some kind is required in order to isolate the offender, place them on teams with hardy personalities, or terminate their employment.

Strategies

Over the decades the work place has become a place where feelings have been pushed aside and ignored. After all, this is work, not the home or church. We have been trained to suppress our emotions and maintain a "professional" appearance. Showing emotions, other than celebrating major company achievements, is frowned upon and is considered unbecoming behavior in some companies. Most psychologists will advocate that continually withholding your emotions is unhealthy for you and may cause an unwanted outburst at some point in the future. Indeed, a new term became part of the vernacular for just this problem and it's referred to as "going postal" after the rash of killings within the U.S. Postal service.

A great model for confronting someone who has hurt you is the Befriender model. This model is used in some churches around the country to help comfort people during stressful or difficult times in their life. Many times befrienders will engage when someone has had a major life change or a death in the family. The basic interactional model is one of "I feel X when Y occurs because of Z" (it is also known secularly as the XYZ model). So an example would be as follows: "I feel sad when I see you reprimanding other employees here because I think you have the makings of a really great team leader." The concept here is that you're disclosing your own personal feelings and that you can't really help it because after all, they're just your feelings.

I have enjoyed some limited personal success with this model and I believe that it works largely because of the disarming nature of the engagement. When you open a conversation with the words "I feel" it lets the other person know that you don't necessarily think that way, but rather have been overcome by some strong feelings that you cannot suppress and that you need to express. Ultimately the Befriender model is one of listening and what better way to strengthen relationships than by listening and understanding rather than judging others.

When technical people are in listening mode they may have a tendency, due to their analytical nature, to focus on facts and figures but neglect the higher purpose or significance of the message. In order to accomplish this you may need to ask more questions but also be attentive to people's reactions, tone of voice, posture, speaking rate, etc. Noticing these non-verbal cues becomes much simpler when you have an existing relationship already established with the person. If you have no baseline to judge their reactions, the task becomes much more challenging, especially for those of us already lacking in these delicate social cue detection skills.

Transactional Analysis

Transactional Analysis is the breakdown and further analysis of interpersonal transactions between two people into a Parental, Child, or Adult ego state. Psychiatrist Eric Berne created this method in the Freudian vein. The general idea is that you want your Adult state in control as often as possible, but it becomes easy for people to digress to Child and Parental states. Whether the theory is academically right or wrong is basically irrelevant because the model helps maintain a professional focus during discussions and it's rather easy to classify the responses. Essentially you want to avoid Crossed Transactions, as diagrammed in figure 8.1 on the following page.

While Transactional Analysis (TA) has been around for quite some time, I believe it offers an effective mix of practicality and simplicity and that it may appeal to the more Analytical personality types. Practicing TA is quite possibly the most realistic way for technical people to improve their social skills and standing. After practicing this method for just a short while you will quickly notice when you flip from the Adult state to a Child or Parent state during conversations. It's a great model to use when reviewing recent difficult conversations. If you do happen to deconstruct a challenging conversation you might be surprised to discover just how frequently you actually switch from your preferred Adult state to a Child or Critical Parental state. A great time to enable this sort of communication style is during meetings, a place where many of us struggle periodically.

CROSSED TRANSACTIONS

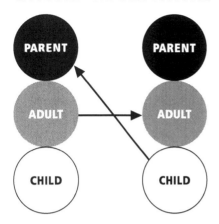

Adult Stimulus: Do you have time to explain those requirements later today?

Adapted Child Response: Why do I always have to explain these things to you?

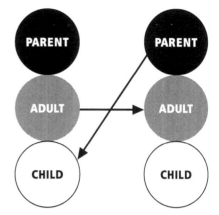

Adult Stimulus: Do you have time to explain those requirements later today?

Critical Parental Response: If you'd have read them carefully, we wouldn't need to do this.

FIGURE 8.1

Dealing with Confrontation

How to Confront Others

When you have a serious issue with someone, the tendency may be to raise your voice or use a hostile tone with them or perhaps just be abrupt and discourteous. This will not endear you with most people obviously, especially the business people. Once someone feels offended or falsely confronted, they raise their defenses and will now resist almost anything presented to them, even well thought out rational ideas.

Disarming someone prior to the confrontation is the key to dealing with it effectively. This requires some planning and consumes more time, but the results can be worth the extra effort involved. For some reason, many of us technical people have difficulty executing on this type of confrontational strategy. We may become excited and blurt out our problem or become accusatory and put our adversary on the defensive immediately. Calming ourselves and engaging our highly capable prefrontal cortex is the key to maintaining control of the situation. Once you realize that your inner brain is in control, then you must either engage your prefrontal cortex or disengage from the situation immediately. One simple, yet effective, way is to just ask for a short break. This will enable you to compose yourself and determine your best alternatives going forward.

Part of the problem here is likely rooted deeper. It is far easier to discuss issues with people when you have a trusting long-term relationship. If they realize that you have been fair and reasonable in the past, there is good chance that they will hear you out fairly and properly. Since many of us are introverted by nature, we may have some difficulties establishing these trusting relationships that can be so crucial to our overall social success. Building these relationships takes time – time that could be used discovering new technologies and skills. This is where us technical people need to make serious choices for our long-term survival in complex and political corporate environments.

So now back to our disarming ways. Starting out conversations with some non-business talk for a few minutes will usually help get everyone in an agreeable mood which may facilitate a mutual resolution of the issue. Another effective way to disarm a hostile or uncooperative employee or client is to display some genuine humility. This is not a trait typically associated with many technical staffers. Numerous business people tell me that they are frequently put off by what they consider arrogant technical people who believe that they have all the answers and therefore become problematic partners in long-term collaboration efforts. A little humility and vulnerability will go an awfully long way towards promoting trust with business team members. Continually butting heads is a tough way to accomplish business objectives and it certainly will not help reduce stress levels either.

A critical point to contemplate here is that talking in a brusque manner, giving up, and stomping away, besides being wholly ineffective interpersonal techniques, is rather easy to do. There is virtually no skill involved in these types of behaviors and we would not expect these types of responses from a technical professional, regardless of his role. Learning to reign in our emotions and engage our prefrontal cortex regions is one of the keys to remaining a viable partner with our business and technical peers. Once you acquire a reputation for being a hothead, or whatever it might be, you begin to lose leverage and power within your organization and others will ultimately use it against you in the future. Certain behaviors are extremely difficult to recover from in organizations, at least from a political standpoint.

Conflict Handling Styles

A major determining factor in how interpersonal conflict is resolved is the approach people use in an attempt to effectively deal with it. Blake and Mouton (1964) defined a model for categorizing modes of handling conflict using five different styles. Later others differentiated each mode based upon two core dimensions: concern for self and concern for others (Domino, 2004).

The five defined conflict handling styles are described here:
(Adapted from Domino, 2004)

Integrating

> This mode involves high concern for self, as well as the other person, and has been described as problem solving, collaboration, cooperation, solution oriented, or a win-win style.

Obliging

> This mode, which involves low concern for self and high concern for the other party, has also been called accommodation, non-confrontational, yielding, or a lose-win style. Agreeable personality types are prone to employing this type of style.

Dominating

> This mode involves high concern for self and low concern for the other person. It has also been called competing, controlling, contending, and a win-lose orientation, characterized by forcing behaviors in order to win one's position. Driver personality types may sometimes use this method in order to keep projects moving forward.

Avoiding

> This mode involves low concern for self as well as the other party and is also called inaction, withdrawal, ignoring, buck-passing, or a sidestepping style. Some technical people prefer this approach because they have less overall confidence in their interpersonal skills and therefore would rather just hope that the problem resolves itself.

Compromising

This mode involves concern for self, as well as the other party, and is also called "mixed motive" style, since it involves give and take, or sharing, where both parties give up something.

Those conflict handling styles where some genuine concern for the other person is exhibited are the optimal styles and allow for the establishment of longer term, trusting relationships. My experience with many technical people is that they exhibit a tendency towards the extreme conflict styles. They seem to either favor a dominating or avoiding style. When they believe they are just slightly overmatched they may employ the dominating style, hoping that their demonstrated aggressiveness displays their confidence along with a warning that they will mount an admirable fight for their position. When they believe they are completely outmatched, they may just avoid the confrontation altogether, as this seems quite logical to people like us. It takes practice for many of us to acquire the necessary skills to successfully engage the business teams. These will not be enhanced by utilizing avoiding and obliging conflict styles.

CHAPTER 9

Problem Solving, Decisions & Creativity

Programming, at its core, is basically about problem solving. I've heard some programmers describe their jobs as one of "solving puzzles all day long." Finding the optimal level of puzzle solving appears to be the dilemma in an industry saddled with tardiness and everyday blunders. Some of the current thinking and techniques in this fascinating field will be reviewed with an emphasis on how it may or may not apply to our software development maladies. Of course, problem solving is also involved in many other broader aspects of software development such as design, team and tool selections, scheduling, estimating and so on.

There are many techniques for solving problems. The research in this area is plentiful and of course there are arguments for and against most of the techniques in question. Since several of the psychological studies in this area are simple lab exercises, it is best to look at some basics first. Later there will be discussions of some more specific techniques and the benefits and pitfalls thereof, particularly as it relates to programming.

PROBLEM SOLVING VS. CREATIVITY

The need for creativity in software development is dependent upon the type of software being developed and the stage of development. I would argue, as a general tenet, that coding of web apps today requires much less creativity than other types of development. With well defined user interfaces and preprogrammed widgets available, it may not always require high levels of imagination. Certain stages of development, such as design and architecture

163

may require a large measure of creativity however. Other non-web based application development efforts may also entail a bit of creativity, especially if there are environmental constraints such as limited amounts of memory in a tiny USB consumer device for example.

While problem solving is very specific, it often consists of periodic small doses of creativity. This is particularly true in software development. Creativity is an entire discipline of its own. For our purposes we will discuss the basics as it might apply to software creation.

CREATIVITY AND PROBLEM SOLVING STEPS

One of the obvious conclusions one might draw from a cursory study of creativity is that it typically involves several distinct steps. Even though the end result may be an "aha" moment, there were most assuredly several precursors to that actual moment of illumination. Two sets of creative steps are illustrated below:

Preparation	**Understanding the Challenge**
Incubation	**Generating Ideas**
Intimation	**Preparing for Action**
Illumination	**Planning your Approach**
Formulation	(List on right adapted from Isaksen, Dorval & Treffinger, 2011)

Another key finding is that creativity is not typically available when it's forced. Mozart, the brilliant composer, said that he could not will creativity but rather it had to come to him, usually when he was in a receptive state of mind.

> "When I am... completely myself, entirely alone... or during the night when I cannot sleep, it is on such occasions that my ideas flow best and most abundantly. Whence and how these ideas come I know not nor can I force them."
> — Wolfgang Amadeus Mozart

Unforced creativity is a reasonable argument for getting started early on a project. The earlier you start, the more time creativity has to percolate and nurture within your mind.

For our purposes, knowing that creativity takes time and can be unpredictable is salient. Procrastinating until the moment you need inspiration likely will not suffice. However, it may be that "tinkering" with new software concepts or techniques may unknowingly initiate the incubation process. So maybe that tinkering time is not completely wasted after all. That's what 3M and other leading innovation companies are banking on anyway.

Unconscious vs. Conscious Thinking

Developing algorithms for computer modules and systems can be puzzling, complex, and sometimes downright maddening. Oftentimes there just doesn't appear to be an obvious answer, much less a graceful solution. And remember, top developers don't just want any old solution, they much prefer the most elegant solution and that usually means a solution with the fewest lines of code (this can cause other issues such as maintenance problems later) or perhaps the fastest performing code.

There are many points of reference here. Some studies will conclusively show that one is better off to use the conscious mind to solve complex problems and yet several other studies conclude that allowing the unconscious mind to work is the better approach. So which is better, unconscious or conscious thinking? Well I'm sure by now you knew it wasn't going to be that simple, right? The answer likely depends upon a combination of the exact problem and the individual. For many people, allowing the possible solutions to marinate within your brain is best, and for others they may need to consciously keep working it. If you've ever forgotten a word and have it on the tip of your tongue, you may have found that later on, without consciously thinking about the word, it eventually comes to you. Your mind continued to work on the problem, much like a computer process running in the background.

The psychological term used to describe the unconscious method of problem solving is called **Incubation**. Studies on incubation show that a period of time spent away from the problem may be more effective for problems with multiple solutions. Virtually all software development related problems involve multiple solutions, so the findings here may be applicable. There are two main theories regarding the underlying processes behind incubation. One is that the subconscious mind has some additional time to "work" the problem, as discussed previously. The other theory is that by temporarily departing the problem, it may free your mind from applying standard solution approaches and allow the adoption of entirely new approaches. Either way, studies have shown that literally "sleeping on it," a form of incubating, can in some instances improve solution approaches dramatically (Eyseneck & Keane, 2010).

My personal experiences lead me to believe that approaching problems with a "clean slate" is sometimes critical. Not being aware of the traditional problem solutions allows you to potentially come up with radical solution designs that other, more experienced developers, may not have considered. One of my first professional programming assignments was the creation of a runtime library for a programming language. These libraries consist of hundreds of complex and esoteric functions. Since I was clearly a runtime library rookie, many of my algorithms surprised my more experienced colleagues. And even though several of my designs were busts, there were a few new and more practical approaches as a result.

Five Step Problem Solving Model

This model is recommended by FEMA, the U.S. Federal Emergency Management Agency. Since the model is geared towards medium to large scale emergencies, it may well apply to our discipline (tongue somewhat in cheek).

Step 1: Identify the Problem

Many times in our hurrying ways, especially in software development, we fall into one of two possible traps. The first is defining something as a problem in our mind and the second is to be sure we really understand what the true problem or issue actually is.

If you're working your way through an algorithm or just some maintenance coding, there are times when you encounter a roadblock of some type. It may be minor or it may be something more serious. When this happens the first thing you need to know is whether this is actually a real problem. Once your mind comes around to "Oh, that's definitely a problem" your subconscious mind can kick-start itself to begin searching for solutions or possible workarounds. This framing of an issue as a problem initiates the "problem-solution" sequence in our mind and gets the process started.

That leads to the second issue with problem identification. Do you really understand the underlying problem? This may take a little time to resolve properly, but it can save you the time and pain of going down the wrong path. A good general example is getting lost while driving. After driving about for a while in that "Sort of know where I am" state, the quicker you can get yourself to the point of "Yes, I'm really lost," the faster you will resolve your problem.

It unquestionably pays to take the necessary time to properly define the problem so that subsequent efforts are not in vain. Any false assumptions made in this first critical step can be agonizingly costly, both monetarily and from a schedule perspective. Multiply this several dozen times in a typical software project and you can begin to understand why projects are perennially late.

Step 2: Explore Alternatives

This step can be rather complicated as it involves generating ideas and evaluating their worthiness. Brainstorming is one common method used to generate "raw" ideas and it is discussed in the next section. One problem here is that many times people get off track and generate a surplus of ideas in one vein and a limited amount of ideas in others. In this way Brainstorming actually acts as an Anchor or a Framing Effect (discussed soon) and may limit prospective ideas.

Evaluating ideas is also burdened with problems. Below are the adapted FEMA recommendations for evaluating ideas:

> **Identify Constraints**
>
> **Determine Fit**
>
> **Verify Adequacy**
>
> **Evaluate Effectiveness and Efficiency**
>
> **Determine Side Effects**

One note of importance here is that many times there are several ideas that may be reasonably implemented but that are not practical or cost effective.

Step 3: Select an Alternative

While this step may seem quite trivial, it's actually packed with many perils. These will be discussed forthcoming in the Decision Making section later in this chapter.

Steps 4 & 5: Implement and Evaluate

The last step sequence is one that is typically not fully completed by many software teams. While obviously we implement, we many times do not evaluate. This is typically where the real learning opportunities lie, but many times they are wasted. This is usually the result of how busy development teams are and "if it ain't broke don't fix it." And while this old adage is actually great advice for software development, it may still provide some useful training for junior developers. Perhaps "fixing" is not required, but reviewing what techniques were particularly successful might be useful.

Brainstorming and Process Loss

On the surface, brainstorming certainly seems to make a lot of sense. Eliminating critiques, especially among an audience who can be quite critical seems to be the prudent approach to take. Attempting to capture as many possible resolutions to a problem also appears to be of sound judgment. However, a preponderance of research has shown that people working alone generate more and better ideas than the group as a whole. Software teams may be assembled specifically to address emergencies, such as recovery from a botched release. In some cases they will resort to implementing some form of brainstorming in an attempt to remedy the issues. However, brainstorming looks to be least effective when you need it most – in a crisis. There are at least two possible explanations:

Evaluation Apprehension

Even though ideas are not supposed to be evaluated, per the rules of brainstorming, participants realize that they're obviously still being scrutinized, especially in a group of highly intelligent and analytical people. Therefore, they end up suppressing ideas that they might normally wish to promote. This is particularly true of junior or new members and these members must be strongly encouraged to participate freely in order to realize the optimal benefits.

Process Loss

According to Aronson (2007), "Process Loss is any aspect of group interaction that inhibits good problem solving." There are a number of logistical issues with groups that limit their overall effectiveness. One is the issue of coordination. People typically are expected to wait for others to finish speaking before proffering their own suggestions. This may cause them to disregard their idea, based upon how others may have reacted to similar ideas, or never propose it in the first place. Depending upon the cultural makeup of the group, some members will contribute proportionally more than others. This means that in some groups, at least one group member may have had a better idea than the ideas the group as a whole generated (Kraut 2002).

Modified Brainstorming

One possible way to improve brainstorming results and surmount the problems just described is to have people generate ideas on their own prior to the meeting. Then the group moderator can collate these into several common themes for later debate. Besides generating a significant number of ideas, the process is much more efficient. The only potential downside of using this method is that other's ideas will not create the springboard effect, where someone else's ideas create a related but different idea in another.

PROBLEM SOLVING PROBLEMS

It turns out that determining how best to solve problems is a significant problem in itself. The bottom line is that in order to provide the most exhaustive and optimal solution decision, a comprehensive and lengthy process is required. Obviously this comes as no real surprise, however people are convinced that viable short cuts exist and may take them in weaker moments.

Satisficing

Satisficing is a term coined by Herb Simon that refers to people's tendency to find a solution that's "just good enough" and to not be remorseful about the chosen solution. Rather than digging extensively for the optimal solution, one makes choices that are deemed adequate, since it may be either impossible or infeasible to determine the most favorable resolution. It seems to me that this might be just the alternative many development managers have been searching for all these years. With developers wanting to Gold Plate and business leaders' continual attempts at Feature Creep, Satisficing may be just what the doctor ordered. The concept of Satisficing is closely related to Heuristics.

A possible example of Satisficing (I say possible because I wasn't there while the decision was finalized) occurred at a local chain restaurant our family patronized to celebrate a recent graduation. My in-laws were present and we were intending to share a bottle of wine. To our surprise all of us were required to present our IDs to confirm that we were of legal age. My father-in-law was getting set to commemorate his 83rd birthday in a few weeks. While he's in excellent condition for his age, he was visibly over age 50, much less 21. How does a management team arrive at a decision to card every guest, including senior citizens? Perhaps Satisficing was involved in this situation. It clearly solved their carding dilemma rather handily, even if it continues causing undo frustration for many of their clientele.

Satisficing Risks

While Satisficing may help reduce the cumbersome and time consuming search for optimal solutions, there are some notable risks involved when pursuing this approach as noted below.

Order of Alternatives

How one selects among the perceived choices available to him may have a profound impact on the decision (Hastie & Dawes, 2010). Many studies have shown that the order in which choices are presented will have strong influences on the decision making process and may cause people to eliminate reasonable choices in their haste to make some type of choice. In extreme cases the perceived order of choices may be negatively and intentionally influenced by another party in order to affect someone's decision.

Either / Or Decision Making

A trap that some analytical thinking people may become victim to is feeling compelled to choose between one option or another, when both options somehow combined may actually be a reasonable choice. Tool selection is one area where this may occur. Sometimes it may work to mix tools from different manufacturers, or even tools of different types to create a unique solution for a challenging project. Too many times we think "all or none" and rule out many potentially attractive choices in between.

One small example involved the signature on my credit cards. Some attorneys have suggested that not signing your cards, but rather using the words "See I.D." is safer, since if someone steals the cards they will need to show YOUR ID. So for many years I did not sign my name on the back of my credit cards. Then one day, while standing at the car rental counter in an airport, I was not allowed to rent a car unless my credit card was signed. So what was the ultimate decision that solved both my desire for security and the merchants' requirement for a signature? I now both sign my credit cards and print the phrase "See I.D." in the signature box. Now merchants still ask for my identification but they also have a signed card.

Suppressing Solutions

Many times a practical solution has been right there for the taking all along. I'm sure if you think back on previous projects you'll come up with occasions where this has been the case. Unfortunately, this occurs because of our political nature and stubbornness. Potential solutions are sometimes weighted according to who it is that originally suggested them. This nearly always takes place within a group setting where other members may flex their technical muscle or positional power. This tends to happen in groups that have members with large egos or members who feel a strong need to contribute or prove that they know more than their subordinates or junior peers. Only certain people are "allowed" to discover the proper solutions. There have been studies which sadly prove this can be the case. Managers and group leaders must be cognizant of these behaviors and encourage younger and junior technical professionals to contribute. Lower status group members may wish to discuss their ideas beforehand with their supervisor or other more senior members. The senior member may present the idea and only when it has been accepted should he acknowledge the originator of the suggestion.

Over Architecting

Many analytical and highly open individuals (review the Personality section) will attempt to architect solutions that are so complete and so elegant, in effect a masterpiece, that it becomes untenable. Striving to account for every possible condition impedes software design and therefore software development. Some features and conditions just need to be designed out. This doesn't mean that these special features or conditions are not accounted for; rather these mundane features and states will be relegated to "not supported" status. The standard error processing protocol will be implemented to handle conditions caused by these features. This is one of the key early management decisions that must be made for the sake of saneness in our industry. Architecting, developing, coding, documenting, and testing features that add little value or that will be invoked extremely rarely do not merit consideration other than to elegantly design them out. Of course there are some situations where features will not be able to be designed out of the system. In this case care must be taken to simplify solutions, even if it isn't the most elegant one. This can be difficult for many software designers and architects.

Leaping to Solutions (that laziness thing)

One of our budding societal problems today is that we've come to expect results instantaneously. With always on internet, smart phones, movie downloads, and internet searches, we just assume that the information we want is readily accessible. And it's not just the younger generation either. Many of my colleagues, associates, and friends that are well into middle age are becoming accustomed to getting their information promptly too. They just can't wait to find out whatever it is that they need or want to know.

This can pose a serious problem when dealing in solutions. It's very tempting for software staff to quickly define the supposed ideal solution so that programming can immediately commence. After all, coding is what we prefer to do. As a people, it seems we're becoming "unadapted" to waiting for answers and that includes software solutions as well. People rely heavily upon previous experiences to solve problems. That makes good sense. Without this, we might spend inordinate amounts of time on regular, everyday mundane problems. Many lines of code are a result of "cut and paste." That's because you know it works or at least it worked once before.

The concern is that sometimes as soon as we detect what we think is a familiar pattern to us we jump to conclusions without even considering other possible alternatives. This is the battle with human nature and this type of behavior may be much more prevalent when we're behind schedule, which is quite often. This may be one of the main threats of late development – scraping together a bunch of code from other modules that performed similar functionality. Sometimes it works out just fine and other times, well…

DECISION MAKING

I'm assuming that you're familiar with the illustrious good news – bad news jokes. They go something like this: The ship's captain (of a huge 1500s style Viking row boat) has some good news and bad news to share with his crew. The captain announces the good news: "all of you will get the day off tomorrow;" the bad news is that the captain wants to go water skiing later that night. So I have something similar for you, but it's called bad news – bad news and unfortunately for us it's not a particularly amusing story.

The first bit of dire news is that individuals, all by themselves, can make some very poor decisions in many different, yet expected, types of situations. The other ghastly news is that group decisions can be just as bad, but in different ways. There's really one more bit of unpleasant news here and that is many times, even when people know the tendency, they will still make the wrong decision. Obviously this is not a good situation and since there aren't any other ways to make decisions (at least that I know of) we need to do some serious exploring of these issues. We need to acquire a better understanding of the traps and pitfalls in the decision making process to determine which ones might apply to the software development process and how we can mitigate them, at least to some degree.

In psychology, many times just knowing the issue exists is all it takes to help mitigate it. Once you become aware of something it seems to come up quite frequently. A good example would be when learning a new word. Once you understand the meaning, it then seems you suddenly begin hearing it all the time.

Before we jump into decision making consequences, there is one key point to be made. I realize it's apparent, but it still needs to be stated. Decisions made early on in a project will usually have a greater impact on the project than those made later. This may seem exceedingly obvious, but we need to keep this in mind. Decisions made regarding platforms, tools, schedules, and staffing are all made very early on in a software development project and they are very cumbersome to change later without having a significant impact to the project and its stakeholders.

Individual decision making will be discussed here and you may refer to the Teams chapter for a more detailed review of group based decisions.

Individual Decision Making Pitfalls

There has been a significant amount of research on human decision making. For starters, individuals make decisions in two very basic environments. One is by individuals in private, although private decisions are also influenced by others even when made in complete privacy (more about this later) and the other is as part of some type of group consensus activity. It's difficult to assess how much influence other people have on decisions made by a single person. Once a decision is made, others will eventually find out about it and it may need to be explained and justified. We've already discussed two of the decision making pitfalls: Anchoring and the Planning Fallacy. We could see how outsiders may be able to influence our decisions. In one case it could hurt us (Anchoring) and in the other case it could possibly help us avoid a bad estimate (Planning Fallacy). Following is a more detailed review of some additional common decision making hazards and their application for our industry.

Gambler's Fallacy or The Monte Carlo Effect

The Gambler's Fallacy was mentioned earlier as one possible explanation for software project escalation. This is closely associated with the Planning Fallacy, also discussed, in that people are not necessarily learning from their previous experiences and believe that outcomes will be improved in the future, even when there have been no material changes in procedures. Planning for failure seems to produce the thought that one is also expecting to fail as well. If one is not expecting to fail, and most technical people do not anticipate failing, then "why waste any time on contingency planning" could well be the thinking here. Regardless, decisions that are made based solely upon the idea of "things getting better on their own" are not rational. This may be one of the primary reasons that many people in software engineering believe that those who are more pessimistic are better suited for the industry.

Prospect Theory

"In short, those faced with gains tend to be risk averse, while those confronting losses become much more risk seeking" (McDermott & Fowler, 2008). As mentioned in our discussion of Project Escalation, this could be a possible rationale for much of the project escalation tendencies in software development. It seems as though we are continually facing losses and the urge to make it all up can exacerbate the problem. Clearly it can precipitate unusually risky behavior when you combine it with the Overconfidence Barrier.

Daniel Kahneman won the Nobel Prize in Economics in 2002 for his work with Amos Tversky on what is now widely known as Prospect Theory. This new theory contradicted many of the older theories of decision making, creating significant interest in behavioral economic studies designed to review irregularities in how people make decisions.

Prospect Theory comprises two phases, the editing phase, which constitutes framing effects, and the evaluation phase. Framing effects prove that people will make significantly different decisions when facing alternate outcome framings (Tversky and Kahneman 1981). As an example, people will make different choices about medical treatment when options are phrased in terms of "survival" or "mortality," even when the objective results remain the same. Specifically, people are much more risk averse in the "gain frame" when outcomes are expressed in terms of the probability of living (survival), than in the "loss frame" when outcomes are expressed in terms of the probability of dying (mortality) (McNeil, Sox, and Tversky, 1982).

The evaluation phase has both a value and a weighting component. The value function predicts risk aversion in the area of gains and risk taking in losses. Weighting shows that individuals have a strong tendency to overweight small probability events while also underweighting the more medium and high probability events. Normally, people overweight certainty, so that they are likely to think of highly probable events as near certain and highly improbable events as though they are impossible.

This could mean, in our domain for example, that a Project Manager might believe that the product schedules will be considered highly likely to be attained at first, since he created them. Subsequently he may convince himself that it is all but a certainty they will be accurate. That is, he is overweighting the possibility of a successful schedule because he believes that schedule failure was a small probability from the outset. Again, this is just one more example of the flawed ways in which people have a tendency to think. This doesn't mean that this will always be the case for any one individual in any one defined circumstance of course, but only a general tendency.

Prospect Theory might help explain why once a software project gets into trouble, team members start coming up with unlikely (read as risky) solutions because they are desperate as they are facing a potential loss. Yet they may actually believe that these unlikely solutions will correct the project and allow it to get back on track. What's more likely to happen is that the proposed risky solutions will further endanger the project eliciting perhaps even more subsequent risky solutions.

Expected Value Theory

Much of our previous understanding and thinking concerning decision making has been rooted in economic theory. Economists, and scientists from other disciplines, generally assumed that people would naturally make decisions that were optimal for them economically, regardless of the other factors involved. Subsequent research in this realm has shown that people do not necessarily think this way much of the time. Several other factors come into play when decisions are contemplated, such as perceived fairness, levels of emotional attachment, and how available options are positioned or framed. Furthermore, people are constantly resorting to short cuts, or rules of thumb (referred to as Heuristics by Psychologists), when making a variety of decisions in order to avoid over thinking or consuming too much time, often times without realizing it.

The way decision making is viewed in the Expected Value model is that users will make choices that yield the optimal return by conceptualizing a mathematical model of sorts in their mind. They will review the various choices they perceive (a key concept here is the person's perception of their available options) are available to them and attempt to associate both a probability of that event occurring and the resultant payoff. The probability of the event multiplied by the resultant payout yields the expected value. So choosing the option with the highest expected value would be the most logical choice. As it turns out, decisions rarely play out this way because of the aforementioned issues further examined below.

Framing Effects

Decisions are strongly influenced by how a problem is framed or perceived by the decision maker. Once a person becomes locked into a particular framework it becomes immensely difficult to view the problem in any other way. What's even worse is that these frameworks may not even be of our own making. They may be suggested by other influential people or just a normal part of our cultural thinking, the way things have always been done.

A pertinent example from my past will illustrate framing more succinctly. In the 1990s I worked for a company that designed and manufactured Light Pens. I'm not referring to a writing instrument with an attached light, but rather a mouse-like device used to navigate a computer monitor. The pen detects the screen refresh cycle and is able to calculate where it is on the screen in terms of X, Y coordinates. These devices were designed to be used in manufacturing and other environments where a mouse wasn't optimal. However a tricky problem emerged in conditions of high static electricity that caused the pen to receive false reads from the monitor. The result was a mish mash of zigzag lines all across the screen and it essentially rendered the device useless. The hardware engineers' solution was to focus on the pen materials that came in contact with the monitor and would therefore reduce the amount of static electricity created. They spent weeks in a vain attempt to come up with suitable materials. Once the software people (including me) discovered the problem we quickly realized it might be resolved via a special software algorithm in the driver; after all we didn't know much about material attributes. By throwing out virtually impossible reads (a person couldn't realistically move their hand several inches in a millisecond's time) the problem was solved (well it was a little more involved than described here). This example highlights some of the negative impacts that framing can have on decision making and problem solving. The hardware team and management, both having hardware backgrounds, were convinced that the only practical solution was a different material for the tip of the pen. Due to their lack of software understanding they went down the only path they thought viable. Their frame of reference limited the solution options they pursued.

The problem here is that once you begin down the wrong path you may become doggedly determined to solve the problem and then it becomes even more difficult to change your approach. A little cognitive dissonance and sunk costs may come into play here also. The longer you've pursued one approach to the problem, the less likely it is you'll be capable of admitting your mistake or believing that you'll soon prevail. This is a case where the "99% perspiration" rule doesn't apply and may actually impair progress. People with Driver personality types may be at risk for continuing down the wrong solution path for too long when they might be better served by reevaluating the situation. One effective way to re-examine lingering problems is by bringing in people with completely unrelated backgrounds and viewpoints. These parties may come up with an approach that would otherwise never have been considered.

Heuristics

It appears as though the majority of people will take cognitive shortcuts most of the time. This is my conclusion from researching dozens of sources on this topic. When people employ rules of thumb, or other thinking short cuts, it's referred to academically as Heuristics. And while I'd like to think differently,

I'm guessing that technical professionals are not much different from everyone else in this regard. Assumedly we will fail less frequently when deductive logic is involved, but I'm not quite sure I'm ready to bet on that outcome either. Study after study reveals that people will make common mistakes due primarily to the use of heuristics even when there is no time constraint involved. It also appears as though cognitive ability is unrelated to outcomes on most judgmental tasks (Stanovich & West, 2008). This does not bode well for our industry and indicates that people are very likely to fall into regular patterns of thinking. While this may almost assuredly save us time over the long run, errors are virtually certain to occur in isolated incidents. This is why even senior developers should participate in code reviews and other quality control practices. While they have more experience, they also have encountered more patterns that they will attempt to apply to similar problems.

During the regular course of life, we become conditioned to using heuristics on a daily basis. If you had to logically analyze every little thing you did over the course of a single day you'd be exhausted or at the least, you'd be very tight for time. So instead, we exploit mental short cuts that work out just fine for us on most occasions.

COMMON HEURISTICS

Two of the more commonly engaged heuristics are Availability and Representative heuristics.

The **Availability Heuristic** is the assumption that the likelihood of an event occurring can be precisely estimated by the ease of which it can be recalled by one's memory. People tend to believe that some rare, yet sensational, events occur more often than they really do, like system outages versus system performance issues. This is because it may be easier to remember a system that was completely unavailable than a slow performing one.

The **Representative Heuristic** is the inclination to judge the probability of an event based on how closely it resembles the typical case one has in mind. When I was attending college many people thought I was from California because I had a dark tan and blonde hair from working outdoors all summer. They believed this even though exceptionally few people that attended my small Minnesota college were from California. But since I met their best representation of what they expected a Californian to look like, they falsely assumed that's where I was from.

Dual Process Theory

While it's absolutely clear that we can perform complex cognitive tasks at times but that we also engage in short cuts, a two process theory of reasoning has since evolved. They are labeled simply as System 1 and System 2. System 1 is our more automatic and less taxing mode of reasoning whereby we employ a variety of universal heuristics to make decisions. System 2 is the analytic and logical reasoning system that applies systematic rules and known facts to infer conclusions. System 2 is slower and requires linkages from one thought or construct to the next and may be limited by our working memory capacity. System 2 is much more deliberate in nature whereas System 1 reasoning happens without us consciously thinking about it.

The dual process theory proposes that we will come to a conclusion on a task with each system and when there is a different outcome between the two we then need to invoke System 2 to make the final decision. In many instances System 2 reasoning is never even summoned; however there is nominal evidence to suggest that highly intelligent people make more use of System 2 reasoning. This may perhaps explain their superior intelligence.

Emotions & Fairness

There is much debate about the role of emotion in decision making, but I think it's fair to assume from the research that too much emotion may cloud the decision making process. This is an area where some technical people appear to struggle. My advice would be to ask for more time to review the alternatives when feeling forced to make a quick decision under emotional duress, even if it means getting back to someone later that same day with your thoughts. Once the inner brain seizes control, the prefrontal cortex is shortchanged and that is where critical thinking originates. Giving your brain time to normalize will allow you to make a more informed decision.

In those cases where people feel they have been cheated or treated unfairly, they may resort to decisions that are not in their best interest in order to extract some sort of revenge. It's clear that emotions can impact decisions in many varied ways and making decisions while in an emotionally aroused state is typically not advised.

TWO POSSIBLE METHODS TO CONTROL THIS TYPE OF SITUATION:

Reinterpretation

This is one of several cognitive reappraisal approaches that may be used to reinterpret the meaning of an event in order to modify the resultant response. People who employ some form of reappraisal "express less negative emotions than individuals who use the reappraisal strategy less frequently" (Gross & John, 2003).

Distancing

This mechanism involves taking a detached stance or third-person view of a situation. Pretending that you're watching the scene play out, as if you're watching it on TV perhaps, with yourself being one of the actors.

In both of these techniques, the brain is disengaging with the amygdala, which is involved in emotional responses, and engaging the prefrontal cortex.

Who Makes the Decision Decision

While this section heading may appear to be a typo, having two of the same words in a row, it is actually correct. Determining who makes a decision is also a decision of sorts. First, as you will soon learn, the Group Think quandary featured in the Software Teams section, tells us that groups have a tendency to become enthralled with conformity and efficiency. They prefer to make decisions quickly and move on and I would posit that this is especially so in software development as most of us would much rather be performing the actual work of creating software versus spending the necessary time on prepping and planning components. Group members who dissent are frowned upon and often viewed as trouble makers and they just delay the inevitable group majority decision, whatever it might be. Damaging long standing personal relationships because of a single decision is not comfortable or appealing for most people. They'd rather just go along with the majority and not be thought of as boat rockers, especially when they are new team members, members with junior status, or considered to already be in the minority somehow. When people do dissent, it is many times the same individual and therefore their comments are typically discounted and the dissenting remarks are expected and do not help contribute to a viable solution.

There are also grave concerns regarding the viability of the individual decision making process as previously discussed, such as the regular reliance upon numerous heuristics. Therefore I will present some guidelines for when to employ group decision making versus individual decision making.

Guidelines for Decision Making

This section is adapted from FEMA Decision Making & Problem Solving (2002).

Answer each of the key decision questions below either yes or no.

If the response to question 1 is "No," it may be preferable to make the decision individually or in consultation with one or two key players.

If the response to question 2 is "No," it may be preferable to make the decision through consultation, with a group, or by delegation.

If the majority of your responses are "Yes," group decision making may be preferable.

If the majority of your responses are "No," individual decision making may be preferred.

Key Decision Questions:

1) **Do you have enough time to make the decision?**

2) **Does the group leader have the necessary expertise to make the decision?**

3) **Do the group members have enough knowledge to make a good decision?**

4) **Do the group members share in the organizational outcomes that will be attained when the problem is solved?**

5) **Is the decision complex with many possible solutions?**

6) **Is commitment from members in the group critical to success?**

7) **Is the decision likely to cause serious conflict among the people it impacts?**

8) **Does the decision impact only a few people?**

While this is a good general model, there are some possible pratfalls for use in the technical field. Many technical leaders may feel that they have the expertise to make nearly all decisions within their domain, therefore deciding without sufficient input from outside experts. Also, many technical decisions will typically not directly impact the decision makers, beyond long term job security that is. So while this may be a reasonable guideline, it is certainly not foolproof.

Personality Impacts

Our individual personalities play a fundamental role when we engage in decision making. This probably goes without saying, but many of us still disregard our personal tendencies and most of us renounce our weaknesses. As a group largely dominated by analytic personalities we need to be open and flexible when it comes time to make important decisions. Analytic personalities prefer to have all the facts and data in hand prior to making decisions while also reviewing all probable outcomes. Achieving all of these conditions is somewhat rare and therefore overcoming the desire to make a mathematical type of choice may be required.

Risk Propensity and Personality

With all the potential that exists for calamity within our profession, it would be prudent to better understand the personality tendencies that may support risky decisions.

In a study of risk propensity and personality (Nicholson, et. al., 2001) it was found that several factors may influence risk taking. Young males generally tend to make riskier decisions, though many of these may occur outside the professional domain. From a personality standpoint it was found that some people are consistently risk takers where others are consistently risk averse. Because someone takes risks in one area does not necessarily imply that they will be risk takers in others.

In terms of the Big Five, their study yielded the following results: High extraversion and openness supply the motivational force while low neuroticism and agreeableness protect people from negative consequences. However, the biggest finding, according to the researchers, was that low conscientiousness would lower the cognitive barriers to excessive risk taking. So it appears that a well defined blend of personality attributes, along with being younger and male could potentially be a formula for unwarranted risk taking.

PART III

People

CHAPTER 10

The Talent Pool

HIRING

It all starts out right here. That very first day when a promising candidate walks into the boss' office and stares across the desk in one of the most dreaded of activities for technical people; the infamous job interview. In some cases it may consist of two male introverts who don't prefer to talk all that much gaping at one another and wondering how to get through the next hour or so. It doesn't have to be this way for either party, so we'll further explore some interviewing techniques for both sides of the bargaining table later in this section.

Good software is a direct result of quality developers. There are some tasks that average developers will never be able to accomplish and then there are the myriad tasks that average developers will complete an order of magnitude slower than a high caliber one. This is another major difference between software developers and housing construction workers, a profession often times compared analogously to software engineering. I doubt if the best carpenters are ten times faster at framing a house than an average one, but yet this is the declared difference in ability that many claim exists in our profession. There are some even bolder claims that this difference may be significantly larger, such as 100:1.

If this is even partially true then the emphasis on hiring is immense and companies must create bullet proof methods for weeding out weak talent. I'm not saying that every development team member must be an A player. But it's certainly important to know who your A players are and which B players have the aptitude and attitude to become A players at some future date.

Here is the real conundrum however. You want top flight developers, PMs, BAs and DBAs but you also want people who can work together as a team and who are capable of remaining focused on the work while also resisting the decoy of group politics. You would prefer to have staff on board that has good social and emotional intelligence (review Chapter 8, Analog Intelligence, for more on this topic), is properly motivated and works hard every day too. It can be challenging to ascertain all of these traits in one person, especially a technical person (remember, I'm one too) in the course of an interview. So your hiring methods must include techniques for determining if candidates exhibit at least some of these other traits beyond the required technical ones.

I distinctly remember an interview I once had with the CEO of a fairly large company. I was surprised to be interviewing with the CEO for a development position and had little time to prepare, as it wasn't on the days' agenda, and as it turns out this was a part of the plan. While en route to his office, my escort warned me that this CEO was famous for asking a trick question or two of the candidates. He suggested that I be ready for this type of question if indeed it came up. Well of course it came up and I remember the question still today, even though it was asked long ago. The question was this; how do you determine, in an interview, if someone is a good developer? Great question I thought as I fumbled for that well deserved clever retort. My answer, though not really all that clever, was that he would find out in about 3 months or so. I did get the job, so I guess my answer was at least plausible. The point behind this question was really to determine a little about my social skills. Of course, while he would like the real answer to the question, it was really just a way to test my response in a pressure situation. Would I get flustered? Respond with humor? Make something up? These are the answers he was really after. He was letting the others evaluate me technically, he just wanted to see if I could think and speak clearly in an ambiguous situation.

Another issue with interviews is that they are known to have low validity (Statt, 2004). That is, the interview itself is not a good indicator of an interviewee's abilities to perform the duties of the job in question. The same holds true for personal references. In fact when hiring technical people, the classic job interview may be better suited for assessing social skills than technical ones. According to Hogan and Kaiser (2005) psychopaths and narcissists excel during job interviews. It's only later, after they've been on the job for a while, that you find out about their hidden personality flaws.

Interviewing Guidelines for Technical Staff

Preparation

Many technical people may only arrive partially prepared for an interview. They may be well aware of the technical requirements of the position, but not the broader business objectives. Educating oneself on the company's history and reputation will often times be helpful and it also provides a good opening introduction for the interview, one that displays both a little class and social awareness. Most people conducting interviews like to start things out with some lighter conversational fare rather than jumping right into the meat of the interview. Some of us technical people prefer to cut right to the chase, usually a result of nerves. Initiating the interview with some small talk will typically earn you some respect. One favorite tactic of mine is to pick up on any cues in the office relating to the interviewer's personal interests, perhaps from a photo, and start out with a related question.

Answering Interview Questions

A classic answer to a question from software professionals is "Yes" or perhaps "Yes, I have done that before." Instead of just countering with a straightforward "yes" or "no" answer, strive to highlight relevant examples of your past work that make the most sense. Elaborate on when and why you've used some particular technology or tool and the ultimate outcome. Real life examples are the most pertinent. Remember, the interviewer is not just interested in your technical accomplishments, but also how you interact with others and what type of personality you bring to the team. It certainly doesn't hurt to show a little excitement as well, assuming it's genuine. Another useful tip is to ask the interviewer if you've successfully answered their question. This also exhibits maturity and may catch the interviewer pleasantly off guard.

Attire

Many of us insist on donning a decent shirt and tie for an interview, only to accompany it with wrinkled slacks and scruffy shoes. Now I will admit that some software development cultures frown upon overly dressed technical professionals. It's nearly always better however, to over dress for an interview. If you're not sure of the dress code, check with someone familiar with the organization beforehand. I've found that business casual attire works best for most technical interviews. Some will frown on jeans and tennis shoes and others will be surprised if you show up in a suit. For women, I believe it's a bit simpler; dress pants and a nice top will usually suffice. My personal rule of thumb is to dress one notch above the standard for the position in question.

Interview Protocol

Nearly every interview is unique. There seem to be few existing standards for interviewing technical candidates and virtually no training for the interviewer in the process in most cases. Many insist on asking hypothetical questions, which glean little practical information (Statt, 2004). For as much job interviewing that takes place, you wouldn't think this would be the circumstance we find ourselves in.

If the interviewer is slowly meandering and not getting to the point of the interview, it's generally best to just go with the flow and not blurt out all of your technical expertise. He may just be attempting to get to know you better or in some cases, for technical interviews, letting you become comfortable in the interview process so he can attempt to discover the real you.

It's acceptable during the course of an interview to say those words every technical person utterly dreads; "I don't know." Some interviewers will actually test candidates specifically for this capability. They want to know if a candidate is humble and will openly admit when they don't know something versus making something up. It's more of an integrity check really and I think it's a reasonably sound tactic and one that I advocate.

People Skills vs. Technical Skills

Many companies today are much more focused upon candidates' interpersonal skills than they were 10 or 20 years ago. Organizations have come to realize that it's better to have a highly cohesive group of above average technical people than a dysfunctional group of geniuses. My personal rule was that more than one "genius" can spoil the software broth and in fact a single "genius" may be enough to sufficiently obstruct the wheels of progress. At SWAT Solutions, we now consider people skills at least half the equation. When interviewing candidates for consulting positions this is even more imperative today than ever before. Consultants must sometimes enter difficult conditions where tensions are high, so they must be highly adaptable and have strong social skills to help guide them through tense situations. See the section on Consulting Skills for more details.

Of course, many technical people disregard social skill upgrades and would much prefer to acquire more and greater technical skills. It's somewhat difficult to blame us really, because of the torrid pace of technological advancement that's taken place these past three decades. With Moore's Law and the relatively newer technologies, such as wireless, progressing so quickly we'd be fools not to attempt to keep pace. That being said, I still believe that most software engineering professionals would benefit even more from social skill improvements. Of course, a certain level of technical competence and dexterity must be maintained for any good technical person to keep on advancing and in many cases just to break even. My advice is to stay current technically, but to also make continual investments in your social skills.

Screening Candidates

Resumes, unfortunately, are not a great way to screen candidates. I've reviewed thousands of them over the last decade alone and I don't believe that I've seen a single resume that didn't contain the phrase "Excellent verbal and written communication skills" or something very similar. Now I might actually believe this in some cases if I were in the Journalism profession, but since I'm working in the high tech field, where many of us are introverted males, this is somewhat concerning. While many people in our profession do indeed have excellent interpersonal and communication skills, this is undoubtedly not the norm. In fact this phrase is now so worn-out and clichéd that we've become immune to its intent and not just in the technical disciplines.

Another major pitfall of many resumes is the list of technologies one is supposedly proficient in. This inventory is usually just a laundry list of everything someone has seen or heard of and maybe touched briefly at one time or another. So that too becomes rather insignificant. In some ways a very long list is a yellow flag for me. It's really challenging to become an expert in nearly every technology and tool in the market. I would strongly advise technical professionals to have a professional review and prepare your resume with you. Based upon my extensive experience reviewing resumes, it would help you stand out from the crowd and provide you with some credibility.

The last piece of information to ignore on most resumes is the reference list. These are almost always people who will say wonderful and amazing things about the candidate. The best reference is the one who isn't on the resume. That will require a little more effort to obtain. Social networking sites, like LinkedIn and for other people perhaps Facebook, can be helpful in finding connections to your candidates beyond those listed on the resume.

Technical Proficiency Tests

There are businesses that run websites to administer tests in many of the common programming languages and tools. These tests can be an objective means of determining someone's skills. Besides ranking their technique, these tests will record the time it took for the candidate to complete. These are not 100% bullet proof tests, but I believe that they are worth serious consideration. eSkill.com is one such organization that provides pre-employment technical testing. The one nice feature of these tests is the consistency of the results compared to someone's opinion of a candidate's skills based upon a 15 minute discussion.

Successful Interviewing Techniques & Pitfalls

Order of Interview

There are a number of minor psychological impacts that occur during an interview process. One of these is a result of the order in which candidates are sequentially interviewed. There are two effects that come into play, the **Primacy Effect** and the **Recency Effect**. For candidates who interview last they would have the benefit of the recency effect because the interviewer will be prone to remember more about the most recent candidate and have a tendency to favor them, particularly if the decision will be made imminently. Candidates who interview first also have an advantage in that they've had the benefit of first impressions and have a leg up on subsequent candidates, especially if hiring decisions are prolonged and the interviewers' recency effect has diminished.

Halo Effect

When people attribute a host of positive personal traits to an individual based upon an irrelevant trait, it is referred to as the **Halo Effect**. It is normally associated with attractive people, but may also be associated with other traits. Multiple studies over many decades have proven beyond a reasonable doubt that attractive people have numerous advantages in life. They are regularly thought of as smarter, more capable, and more honest. In our situation other factors may possibly yield a halo effect as well. These would include certain former employers that may have a reputation for hiring top talent (or lower tier talent) and work completed on certain projects that may have an aura about them, such as a NASA project perhaps. It's reasonably difficult to moderate this effect in one's mind once it's been lodged there however. That's why in these cases you may opt to wait a day or so before making a decision regarding the candidate in question.

We Like Ourselves

While generally it's healthy for us to like ourselves, during the interview process it may work against us. Research has revealed that we tend to like candidates more like ourselves and will actually spend more time and engage more with these sorts of candidates. This is not a surprising finding but one that ought to be guarded against during the interview process. As software development has become a global endeavor, more and more qualified candidates are coming from all corners of the earth.

Identifying Positive Traits

When interviewing a candidate for a software position, one approach is to separate technical assessments from social and personal assessments. The other is to attempt to mix the two approaches with one set of questions. One handy way to engage a software professional is to ask them to critique something (Venners, 2003). This gets their cognitive juices flowing and plays into their personality somewhat. Asking them to identify the benefits and pratfalls of some particular language or tool is a great way to really understand what makes them tick and establish how much software engineering acumen they possess. As we know, this type of activity will engage their prefrontal cortex and allow them to share with you their knowledge and interests.

You should also consider asking them how they deal with team dysfunction by having them provide an example where they were able to overcome a difficult situation. Better yet, ask them to describe their conflict coping styles, again preferably using a real life example.

In my interviews with candidates I always start by asking them what they like doing. If they could write up their own job description, how would it read? One of my colleagues likes to ask people what they would prefer to be doing on a Sunday afternoon. This affords a little glimpse into their personal life and perhaps what motivates them.

Consulting Skills

Various people falsely assume that working as a consultant or contractor is identical to being an employee of an organization. There are some psychological nuances that consultants must be aware of so they can perform at their absolute best.

Employees may resist consultants

I've found that there are several possible reactions employees have when a consultant shows up on a Monday morning for a new assignment. Some employees believe that consultants are overpaid, erroneously assuming that the rate charged for the consultant is their pay rate. While this may be the case for truly independent consultants (even though it doesn't include payroll taxes), this is extremely rare. Most consultants are paid comparably to the people they're working with or perhaps just slightly higher. After all, they are consultants for a reason. This leads directly to the next issue and that is unreasonably lofty expectations. If you believe one is overpriced you might naturally expect them to perform miracles of some sort. Many consultants do have two distinct advantages: a small army of fellow consultants backing them up, and the benefit of experience on other similar projects at other companies. However, even with these advantages they still have their limits.

Another, and possibly more serious issue, is that employees may feel threatened by these types of workers and may sense that they have personally let the company down because a consultant was required to be brought on board. "I could have solved that problem if only..." may be the thought process here. These employees may attempt to undermine the work of the consultant and this can escalate into serious problems. Behaviors as a result of this type of thinking include the **Not Invented Here Syndrome**. Unfortunately, this is a common condition where people only support their own ideas or creations due to their sensitive egos, and it's especially prevalent in Individualistic societies such as the U.S. (see Chapter 13). This may in turn result in the rejection of some potentially high-quality suggestions for improvement. As mentioned previously, technical people are exceptionally proud of their work and suggestions coming from others may feel threatening to some.

Of course, the majority of employees welcome with open arms the additional help and the outside perspective consultants often provide.

EVALUATING PERFORMANCE

This is an area where corporate standards appear to deviate fairly significantly. I've worked for ten different organizations ranging from those very large global corporations to those with as few as a handful of employees, and everything in between. All ten of these organizations utilized a different system, although somewhat similar of course, for evaluating performance. Some were unconventional and did not coordinate performance reviews with salary adjustments, although most companies do make their salary updates as part of the performance review.

Self Review

One popular method of performance evaluation is to have the employee perform a self review first and then the supervisor will share his review and compare the differences. I've never particularly cared for this method of review because it forces the employee to make the first move. Now it's possible that the supervisor has become anchored, either too high or low, in an area of the performance rating. The reason this method is employed is to limit the number of "shock" reviews where the employee's view of himself is drastically different from those of his supervisors. This does make a certain amount of sense when working with delicate technical egos.

People may also have concerns that other areas of the review may have been compromised as well. Perhaps a supervisor, after reading the employee's self-review, now elects not to highlight an area of accomplishment not mentioned by the employee. While this is unlikely, it could theoretically be used to reduce the employee's annual compensation adjustment. These are concerns I have personally heard from technical staff in the past. Another potential problem with self-reviews is the possibility for gamesmanship. The employee nearly always inflates their self-review and I believe this is to be somewhat expected. They're hoping that this may leave some room for negotiation with their supervisor and perhaps they can meet somewhere in the middle.

360-Degree Feedback

360-degree evaluation systems solicit feedback from the employee's peers, supervisors, and subordinates. It's a more comprehensive system because people on all sides of the employee are rating his performance, thus the name 360-degree. Also referred to as multi-rater systems, this method of performance evaluation seems particularly well suited for use with technical staffers. For starters, virtually all of these systems are now web enabled which suites technical people perfectly, and most importantly the feedback is anonymous. Since many of us are not entirely comfortable sharing difficult messages with our colleagues, this method of providing feedback is practically ideal. The 360-degree critics allege that this type of anonymous feedback does not promote an atmosphere of openness and could eventually undermine organizations who adopt it.

The power of 360-degree feedback is that once employees start receiving consistent messages about their behaviors from multiple sources of different types, it becomes much more difficult to disregard the negative feedback. The key here is that people may be receiving similar messages from more than just one person, typically their supervisor.

Some years ago I attended a mandatory HR internal company seminar that essentially performed 360-degree feedback on all of the seminar participants. However, this version had a slight twist. It was done right in front of the other person. In fact, you were required to sit on the "witness stand" while the "jury," your peers, gave you their verdicts one at a time. All of the "jurors" were required to come up with several negative attributes of the "witness." One employee in particular was stunned to find out what many of his co-workers thought about her, some who had been working with her for nearly a decade. According to CIO Magazine correspondent Michael Schrage, "a reasonably good 360 probably could do more for MIS productivity than the latest suite of object-oriented development tools" (CIO Magazine, October 1, 2002). Another benefit of these systems is that many technical people are just not aware of their unacceptable behavioral patterns. When several co-workers deliver a similar message it becomes much more apparent than if it comes from your supervisor alone.

LETTING STAFFERS GO

Your options for a poor performer are generally limited to remediation, finding a better work fit, or firing. Often times however, supervisors find themselves caught in no man's land. That is, rather than take action they just keep muddling along, perhaps hoping it will get better on its own (see the Gambler's Fallacy). Terminating an employee is a serious matter and many technical people will do nearly anything to avoid it.

Once you find yourself unhappy with a subordinate on a regular basis, you must quickly determine the following:

> Can the problem(s) be easily remedied?

> Are the subordinate's skills duly suitable for the task?

If the answer to these questions is a resounding "No," then your alternatives are to either find another position for the individual or terminate their employment, typically in that order. My experience is that many technical managers postpone these types of decisions and resort to incessant complaining instead – which in my opinion is the worst form of management. By utilizing this recommended structure, you'll find that everyone will generally be better off, however it does require having some involved discussions with the subordinate.

Undoubtedly for most people, firing employees is the least desirable part of the job. I would argue even more so for the technical profession where social skills are not at the top of our list. Many times we try to remedy the situation for too long before firing a person who may not have a reasonable chance of working out for the long term. There's a sensible business adage that states: Hire slow and fire fast. This is practical advice and if you hire slowly, meaning carefully, you may avoid having to do as much firing later. However, once someone is causing undue distractions, in addition to not completing their work suitably, waiting too long to terminate an employee can cause considerable morale issues for the remaining good performers. If management cannot resolve the issue in a succinct manner, confidence in the management team may be diminished and other problems may ensue.

Terminating employees generally involves consulting with an HR representative to discuss the proper methods as determined by company policy. Typically HR likes to see a performance plan implemented, with the associated comprehensive documentation, prior to termination. My suggestion is that if you have an employee who is causing team issues or not performing the assigned duties as prescribed, consult with HR sooner rather than later. Have them help you craft a plan to proactively and constructively manage your low-end performers.

CHAPTER 11

Teams

Decades ago a young, relatively unknown psychologist conducted a series of experiments, now famous, that exemplifies the power of groups. The Asch experiments, as they are known today, show just how powerful an influence groups can have on others (see the side bar). As it goes with individual decision making so it goes with groups and teams as well. There appears to be more problems to surmount in teams or groups than with individuals alone. Since software is largely a team activity, at least in many instances, we need to explore the issues and pitfalls with teams and in particular, software teams.

The Real Value of Technical Teams

While the principal benefit of teamwork on most activities is due to the utilization of the differing skill sets people bring to the team, there is one area where teamwork really stands out. Several years ago one of our top tier consultants was struggling mightily on a complex and demanding project. This consultant eventually bottomed out and his productivity sank precipitously low, to the point where the client suggested that we consider removing him from the project. Instead we opted to "parachute in" another top consultant to facilitate a "rescue operation." Once the two consultants began working on the project together the original consultant felt the pressure begin to ease. He started to get his confidence back and realized that the project wasn't hopeless anymore. Soon he was back to his usual productive self and we were able to pull his rescuing companion off the project.

When technical people feel that their project is doomed, their production may abruptly nosedive. Not because they've suddenly lost their overall technical abilities, but rather because they just can't visualize a realistic way out of the situation and some of us are too self-conscious and prideful to ask for help. Every little problem or issue that subsequently crops up now seems overbearing in nature and just adds to the woefulness of the circumstances. At some point very little if anything is accomplished and even though the person may still be clocking hours, productivity comes to a virtual standstill. This is where teamwork really provides value to organizations. The ability to "parachute in" a teammate who can lend a helping hand is truly invaluable in some instances.

TEAM TENDENCIES

Conformity

In order to become a true team there is much conforming that typically occurs. Too much non-conformity by any one member and the team may ostracize that person or, in some cases, even punish them. However, too much conformity also negates the primary reason teams form in the first place. That is, to come up with solutions that any one person may be unable or unwilling to attain on their own. People will conform for various reasons, one being the need to belong and be liked. This is a strong human need that has been verified by numerous researchers over the years. Therefore, there will almost assuredly be conformity of some type in virtually all groups. Ironically, if there is not enough conformity among members productivity will be limited.

THE ASCH LINE STUDY EXPERIMENTS

A psychologist by the name of Solomon Asch conducted a series of clever experiments in the 1950s to determine just how much people might conform to what others think. In the experiment, several participants are shown two cards, one with a single line and the other with three lines of varying lengths labeled lines 1, 2, & 3. Each participant is asked to publicly declare which of the three lines on card two most closely matches the length of the solitary line on card one. For the first several rounds all of the participants are in agreement when all of the sudden the first several participants select a line length match that is plainly wrong. As it turns out, all of the participants but one are experimental accomplices and have been trained to select the wrong line. The subject in question is one of the last people to state their line match. So now you have several other people who have all chosen what obviously appears to be the wrong line match and suddenly it's your turn to make a selection. What would you do?

In the Asch experiments seventy six percent of the participants conformed on at least one trial. Subjects conformed on roughly one third of the trials where the accomplices selected the wrong answer and some small percentage conformed almost every time.

According to Bibb Latane's Social Impact Theory (Aronson pg 251) people will be more likely to conform according to the level of three variables; the importance of the group, how close to them in space or time the group is and the number of people within the group. When group numbers grow, the level of influence per new member will obviously decrease (unless perhaps it's the CIO or other high status individuals). However in software development it's rare to see especially large groups, of say more than 15 members. Therefore adding or subtracting one or two members from a software team may have a fairly significant impact on the performance of the team. Depending upon the personality of the new members, other members that may have been fully engaged and contributing to the group may shut down to some degree. This is where managers must be attentive to these dynamics and intercede when necessary to pull those prior contributing members back into the group.

Adding members to a group can have several possible outcomes. One interesting condition is when a new employee joins an established team within the company. She may have great ideas that are dead on perfect solutions for the problem du jour, but it's very likely that she may be ignored, at least initially. Matthew Hornsey and colleagues (Hornsey et al., 2007) have conducted studies in this vein indicating that newcomers, with the same ideas as established reputable members, will have considerably different outcomes when presenting their solution. The same idea from an established member may be dutifully embraced while the newcomer's exact resolution may be discarded off hand. One possible way to resolve this dilemma, other than waiting for the new employee to become accepted by the group, is for the new member to share her idea in private with the group leader, or another influential member, beforehand. There are experiments where groups were "seeded" with a low power individual who knew the answer to a problem the group was charged to solve. This individual offered the solution many times during the problem solving exercise only to be ignored because of his status. Leaders are often times blind to ideas from the "wrong" people and will keep searching for answers until one of the more elite members is "enlightened."

Resisting Conformity

This can be a hard habit to break. Once someone is well established in a group the others expect a certain pattern of behaviors to occur. A teammate who feels a strong need to refuse the group's decision has two basic options, if they still wish to maintain their longstanding credibility; one is to cash in some Idiosyncrasy Credits and the other is to find an ally. Having just one other ally in the group will help one resist conformity considerably, especially as noted in smaller groups. **Idiosyncrasy Credits** are abstract credits one earns for being a loyal upstanding (read as conforming) part of a team over some sustained time period. This allows someone to occasionally deviate from the group standards without risking their standing on the team, the key word here being "occasionally."

Group Participation

Studies have shown that within groups the speaking which takes place is heavily skewed to a substantial minority of the group. In a six person team for instance, three people do more than 85% of the talking. It wouldn't be a revelation to me if these numbers were even more skewed when it comes to meetings of business and development groups as participation is principally influenced by personality, status, and company culture. Psychologists have discovered that group members who talk the most are more likely to be perceived and acknowledged as leaders. Even those who interrupt others while speaking were perceived to have more influence and in some surprising cases even more influence than those who waited their turn to speak. Who knew that all along Mom could have been wrong!

Group Think

First coined for use in psychology by Irving Janis in 1972, **Group Think** is an illusion of agreement between members, usually found among those in a cohesive group. Close knit groups tend to think like one another over the course of working together and new and dissenting ideas are seldom suggested. Group think is linked with conformity, as described earlier in this section, as rebellious members could feel that they may lose influence or status with other group members and be subsequently ostracized from the group. Group think goes back to the days of the "good old boys" network where groups were famously homogenous and these types of groups could quite easily talk themselves into a crucial decision that they alone would never conceive, support or deploy.

A closely linked phenomenon is **Group Polarization**. This is where groups come up with an extreme solution to a problem only because they had the comfort and safety of others agreeing to do so. They all may be thinking to themselves that "this idea will undoubtedly fail" but no one actually speaks up and everyone falsely assumes that they are the only silent dissenter within the group.

It turns out that polarization can work in both directions; adopting more risk or becoming more conservative. This concept was previously referred to as the **Risky Shift**, but it turns out that decisions may err on the side of being overly cautious as well. The research appears to indicate that polarization will typically tend to influence decisions to become more risky. Basically, it boils down to a "safety in numbers" idea. This is one way overly aggressive software delivery schedules may be created. Many technical people have a fear of appearing weak or incapable in front of their peers and will therefore commit to excessively optimistic schedules, a schedule they may not have come up with or agreed to on their own.

To counter Group Think and to some degree Group Polarization, the team needs what is referred to as authentic dissenters. These people are differentiated from those who role play the devil's advocate in that they truly believe in their dissent. Since groups come together to make decisions and most groups naturally conform over time for practical reasons, it becomes a bit of a thorny undertaking to facilitate dissent. This is an area where strong leadership comes into play and the leader needs to encourage team members to seriously consider alternatives and not just mail in their decisions.

Software people can be very critical and religious regarding platforms, algorithms, and tools. Any dissent in these areas may touch people's nerves. The facilitator can help by siding with the dissenter as we learned in the Conformity section earlier. Having an ally in the facilitator will support the dissenter in presenting his case. Another way to counter Group Think right from the outset is to bring together a diverse team. Diversity may be in the form of people from other cultures or people from different stakeholder groups within the company or even outside experts. If you plan to bring in an outside expert in the software development field it would probably need to be a recognized and bona fide expert and not just a smart friend. This is where outside consultants are employed as they hopefully have seen many instances, in other like organizations, with the exact problem that you are currently facing.

TEAM PERFORMANCE

Team Formation

There are many models available for how to properly assemble and nurture teams. One of the most popular is the Forming, Storming, Norming, &

Performing model developed by Tuckman and Jensen (1977). This model starts out with the basic formation of the group which consists of getting to know each other and establishing some basic goals. The Storming stage is next and it can be a difficult one. People may not agree on specific roles and group processes, and people may form alliances in subgroups. In software teams, a number of problematic issues may arise in this stage. These include team assignments, tool usage, possible scheduling conflicts, the high level technical approach, and so on. Emerging from the Storming stage is critical and some members may seek to drop out at this point. Since dropping out of a software team is not always an option, these team members may cause trouble as the rest of the team begins to gel. Keeping a close watch on these members may be critical to the ultimate success of the overall team. However, once this stage is complete, and these stages aren't defined in black and white, the team will usually be stronger. The Norming stage is usually less dramatic and the team is establishing some ground rules and relationships between many members are strengthening. The team believes there is light at the end of the tunnel as this stage winds down. The next stage is that of Performing, where the bulk of the actual work is completed. Some groups never make it here as conflict and norms are not fully established or followed by all members. This is one potential reason why adding new members to a failing team may be like adding gasoline to a fire (according to the venerable Fred Brooks).

The real key to this discussion is that effective groups don't just magically form over night. It takes time to meld a collection of different individuals into a truly cohesive team and management needs to understand the approximate phases a group must endure to be successful. Using this model is helpful in that management can see the bigger picture of teamwork and determine if the group is stuck in a pre-performing stage and what the cause of the obstruction might be. So the next time that you're tempted to hastily assemble an Agile team, remember that meaningful teamwork takes time to establish and sometimes it never takes place, depending upon the exact composition of the team.

CIOs and Teams

CIOs and other high ranking people must be careful when joining teams made up largely of subordinates, especially if they do so randomly and infrequently. If they are there to observe, that may be okay, but contributing even a little here and there may have unexpected and unfavorable consequences. In individualistic countries like the U.S., these executives may be pandered to so that the best ideas and solutions are never proposed. For smaller companies it may be quite common for the CIO or CTO to be part of customary technical meetings, but in large Fortune 500 companies this is probably irregular. While many technical people have strong opinions on software development issues, they may not feel that challenging the CTO in front of others is appropriate, or they may be afraid that the CTO will show them up and therefore they conceal ideas they might normally promote. Other times having the CTO or another high level officer in a meeting may produce some showboating behavior and now the meeting has changed its focus and little will likely be accomplished.

Team Dysfunctions

Unfortunately, there are plenty of team dysfunctions to uncover and therefore only a select few will be featured here.

Redundant Communication

Stasser and Titus (1985) found that people in groups spend much of their time repeating to others what they already know. This is basically a form of **Process Loss** and wastes precious productive time. A related note is that any disruption from technical work interrupts flow and actually costs organizations considerably more than just the time on the clock. See the Task Interruption section for details.

Blaming Others

In her authoritative book, *Creating Effective Teams*, Susan Wheelan identifies one dysfunction that stands out above the rest for technical teams, at least in my mind anyway. That is the tendency to blame others for problems or lack of sufficient progress towards identified team goals. She highlights several tendencies. One of those is the inclination to blame the boss for virtually everything as a result of the **Fundamental Attribution Error** (FAE). The FAE is defined as people's tendency to attribute other's behaviors primarily to their personality and not the specific situation at hand. As mentioned earlier, analytical people like us have a tendency to be critical and to attempt to analyze the circumstances. However, if we succumb to short cuts and jump to the conclusion that the boss (or others) are to blame because they're lazy or otherwise unqualified, this may lead to biased and inaccurate assessments. When you combine the FAE with the veracity of the Confirmation Bias, previously reviewed, you now have a potentially serious disorder to contend with. Once people think that the boss, or any other group member, is incompetent there is a strong tendency to verify one's own opinion. Now everything they do is a failure and the blaming becomes accentuated.

Wheelan goes on to say that blaming is ineffective behavior and starts the nasty cycle of revenge and retaliation as people attempt to uphold their reputations within both the group and the larger organization. Giving people the benefit of the doubt is a good starting point to reduce this type of unwanted behavior and this can be facilitated by spending more time with your detractors rather than less, which is our natural tendency. There's almost always more to an important and complex decision than people realize. Discovering these other facets may lead to a deeper understanding and appreciation for the decision maker.

Gossip

Gossip can certainly be an issue for teams and organizations at large, although not all gossip is necessarily bad for the company or group. It can help knit groups together and provide social support for individuals in some instances. However, gossiping about forbidden subjects such as people's personal affairs or spreading fabrications about others can debilitate teams quickly. One way to handle gossip is to threaten to discuss the topic in public. Gossips prefer to work covertly and watch the damage they wreak from a distance. If gossips are required to discuss or defend their comments in a group setting it may discourage gossip from starting at all.

Team Mix

In other studies (Stewart & Neubert, 1998) it was found that teams having just one individual with an outlying low score on agreeableness, extraversion or emotional stability had decreased overall performance and increased conflict. Interestingly, team members are generally more supportive of people low in g (g is the symbol used by some psychologists to represent general intelligence) than those low in conscientiousness. Apparently they realize that low g is something an individual can't control whereas conscientiousness is more about one's effort. I'm not necessarily convinced that this situation would completely apply for development teams, but generally people are more tolerant of those who provide authentic effort over those who coast on their natural abilities.

Regression Toward the Mean

Sometimes management is disappointed when a top performing team is not able to replicate its previous level of performance in subsequent efforts. They may then begin searching for all of the possible explanations of why this happened, when it may just be a natural result of what is referred to as "regression toward the mean." This phenomenon is due principally to the fact that teams may excel for any number of reasons that may have little to do with the members themselves. Perhaps things just fell into place for them or they just happened to have had the exact right mix of skills and experience for the particular problem that one time. Expecting standout results to continue for the same group or individual, time after time, may not be realistic. Unfortunately for the formerly thriving team members involved, they may be accused of coasting on projects that are not excelling.

Virtual Teams

Compounding the problem in software development is a relatively new wrinkle, that of dispersed or virtual teams. It's not enough that we work with ever changing technologies with people from multiple and diverse cultures. Now we must also deal with team members situated across the globe in various time zones. As a group we already struggle somewhat with detecting subtle social cues of a teammate just across the table and this now becomes exacerbated when virtual teams are assembled for projects.

Virtual teams have several obstacles to overcome in order to be even plausibly effective. One of the foremost obstacles from a psychological perspective is establishing a solid, respectful working relationship with someone thousands of miles (or kilometers) away in another obscure culture. This is why many American firms that outsource technical work to India or other global locations will cross-pollinate their teams. They will temporarily locate U.S. workers in India and bring in Indian supervisors for training and relationship building in the U.S. You are much more likely to cooperate and respect someone once you've experienced some face time together and know them as a person and not as just another cog in the machine. As discussed in the side bar, it is quite easy for groups to become competitive rather than cooperative as demonstrated by

Muzafer Sherif's boys' camp studies. When you separate groups by large distances, who already have trouble understanding each other, you can see how rife this situation is for becoming woefully unproductive. However, some people and organizations believe that with the proper procedures and guidelines in place, these virtual teams have the ability to outperform traditional, non-dispersed teams.

Virtual Team Problems

Researchers have identified several major components of Virtual Teams that contribute to possible disconnects between members (Lojeski & Reilly, 2008). These include the typical geographical and operational concerns that trip up multi-faceted teams. Interestingly enough, another study found that even workers in the same building, on separate floors, suffered from dispersion, or geographical, effects (Siebdrat, 2009).

Of these issues, **Affinity Distance** appears to be the most consequential and is the major issue of concern for us. Two of the major contributors to affinity distance related problems are Social Distance

SHERIF'S TEAM DISCOVERIES

Muzafer Sherif, a Turkish born researcher, conducted some famous experiments decades ago in a boys' camp setting. The participants had no idea they were partaking in a social psychology experiment. What he found was that it was moderately easy to establish an Us versus Them mentality in the camp residents. He merely had to separate them into different cabins and assign them different names (Eagles and Rattlers). The hostilities soon began as they resorted to name calling and other similar bad manners. However, when Sherif added competitive games and other group against group activities such as tug of war, the antagonism escalated even further. This now included physical confrontations such as raiding of each other's cabins and food fights in the cafeteria.

Even when noncompetitive activities were introduced, like movies or social events, the groups still sparred vigorously with one another. It was only when special events were staged to get the boys focused on a common goal, one that had benefits for both sides, that they slowly began to come back together. One such event was when the food truck had become purposely stuck and they all had to pitch in to successfully dislodge it. Eventually, the boys began to intermingle and befriend boys from the other group.

This experiment illustrates just how easy it is to develop friction between two factions. Separate them physically and give them different labels and let nature take its course. It also reveals the means to alleviate this intergroup friction.

and Cultural Distance. Social Distance can be created when the focus is on job titles and positional power instead of people's skills and experiences. Cultural Distance refers to possible value incongruities between members of different cultures. These two issues are somewhat related in that different cultures have different Power Distances (see the chapter on Culture and Gender for more detail) which may create social distance barriers between groups with different status. When these official status differences are highlighted, problems may ensue, according to Lojski & Reilly.

Virtual teams also incur some overhead costs, even though one of the primary reasons for assembling these teams originally is lower overall costs. These costs come from the use of various communication technologies employed to link teams together and the periodic cross-pollination of teams physically, which most people with experience in this area strongly recommend.

Virtual team mitigation strategies

There is no one magic formula for making these dispersed teams function at their optimal level. With Virtual Teams comes diversity of many different types; different cities, time zones, cultures, the problem they're tasked with solving, technology incompatibilities and so on. However, the experts (and myself) have some general recommendations for improving the odds of successful outcomes as highlighted here:

Select teammates carefully

Those high in conscientiousness are a good start. Junior team members may not always be high-quality candidates for Virtual Teams even though they may be the most readily available.

Scheduling of meetings must take different time zones into account

This seems to be a hot button for many participants of such groups. Spreading around the pain of inconvenient check-in times is a good start and knowing how to properly use your electronic calendaring system helps too.

Face time

This is important, even if it's via teleconferencing. People naturally cue to faces and they are also able to detect emotions via facial expressions and build stronger relationships and ultimately trust, one of the key ingredients. This is why many organizations incur the additional time and expense of flying people to various other locations to meet their teammates and acquaint themselves with the culture.

Be sensitive to cultural differences

Don't assume that your culture is the "right one." The more I research cultural issues the more I have been able to appreciate the benefits of other ways of approaching problems, dialectical thinking being one such example (this is explained in Chapter 13, Culture and Gender).

Humor

Since most humor is rooted in culture, I would generally recommend avoiding jokes and puns. This goes against my natural tendencies. However most of my early attempts at lightening up a multi-cultural crowd before a talk with some casual humor have failed me miserably. Since that time I stick to smiling and keeping my lame old jokes to myself. Over time I have discovered that I can relate to some cultures better than others and humor sometimes works in that case.

Communication must be extra clear

It's best to avoid slang and colloquialisms. When I was traveling extensively internationally I found it more difficult than I expected to not speak using colloquial phrases, such as "Nickel and diming you to death." These types of sayings mean nothing to people outside the U.S., yet people from most Asian cultures will not impose on you to explain yourself, but rather they may nod as if they fully understand you. When composing emails and other communications, short cuts are not advised either. It's almost always best to spell everything out clearly so there is less risk of confusion.

Competition & Cooperation

One of the psychological mechanisms that sometimes trips up workers is intra-corporate competition. That is, people competing with fellow employees rather than those from a competing company. Unfortunately, competition usually occurs within teams because it's easier for enthusiastic competitors to stake out their rivals when they're in close proximity and they can more readily assess their performance. This may occasionally result in individual performance outweighing team performance, especially in individualistic cultures like the United States and other Western countries. Team members therefore receive a varied message from management: Do what I ask of you from a team perspective or do what you will be rewarded for, which is typically outperforming your colleague (Levi p77). In many U.S. companies, there is a certain predetermined amount of money set aside annually for merit increases and all team members are in competition for this total pool of money. So standing out from your peers is a justifiably worthy goal. It's rare for all team members to be rewarded equally for a successful project, at least in the United States. But if the goal is to promote team cooperation, this issue must be addressed. My suggestion would be to reward people based upon a percentage of their annual salary because some people are more valuable to the team than others but yet you still want and need everyone working as a cohesive unit.

The trick really, in most of the Western corporate world anyway, is to balance team goals with personal achievements. You must become an admirable team member while also attempting to stand out as an individual contributor. When other team members detect or suspect that certain individuals are trying to make themselves look good at the expense of the team, the situation can deteriorate quickly. If this is allowed to escalate it's very possible that individual goals will overshadow the team objectives and now you have a group of individuals working on a project, and not a team. There is a common saying in the world of sports that refers to the championship team versus a team of champions.

Intergroup Conflict

While teamwork itself can be a problem and some of these issues will be highlighted here, there is also a potentially much bigger issue with groups and that is with intergroup conflict. As we discovered in the famous psychological experiment Sherif conducted in the 1950s, it is really quite straightforward to create opposing groups. In a matter of minutes, in some cases, experimenters are able to establish a strong "Us versus Them" mentality among people that have just met one another. Since this is a major dilemma and concern in software development, these intergroup issues will be further explored.

Development teams working with the business teams are what I'm generally referring to here. My experiences, and that of many colleagues I have interviewed for this book, notice the same recurring problems between these two diverse stakeholders. It has become an "Us versus Them" game in software development for many organizations and efforts must be spent brokering demands by both sides. Technical employees may act competitively when it's not in their best interest to do so because of the "Us versus Them" nature of business teams and technical groups. They might rather score a win for the software team than a win for the company as a whole. In many of these cases it's because they feel intimidated by the business people when it comes to negotiations on crucial technical decisions like feature sets and schedules.

CONFLICT REDUCTION STRATEGIES

There are multiple tactics that may be employed to reduce intergroup conflict and tensions. Three of these are featured here: contact hypothesis, superordinate goals, and shared identities (Collett, Kelly, & Sobolewski, 2010). An additional strategy involving the roles in software engineering is also discussed.

Contact Hypothesis

The Contact Hypothesis is similar to the "familiarity breeds likeness" concept. That is, the more time two parties spend interacting together the more that the stereotypes held by each group begin to evaporate and they can begin making their own judgments based upon their experience. Spending time together beyond just when it's required is also important. People will eventually let their guard down and colleagues can start to know one another as people instead of just workmates. I encourage technical people to have lunches, and other informal gatherings, with people from the business team during quiet times when there is no looming issue that may cause a disagreement. This enables people to build a trusted relationship that is able to withstand some level of conflict that will undoubtedly surface at some point.

Superordinate Goals

Focusing on a higher purpose is another way to keep groups working together effectively. This was the core lesson from Sherif's studies. Many times upper management may need to intervene here in order to keep people focused on the larger prize. When people can rally around a common cause and believe in the ultimate purpose of their project, they may just end up liking one another (Goleman, 2006).

Shared Identities

This conflict reduction technique is closely related to superordinate goals. Team members must realize that they all work for the same organization and the emphasis must be on us and we instead of they and them. This provides support for those companies who create distinct software engineering teams. That is, the most qualified, or available, group of individual contributors is assembled throughout the various departments within the company, and they temporarily form their own department. This means that the business people and the software professionals will now become a team in their own right. "They" will now become the "Us." In order to best accomplish this feat, these teammates must collocate as much as feasible.

Neither Us nor Them

One commonsense way around the "Us versus Them" problem, explored by Sherif, is to engage those who are neither "us" nor "them." These people will not have a strong allegiance to either side, are less likely to become victims of confirmation bias and yet they will have extensive knowledge of all the pertinent issues. You may be wondering just who these special people really are, if there is indeed such a group. They are the Business Analysts, the near perfect go-between for these two groups. They are familiar with the business requirements, have relationships with both parties and yet they can understand the pain the development team feels regarding scope and schedule changes. Using these key resources to broker agreements between the two factions is absolutely worth exploring for most organizations.

Meetings

Effective Meetings

There are some obvious reasons for our less than stellar meeting skills discussed earlier and some deeper ones too. The first obvious issue is that rather than taking the necessary time to prepare ourselves adequately, we may just show up. Preparing ourselves with some detailed meeting strategies and alignment discussions with other attendees prior to the meeting is a good start. People will tend to avoid activities that they don't prefer, and many times what they dislike are those activities where they are not particularly skillful or comfortable. This becomes a downward negative spiral in some instances and soon meetings become absolutely dreaded affairs where less and less preparation time is extended. Some technical people end up spending much of their meeting time working on their primary duties rather than focusing on the meeting topic and would be better off excusing themselves anyway. Managers should take extra effort in determining when technical people are actually required to be in attendance or just have them available on an on-call basis, in case their expertise is required for just a few minutes.

Willpower & Fatigue

It turns out that exerting one's willpower functions very similarly to the operation of one's muscles. That is, the more you "exercise" your willpower, the more fatigued you become. For many technical professionals attending certain types of meetings is an exercise in willpower. As highlighted previously, meetings are not our forte and therefore may deplete our mental resources. This may help to explain why many technical professionals seem to "weaken" as the meeting progresses and eventually we either lose interest or say something we may regret later on. The good news on willpower is that, just like our muscle groups, the more we use it the stronger it tends to become. Some of my technical colleagues tend to wrestle with their willpower during longer meetings. They are able to hold out for some time, but eventually, as the meeting heats up, they may succumb to their true feelings and burst out their opinion on a sensitive topic or person that has been frustrating them.

Other Meeting Thoughts

Here are some insights as to why technical professionals may oppose meetings:

First and foremost, most software professionals prefer to program or design or whatever it is their current duties necessitate. Attending meetings for many is pure drudgery.

Secondly, they are apt to have algorithms or data structures coursing through their minds as abstract work never fully departs the brain until it's somehow resolved.

Some of us, being introverts, would rather not spend our spare time with others, particularly extraverts, regardless of the circumstances.

Their project is almost assuredly behind schedule, or on the verge of being so, and they could desperately use the meeting time to reclaim previously lost project production.

This is one of the advantages of Agile development methods. Meetings are performed in a stand up manner, usually first thing in the morning, because they're intended to be completed briskly and efficiently. Rather than meet once a week for an hour or more it's almost always more efficient and productive to meet for ten or fifteen minutes each day. Meetings that occur weekly or less frequently also lose the immediacy effect. That is, people may have had some nugget of information that someone else could have used three days ago and now that moment is lost.

Practicing Transactional Analysis (featured in Chapter 8) is another recommended approach for successfully handling difficult meetings. If you remain firmly in your Adult state you will be much less likely to find yourself in trouble.

CHAPTER 12

Leadership

Leadership can be a cumbersome and controversial topic. The concept means so many different things to different people and groups. It almost seems to fall into the category of philosophy. Leadership is most definitely a very broad topic with many implications and stereotypes. There are actually tens of thousands of books and articles espousing various leadership models and techniques that you can explore and ponder. Leadership may well be the one business topic that has been researched and written about more than any other. However, much of the content has little to do with experimental research as discussed in Chapter 1 (Hogan & Kaiser, 2005).

Some people aspire to the theory that everyone can lead. Then there's the common age-old adage that leaders are born not made. There might be more folklore (and clever sayings) regarding leadership than any other topic you could choose. Think of all those workplace posters you've seen over the years with a leadership or motivational theme. However, it's possible that leadership within software development is somewhat distinct from many other fields, primarily due to the abstract and complex nature of our vocation.

For starters, if you haven't developed software yourself, I find it hard to comprehend how you might lead and coach a development team. It's like asking a diplomat to lead you into a battlefield during warfare. Would you follow them? Do they understand your issues and needs? Will they know how to react to different circumstances? In a nutshell, have they been there before? I have known a select few people over the years that have done a reasonable job leading development groups that had never programmed themselves. Still, I truly believe it puts you at a distinct disadvantage on a number of fronts.

Ironically, development managers who have never developed software, and others who have never coded before, often seem to imagine that the simple everyday tasks of development are difficult and vice versa. I'm not sure exactly why this is so, but I've witnessed countless examples of this type of thinking throughout my career and have seen some programmers take advantage of this potential schedule blunder. However, there are also a few advantages of leading a team having never programmed before, which will be discussed later in this section.

FORMAL LEADERSHIP THEORIES

This section is intended to provide you with a small flavor of the variety and scope of leadership models and theories that have been derived over the past several decades. Perhaps you will be able to observe some of these in action or decide that one of these approaches are better tailored for you or your organization.

Transactional vs. Transformational Leaders

One formal, or academic, theory of leadership differentiates between transaction based leaders and inspirational leaders. Transactional leaders, are those who keep their subordinates focused on well defined, short term goals and outcomes. These transactional leaders may well be suited for work in the world of software engineering as ours is one of many transactions. This model works well for PMs and other more supervisory leaders, such as a Lead Developer.

Transformational leaders on the other hand, have vaguer, higher level and longer term goals. They're usually the ones who make the grandiose speeches and are more focused on the goal than how to actually achieve it. This style of leadership is one that typically doesn't resonate well with many analytical software professionals and other technical people. This type of leader is more likely to be a CEO or possibly a CIO in a larger company.

Task vs. Relationship Orientation

The idea of classifying leadership skills into those which are task based and relationship based is referred to as the **Contingency Theory of Leadership**. Supervisors who are primarily focused on the task specifics and schedules are deemed task-oriented. Those supervisors whose central focus is on maintaining a healthy relationship with subordinates are considered relationship-oriented leaders. For well defined work, task-oriented approaches seem to work effectively. For moderately structured environments, relationship-oriented supervisors may excel (Aronson, 2007). Social psychologists suggest that leaders should be able to utilize both of these methods of leadership, as the situation dictates (Baumeister, 2011). My educated guess is that many software supervisors will be predominantly focused on tasks and schedules. After all, that is the basic training regimen for Project Managers in our industry. Focusing on building solid and trusting relationships with subordinates may not come naturally to many supervisors in our field.

Leader-Member Exchange Theory (LMX)

One of the more prominent theories on leadership, LMX as it's known, states that leaders develop different relationships with different employees. This is probably not a shocking revelation to anyone who has worked in a corporate setting for any length of time. Essentially there become in-groups and out-groups with any one supervisor. Oddly enough, these groups are established rather early in the relationship with the supervisor, possibly based upon some of the constructs featured earlier in the book (halo effect, fundamental attribution error, and preferring others like ourselves, (Levi, 2007)). Once this leader-supervisor relationship is established it is somewhat complicated to reverse, especially when the relationship is negative in nature. This may be reinforced by confirmation bias and cognitive dissonance. After all, a supervisor surely has material reasons for one of his subordinates being looked upon unfavorably. This may sometimes manifest itself in low performing in-group members receiving positive performance ratings and conversely, solid out-group performers finding themselves with lower performance rankings.

The quality of an LMX relationship can determine the fate and job fulfillment of the subordinate employee. Out-group members will typically be less productive and may cause other troubles throughout the organization besides. From a FFM perspective (Five Factor Model of personality – see Chapter 2) those supervisors who are more extraverted, emotionally stable and agreeable foster more satisfying subordinate relationships (Sias, 2009). This is one of the challenges in software engineering as there are fewer extraverts to choose from for supervisory roles. Also, many software engineering supervisors who rise up through the ranks may have strong opinions on technology and methodology. This may stifle the relationship and flow of ideas with subordinates.

TECHNICAL LEADERSHIP QUALITIES

Many researchers in both Industrial/Organizational psychology and business discern between leadership and management. Leadership can be a rather broad topic and many ideas float around in people's minds when the term is evoked. So here's a quick review of some the different aspects of leadership. True leadership, some claim, is more focused on what an organization sets out to accomplish, whereas management is primarily focused on how the chosen path, whatever it might be, is traversed. In summary then, you can think of leadership and management in terms of strategy and tactics, respectively. Leaders lay out the road map and managers drive the bus.

While I generally agree with this model, it seems that leadership within software development is more focused on the management side. Upper management will likely be making decisions around which products to build, how to position and price them in the market, optimal organizational structures and so on. Leadership within the development teams will be concerned primarily with how best to meet the dictates of the corporate leadership, which is essentially a management task. This will include motivation and teamwork concerns as well, which are discussed in more detail in other sections. Leadership in technology comes primarily from the CIO or CTO. They are tasked with selecting technology platforms, defining staffing models, etc.

Credibility

It really starts here for most technical people. If you're uninformed about the technology you're managing, most technical people will have little or no respect for you, at least from a professional standpoint. If you're constantly hounding subordinates to explain themselves, they may eventually become annoyed and truculent. It's not necessary to know everything to be a technical leader and it's not required to earn respect either. Many technical leaders fail because they imagine their calling is to know absolutely everything about a particular technology or tool so that they can answer virtually any question that could possibly arise. Technical people brutally detest having to utter those three most dreaded words: "I don't know." While they might earn some credibility points with their team, they usually lose site of the bigger picture. Remember this: credibility is one of the foremost keys to leadership for technical staffs. Expertise is necessary for legitimacy and respect in virtually all circumstances (Hogan & Kaiser, 2005). If a technical person doesn't believe that you're technically credible they will have a difficult time doing almost anything for you. Once you lose your credibility then the Confirmation Bias will work forcefully against you and you'll constantly experience trouble and quite possibly insurmountable challenges with your team. The key here is balance, knowing enough about your domain, but not coming across as knowing absolutely everything.

Passion & Vision

Once you've passed the credibility test, it's now on to passion and vision. A cornucopia of passion won't go far if you're not sure where you're going and how best to get there (although some technical people seem to have little concern for the vision of the organization, as long as they are working on exciting and challenging projects where they're learning new techniques and tools.) Much of the vision required for software teams is determining the best way to attain an already existing vision or goal. This is where the transactional leadership approach, previously mentioned, comes into play. There are many roads to success, some more treacherous than others. Selecting the proper road, in many instances, requires as much vision and foresight as choosing the destination in the first place. Many times the vision for a technical leader is the exact approach chosen for solving the problem, but beware of getting too deep into the "how" of the solution or you'll risk alienating your team. Staying focused on the requirements and letting your team determine the optimal solution is normally the ideal path.

Leadership Involvement Levels

At the highest level there are basically two generic types of leadership styles; autocratic and democratic. Autocratic leaders leverage their positional or one-up status within the group or organization to achieve their ends. Democratic leaders use more participative techniques and their personal charisma to engage with team members to determine, in a more mutually acceptable way, what team strategies will be implemented. These two styles are polar opposites and therefore alternative approaches may be more adaptable to specific situations as they arise (Erven, 2001).

One such leadership style is the Hersey-Blanchard Situational Leadership Model. This model is based heavily upon the attributes of the followers and is much more flexible and suitable for professional work environments. There are four distinct leader styles defined in this model as outlined here:

Delegating Style

This style is where the leader permits the group to take primary responsibility for their tactical decisions. The team members must be willing and able to accomplish the various tasks required of the project. This is the preferred style to be utilized whenever possible, in my experience, and the leader can then act as a sounding board for members when they become hung up on a problem.

Participating Style

Here the team members are able but not completely sure of themselves. This style focuses on shared ideas and combined group-leader based decisions as to how they should proceed. The leader may choose to make suggestions as to how to best proceed and provide resources for the team to learn more on their own.

Selling Style

This style is where the leader helps to explain the task plans in a supportive and persuasive way. This style should be considered when the team is eager but technically incapable of fully performing the entire task. That is, they need some convincing of their efficacy.

Telling Style

This is the classic top down style where the leader provides specific task directions and personally monitors the work. This may suggest that you have the wrong team for the given project and should only be used where there are no other viable options.

In most software development environments, the first two methods will almost always yield the most favorable results. For analytical, logical and intelligent people, selling and telling may be futile methods unless your track record and reputation are impeccable.

Time Management

The proverb about time is that everyone has the same amount. While this rings true for us logical types, we still have tendencies to fritter away time like everyone else.

It's almost always better to spend the majority of your time with your most important staff members. People need attention and while it's logical for many analytical personality types to feel compelled to spend more time coaching B players, because after all they need the most help, it's actually the wrong policy in most situations. You must really stay focused on your A players in order to keep them plugged in and fully motivated, since they're the driving force for your team. Exceptions would be to spend significant amounts of time with your up and coming B players who you believe will one day flower into those elusive A players we all seek.

As anyone who has spent much time in software development knows, time has a sinister way of getting away from us. When the project first commences, everyone is giddy and excited. There's ample time to worry about requirements and design later. However, we all know that come time for release one, we're almost always wishing we had better managed our time months ago. A strong and experienced software leader understands this and knows that good leadership (or management) requires prudent time management techniques on a regular basis, not just near the end of the project.

Humility

The best leaders of software development groups are probably not the brightest technical people or the top tier programmers. My experience has shown that for starters, the brightest developers and other technical staff should ideally be engaged in doing what they excel at most and this is likely what they prefer anyway. And secondly, the sharpest technical people may not have the patience and soft skills required of management. Top leaders, who have gotten over the thrill of freshly anointed power, are humble and respectful. They will be looking out for the good of not only the project, but for the team members as well. These leaders respect the talent and hard work their team delivers and the team, in return, appreciates the respect they deserve and leaders who share the glory.

It turns out that it's quite easy for a disgruntled team member to bring a manager down. Psychology research shows that sometimes certain individuals will hurt themselves (and hence the company and their supervisor) when they feel they are not being treated fairly, in order to demonstrate their disgust of unjust conduct.

One of the top selling business books of recent years, *Good to Great* (Collins, 2001) studied the personality traits of those CEOs who helped their companies achieve the highest stages of corporate performance. It turns out that the CEOs of the best companies were those that exhibited humility and who attributed most of the credit to their workers. They were also highly persistent, a trait that is an absolute must for anyone working in the software business.

Autonomy vs. Control

Autonomy versus control is the classic management tight rope walk, especially when dealing with business professionals. Too much control and highly educated, deep thinkers may rebel. Too little and the problem could be even worse. This is where finely honed management and leadership skills become highly valued assets in software development. Disrupting your development team in the midst of a project can be devastating.

It's just this type of issue that makes leadership as much an art as a science. Each person on your team will need to be treated and handled differently, yet you must also be fair across the team. Technical people are quick to detect favoritism and may react defensively if scorned. I like to handle this issue up front as much as is reasonably possible. Define with your team the goals for their "exploratory" time versus the time they must focus on the outcomes for the project deadlines. Make a pact with them where you agree to find the time for them to research and apply some new techniques if they in turn will commit to the larger goals of the organization. I find technical staff very receptive to these types of arrangements. They are smart people and understand that the company's goals must be achieved in order for them to have a playground to play within. We must remember that we are working with creative people and having them constantly performing factory line assembly duties is not particularly appealing. This is the one card as a manager that you have to play, and developers, as a group, are more than willing to go along.

Big Picture Focus

As mentioned in the Motivation section, developers are notorious for losing track of time because they've embarked on a deep technical dive. In the past thirty years I've had technical people dive deep on me on a weekly basis, if not more frequently. They're quickly in the midst of myriad technical details that their audience generally has limited understanding of. My solution for this, depending upon the situation, is to let them go for a while. Many times when people are explaining issues to someone else, they are capable of coming up with a new and unique solution in the process. Perhaps it's the verbalizing of the problem that triggers different brain regions to perform more analysis and therefore come up with a solution. The one exception to this rule is when there is a larger group of non-technical people involved. Then it's important to keep these ramblings in check so as not to waste everyone else's time.

So to help technical staff keep the bigger picture in mind, I suggest summarizing their findings back to them within the context of the overall project. I will ask them if my boiled down understanding is basically correct. If so I will then attempt to insert this finding into the overall context to see where we now stand.

Trust

You must build a trust and a bond with technical people to be effective in managing their activities successfully. If they don't fully trust you, they may perform their assigned duties half heartedly and go back to what they really like, learning new technical tricks. Due to their personalities (and probably yours too) this can be rather challenging. Our overriding sense is not to trust others and we prefer to have things proven to us in order to really believe in them. To endear yourself to other technical staff, you need to prove your ability to go to bat for them when it's really needed. This is probably the quickest way to kick start the trust building process. However, trust is a bit like its homonym, rust – it takes time to form and once it does it tends to stay. It will usually take longer to build genuine trust with a technical person, but when you do it will likely be very solid and enduring.

Proactive vs. Reactive

WAM Works

WAM is an acronym for Walk Around Management, something I believe in quite fervently – when it's a personality fit for the practitioner. Many technical people have a very limited understanding of how their work impacts the larger organizational goals, especially in companies or divisions that are somewhat bigger. Managers who walk about and talk briefly with their subordinates on a regular basis can help explain their role in more detail as well as provide subliminal signals to employees that "gee, I must be important if the boss comes around to see me all the time." People who work for managers like this feel very engaged in their work. My personal experience has been that their loyalty and sense of purpose is vastly improved. They feel that they're truly a salient part of the solution, which of course they must be or they wouldn't be on the project team in the first place. Technical professionals need to have a comprehensive understanding of their exact role and why or how it's critical to the overall success of the project. This helps them contribute in more meaningful ways, ways that managers may not always completely understand. It's an opportunity to get those vital creative juices flowing that can lead to real bona fide project breakthroughs and innovation.

While WAM may not work for every manager or leader, my personal results have been rewarding. When I become excessively busy and preoccupied, I begin to feel that I'm neglecting my subordinates and it really does have an adverse effect on the organization. Of course, once you start down the WAM path, it's hard to go back. People then wonder why the boss never stops by anymore and lack of communication will get some technical people thinking the worst. In my opinion, WAM is a type of leadership style and using it just to use it will probably not yield satisfactory results. People, even those of us with lesser social skills, can detect someone who isn't genuine and then WAM has become a detriment to the team instead of an advantage.

Another reason the WAM technique makes so much sense in our profession is that many technical people will not initiate a conversation, yet they may have many questions or concerns. So unless the manager speaks up first, there will likely be fewer conversations and therefore the possibility now exists for assumptions, mistakes and misinterpretations.

I have one final word of caution on using the WAM technique. Once you begin having ongoing discussions with your staff, it may lead to having to share more corporate information, some of which may not be appropriate for certain groups. You need to be honest here and let people know when you can't share specifics, and why, and to be certain that you are consistent with all team members so favoritism doesn't become a problem.

Persistent & Consistent

One of the foremost attributes required to be a leader in software development certainly has to be that of persistence. With software projects perennially behind schedule and unwavering pressure for more features in shorter time frames, persistence is the key to completing tasks on time and within budget (it can happen!) This type of personality trait, and I believe that's what it is, is found in those people who are classified as Drivers in the Social Styles personality model. This model was described in more detail in the Personality Chapter.

While those with Driver personalities can regularly deliver the goods for organizations, they also pose some risks and challenges. Knowing exactly when to push somebody to accomplish a task or how to better deal with one person over the other, based upon individual personality differences, can sometimes be missing in their repertoire. The wrong Driver can lead to a car wreck in some cases, as developers many times become defensive, stubborn, or theoretical in these situations. Approaching developers in an understanding manner, that is seeking opinions from them on how to solve the dilemma, is a much better solution. Developers are intelligent people and therefore prefer to be dealt with in a consultative manner. They can generally solve a problem in an optimal manner if they know and understand the goals and the surrounding situational circumstances. As highlighted earlier, a Drivers' weakness may be in persisting for too long before considering other alternatives. A close friend of mine (a Driver) was helping me install a coat rack on a wall in my home some years ago. After numerous futile attempts (and absolutely refusing to give up) he punctured a water pipe while trying to drive the final nail for the rack into what we assumed was the stud inside the wall.

LEADERSHIP DON'TS

A friend and colleague of mine, let's call her Shelly, was an executive vice president for a huge, well known global American consumer packaged goods company whose name you'd recognize in an instant. Shelly held this position some years ago and relayed the following story to me that symbolizes poor leadership and highlights one of the many negative traits that seem to come standard with many leaders. Shelley's boss was the CEO of the company and every year they would launch a major new marketing campaign. The big time

New York ad agencies would parade through the board room touting their clever themes and strategies to help move the needle a point or two. This CEO would listen to the campaigns and then instantly exclaim his like or dislike of the presentation and concept for all present to notice. He would then go around the table and ask all of his direct reports what their thoughts were. Of course, whether he liked or disliked the campaign made no difference. The direct reports would mirror back the CEO's thoughts almost verbatim, meaning nothing was really accomplished in these sessions other than determining where Shelly stood on the topic. This is a classic example of poor leadership and one of the leading causes of mismanagement in America, a big ego. It also displays a lack of Social Intelligence.

When the importance of the leader becomes more important than the task at hand, something has gone woefully amiss. Unfortunately, the leader in question has probably always been this way and weeding out these people should be possible by rigorous background checks and possibly some personality testing. Leaders with controlling egos have a penchant for wasting the talent that lies within their organizations and this is where good governance boards can come into play. It is very difficult to deal with this type of leadership style and there is little that subordinates can do other than play to the ego. Give the ego the credit, even if it's not his for the taking, and you'll be better off in the long run, politically speaking.

Another trap which some significant percentage of technical leaders fall prey to is that of being the technical solutions provider on every single issue. I would estimate that somewhere between one-fifth and one-third of the leaders in our industry exhibit this weakness. Having technical solutions dictated to them really hurts most technical people to the core, at least when they haven't sought out the advice themselves. As business guru and legend Dale Carnegie sums it up; feeling important is the most basic human desire. When you dictate solutions to smart and capable people there are really two problems: one is that developers will likely feel controlled instead of having the autonomy to solve their own problems; secondly they don't feel like they're a vital part of the team if they're just taking orders from their supervisor.

Earlier I mentioned that there are some benefits of having technical leaders who have a limited technical understanding and background. The benefit is that they aren't typically capable of falling into the "dictating solutions" trap. They effectively become good sounding boards for the ideas their staffs generate and they really just need to listen. Good leaders will listen intently and lightly challenge their development teams to be sure that they are covering all of the important bases and meeting all the requirements. They will look for risks to the project, including the budget and the schedule. They want to know the pieces of the project where they can give up a little, so they can recover from other problem areas if needed. While their developers are diving deep, this is what good managers are trying to ascertain. They will ask questions for the benefit of both parties. A good question might challenge an assumption a developer has made or it may also clarify if the project may be in trouble.

CHAPTER 13

culture & Gender

There are several risks when discussing topics such as culture and gender. It is rather easy to succumb to the lure of stereotypes when considering these subjects. One imperative point to keep in mind is that behavior is comprised of several core elements. These include human nature, our cultural grounding, individual personality and our specific situation or environment. Human nature and our cultural upbringing will determine much of how we collectively interpret our surroundings and react to workplace and other events. Personality and environmental factors will influence how we will respond on a more personal level. Therefore, how any one person, regardless of their culture or gender, will respond to various proceedings in the workplace is not predictable. However, this does not mean that striving to better understand these elements of human behavior is a pointless endeavor.

When I first began my professional programming career, back in the 1980s, most of the other programmers and staff were pretty much like me. They were all Caucasians and they were by and large males. Of course since I was the new guy there were some staff members that were older than me, but other than that we were all reasonably similar. After a year or two on the job, the company hired a candidate from another culture and in my estimation he did have a hard time assimilating into the group. Even though he was a wonderful person, most of us had a challenging time connecting with him, particularly on a social level. However, on a staff of about 40 people it was basically a very homogenous group (Minnesota is not extremely culturally diverse anyway and that was especially true in the 1980s).

Today it's an entirely different story, even in Minnesota. There are more women in software development now, but not significantly more — this topic will be discussed in more detail later in this chapter. On the other hand, there has been a huge spike in the number of non-Caucasians in software development. This varies according to the different geographic areas throughout the country of course, but the number of developers and other software staff from Asia and India has really exploded. This has been due to several reasons. The U.S. Federal government's H1B Visa program, updated in the 1990s, has allowed many temporary technology workers into the country to alleviate the shortage of technical staff that occurred, partly as the result of the Year 2000 software issue. Secondly, many Asians, Indians, and others have immigrated here through other more traditional means to become legal U.S. residents, just as northern Europeans flocked here in the 1800s.

One of the primary reasons that more types of people have come into the software development fold has been the maturation of the development tools. The progress of visual web programming tools and established SQL database technologies along with the ability to quickly link the two together with powerful CGI tools has made it much easier to create powerful and dynamic web applications. Now countries that previously had limited access to mainframe programming environments in the 1970s and 80s suddenly had serious development platforms available to them, in the mid 1990s, with the evolution of the personal computer and the associated programming tools. Costs for these development platforms dropped significantly and now anyone with a PC, Visual Basic, and an Internet connection could potentially be in the software business.

Of course there are other valid reasons too. Many other countries are emerging by bootstrapping themselves, so to speak. Countries such as India and China are establishing themselves in the international community as economic powerhouses. Various other countries and regions throughout the world are also advancing rapidly; places such as Malaysia and Russia come to mind. These other countries will soon be inventing the next generation of technologies along with the traditional Western powers, and this will be a significant change for countries like the U.S. who are accustomed to leading the pack. That is why virtually all of the major U.S. players are investing heavily in other parts of the world. Microsoft, Apple, Google, Oracle, HP, Dell, and IBM all have significant operations across the globe, and I expect that to continue for the foreseeable future.

CULTURAL IMPACTS

Culture has an impact on almost every interpersonal factor you can think of; emotions, social behavior, personality, work ethic, health, and even how people get along with their superiors and the opposite sex. Now that our field has become much more diverse, there are more issues to deal with on a regular basis. These people will all need to work together effectively as a team to get release 1.0 out the door.

However, this area of psychology, termed Cross-Cultural Psychology, appears to be somewhat questionable at this point in time, at least from my perspective. It's apparent from my research that many more years of studies will need to be conducted in order to reach some reasonably useful conclusions in this field. Some of the problems involve studies of other cultures by foreigners, converting personality and other measurement instruments to another language, and the extreme difficulty in generalizing about large cultures such as India and China. Both India and China have many regions that have subcultures of their own, not unlike that of the various regions within the U.S. In addition, much of the current research in psychology has been the result of studies designed and conducted in the U.S. and other similar Western countries.

This highlights one of the trouble areas within Cultural Psychology and that is that there is a tendency to exaggerate cultural differences within any one culture. Social psychologists refer to this as the **Outgroup Homogeneity Bias**. This is where one's own group logically seems to include many individuals who have significant differences from each other, but other groups all appear to be essentially the same (Funder, 2007).

Cultural Issues

One of the more influential and well known cultural researchers is a Dutch professor named Geert Hofstede (see Hofstede, Hofstede, & Minkov, 2010). Through his extensive IBM surveys in more than 50 countries around the globe, he has identified several intercultural dimensions. Those most pertaining to software engineering, in my judgment, are defined as Power Distance, Uncertainty Avoidance, and Individualism versus Collectivism.

Individualism vs. Collectivism and Power Distance

While the research here can be a bit muddled, the basic concept is that within certain societies members are more concerned with themselves (individualistic) and in other cultures people are more focused on the community as a whole (collectivist). Most of the societies in our world are considered collectivist. That is, their identity is with the in-group in which they exist. In contrast, people in individualistic societies are focused on the specific traits and achievements of individuals and there is less dependence upon a larger group. People are expected to make a go of it on their own in the world and have smaller support groups to rely upon. People from individualistic societies value freedom, personal time and accomplishments. The notable countries high in individualism are the United States, Britain, Australia, and Canada.

Another factor added to the mix, when discussing workplace culture at least, is that of Power Distance. This refers to the authority gap between supervisor and subordinate. In the U.S., Power Distance is relatively low. That is, in most circumstances an individual feels empowered to stand up to or confront his supervisor, or at a minimum feels empowered to at least approach him. In countries with a high Power Distance subordinates would never even consider confronting their supervisor, and many times they may even avoid speaking with them. These two dimensions turn out to be closely correlated.

Individualism is generally inversely related to Power Distance. Those countries that have a culture of respect and that nurture the influence of the individual employee have a lower Power Distance ranking. You can now readily understand how people from different cultures may have completely different viewpoints and reactions to the same proceedings. A summary of Power Distance differences, from Intercultural expert Kwintessential, a company based in the United Kingdom, is listed below:

High power distance cultures exhibit some or all of the following:

Those in authority openly demonstrate their rank

Subordinates are not given important work and expect clear guidance from above

Subordinates are expected to take the blame for things going wrong

The relationship between boss and subordinate is rarely close/personal

Politics is prone to totalitarianism

Class divisions within society are accepted

Low power distance cultures exhibit some or all of the following:

Superiors treat subordinates with respect and do not pull rank

Subordinates are entrusted with important assignments

Blame is either shared or very often accepted by the superior due to it being their responsibility to manage

Managers may often socialize with subordinates

Liberal democracies are the norm

Societies lean more towards egalitarianism

This is closely related to another concept proposed by researchers Peng & Nisbitt (1999) referred to as **Dialectical Thinking**; generally described as the ability to see both sides of a situation relatively equally. This is distinguished from the thinking process of most Westerners which is described as positive logical determinism, whereby we tend to agree with one position or the other, but not both concurrently. Peng and Nisbett suggest that East Asians utilize dialectical methods where Westerners, particularly Americans, prefer logical deterministic thinking approaches. There is considerable debate swirling around this topic but there appears to be at least bits and shreds of evidence, both in and out of the laboratory, that support this conjecture.

Implications of this type of thinking are readily apparent in software teams comprised of Eastern and Western cultures. Westerners will typically attempt to make a choice for one solution or side versus the other, whereas Easterners may likely see some merits of both sides and perhaps suggest a compromise of some sort, thereby keeping everyone at least partially satisfied.

Westerners should also realize that it is exceptionally imperative that people in collectivist societies be able to save face in front of their peers. Coercing them to admit mistakes and forcing an abrupt change in positions is not a realistic strategy for successful resolution of issues. A better alternative would be to approve of the final terms of an agreement in private so that they may be able to save face in a means more palatable to them.

These cultural issues, if not addressed properly, can undermine software team efforts rather quickly. Team leaders must be cognizant of these broader issues, and expecting people from other cultures to just automatically adapt to your way of thinking is not realistic. It is only relatively recently that we are all beginning to become aware of these issues in our field, and it is quite probable that the people of the minority culture will know more about the majority culture than vice versa. This is just as true for an American working in China as it is for an Indian working in America.

Uncertainty Avoidance

This cultural dimension involves how people respond to ambiguity. It involves domains such as technology, law, religion and customs. It is defined by Hofstede as "the extent to which the members of a culture feel threatened by ambiguous or unknown situations." It makes me grin just a little when I hear a term like Uncertainty Avoidance in conjunction with software engineering. Anyone who originates from a culture high in Uncertainty Avoidance may well struggle in the software industry. Developers from countries scoring high in uncertainty avoidance (Russia and Japan for example) may have a slightly increased tendency to make riskier decisions. This claim is not backed by any specific studies but rather it is based solely upon Hofstede's cultural dimensions. It may also explain why people in weak uncertainty avoidance societies are less concerned with long term employment with the same company. These societies are less anxious about change and therefore do not need the comfort of long term employment.

Figure 13.1 compares Hofstede's cultural dimensions across several prominent countries involved in software development outsourcing by many Western organizations.

	POWER DISTANCE	UNCERTAINTY AVOIDANCE	INDIVIDUALISM COLLECTIVISM
USA	Low	Weak	Strong I
INDIA	High	Weak	Weak C
CHINA	High	Weak	Collectivism
RUSSIA	High	Strong	Collectivism
INDONESIA	High	Weak	Collectivism

FIGURE 13.1

You can readily see from figure 13.1 that all of these countries have some cultural differences from the U.S. This suggests there's a reasonable probability for occasional misunderstandings and conflicts to occur during a highly abstract and complex activity such as software engineering. When you consider the fact that many development efforts involve groups from several different countries, the problems may be compounded.

Culture and Software Ability

This is a fascinating topic, at least for me. For decades, starting in college, I was convinced that Asians were superior in mathematics and software development, and now the emerging statistics appear to support this conclusion. Virtually all standardized tests, and other indicators, strongly suggest that Asian countries such as Korea, China and Japan are all superior in math scores as determined by agencies such as the International Association for the Evaluation of Educational Achievement (2003). American students score above average worldwide, but are significantly below most Asian countries in this area of academics.

The real intrigue for me has always been determining why this is so. Are they naturally more gifted in this arena for some particular reason or is it something entirely different? Elliot Aronson and Carol Tavris, noted social psychologists, suggest in their engrossing book *Mistakes Were Made (but not by me)*, that this phenomena may actually be rooted in culture. They assert that the American culture is failure phobic and that Americans will do almost anything to avoid appearing foolish or being marked as inferior in any way. They go on to describe Japanese students, who when confronted with a difficult mathematics problem, are encouraged by their peers and expected to work through it. For many Asian countries, success in these domains is a result of hard work and persistence versus innate ability. The failure averse culture of the West may at least partially explain the difference in mathematical test scores.

Team Work

Teamwork in the United States can be somewhat of an oxymoron. Numerous team members in the U.S. are more interested in individual achievements. However, many software teams are now multi-cultural, or there may be several sub-teams assembled around the globe that may consist of unique cultures. As an individualistic culture, for the most part, we in the U.S. focus on individual accomplishments and revere independence throughout our society. Yet, many business place activities, particularly software development, have become heavily team oriented over the past decades. When it comes time to reward workers, U.S. companies normally tend to favor individual accomplishments over team achievements as this is so embedded within the culture. So now the employee is potentially receiving some mixed messages – "Do what I say and not what you will be rewarded for during your performance review." Most employees will then choose to focus on the individual goals and only pay lip service to the teamwork aspects of their job. To make this situation even worse, managers in high tech companies are probably some of the most competitive and extraverted employees in the company and they likely rose through the ranks by highlighting their individual successes themselves. Thus, they may not fully believe in the merits of teamwork either. In the U.S. one needs to be both a team player while at the same time attempt to stand out for individual accomplishments – a tricky and continual balancing act. Too much "me first" and you may get the dreaded reputation of being a Prima Donna. Too little of "just you" and you might get passed over for a long awaited promotion or salary increase.

Within the U.S. most employees would prefer to be rewarded for their individual achievements rather than group based activities, as is suggested by Hofstede's research. This may end up discouraging effective team work and certainly seems to be detrimental to the high performers (Levi p316). My experience is that quite a few developers and other software staff are what people sometimes refer to as "lone rangers." They prefer to work by themselves for the most part and they contribute as constituents of the team to the minimum extent possible. This makes team work all the more cumbersome and ineffective.

Other countries, especially Eastern ones, have more of a collectivist culture and really have a much better likelihood of making teams work efficiently and smoothly. Mixing of teams with members from Collectivist and Individualistic countries may have several undesirable consequences. Those members from Collectivist cultures may have some difficulty understanding the selfish motives and actions of those members from Individualistic cultures, while those from Individualistic cultures may end up taking advantage of the more team oriented members.

Communication

There are two primary issues when intercultural teams attempt to communicate. The first glaring one is the language barrier. Virtually all countries that provide software development outsourcing use English as their primary language for all technology related activities. That is essentially a forced issue, as English has become the unofficial language of high technology. Often, team members from different non-English speaking countries end up using English as their mediation language. In this case neither party may be fluent in the language, which may further accentuate communication problems.

There are certain additional language barriers that are not completely evident. One of the most prominent problems is the ability to master all aspects of a second language. Most people learning a new language are first able to read, then to comprehend spoken words, and the last skill typically mastered is comfortably and confidently speaking the new language. This model typically works fine for most of the routine tasks in software development. However, when conflicts arise between teams from different countries, listening skills may be more critical than reading proficiency (Huang & Trauth, 2007). When you are debating complex technical issues, having limited communication abilities puts one at a distinct disadvantage.

Another potential risk with language issues is that they may cause certain team members to limit their contributions. Remember, technical people pride themselves on their technical accomplishments and talents. If they perceive that a language hindrance could cause them to appear incompetent they may not elect to fully participate. Their participation may be reduced to email or other written documentation only.

Communication styles vary from culture to culture. Some, like in many Western countries, use a more direct form of communication while others use an indirect style (Brett, 2006). Indirect communication styles are used in some cultures so that people do not come across as arrogant. It's a way to honor others that may be older or in superior organizational positions (Huang & Trauth, 2007). It can be confusing at times for those engaging in direct styles to understand what the indirect communicator means. Are they asking questions because they don't know the answer or just being respectful? Many Americans are isolated from other cultures since most of what they need can be found at home, and because most Americans have not spent significant time living or working in other countries.

Indian Culture

People from India have become extremely influential in the global world of software development. In fact, you might say it was the Indians who initiated the global aspect of software development. Their dominance and pervasiveness merit a closer look at how to better understand the Indian culture.

A few caveats before we begin are in order. Cultural differences will vary considerably based upon several factors highlighted below:

Whether or not the individual was raised in their native culture

How long they have been working with people from other cultures and their overall level of acculturation

Individual personalities

Gender

If you happen to be an American living in California who is working with an Indian, that in itself doesn't mean all that much. If your Indian colleague grew up with you in California he may be very similar to you and that he's of Indian descent will not particularly matter. However, if he just recently relocated here from India, and is a young adult or older, that is entirely different. That, coupled with his level of acculturation in America will determine how well you are able to understand and work with each other. Individual capabilities and personalities also play a significant role along with the gender of the person. Some Indian cultures view women substantially differently than most Western cultures view women in the workforce.

The major differences in working with Indians, again depending upon the individual, are threefold from my experience and research. First, Indians are an agreeable people. They are raised to conform and this is why they will respond with the word "Yes" on a regular basis. India is a country with a high Power Distance so they will tend not to disagree with superiors of any type. The word "Yes" has a broader meaning for most Indians. It usually means what Americans refer to as "okay." That is, they understand and have heard you, but they don't necessarily agree with you. This is why it is imperative that you avoid engaging them with Yes-No types of questions. Ask them to expound on a subject and explain themselves and you will probably discover all the information you need without any difficulty.

Their relationship with superiors is somewhat complicated for Westerners to comprehend. Being a subservient subordinate is an important part of the Indian culture in most regions. Even though Indians generally will have difficulty disagreeing with a supervisor, many Indian software professionals have come to understand how this relationship works in America and have adapted accordingly. Lastly, some Indian males may experience mixed feelings when working for a women supervisor, especially if she is also of Indian descent. My personal experience has been that Indian males are accustomed to reporting up to American women and they effectively treat them as they would a male supervisor. However, when it comes to reporting to an Indian woman, which I find somewhat rare, this may create a distinct hardship. For much more in-depth information a must read is Craig Storti's book entitled *Speaking of India*.

Learning Differences

In America, making mistakes is seen principally as a weakness and not as a golden opportunity to acquire supplementary knowledge and experience or improve oneself, as was highlighted earlier. This is essentially taught to us while growing up, but it is not necessarily this way in other countries. In many countries, students learn that it is okay, even expected, to make mistakes as long as one learns from those mistakes and eventually succeeds. Persistence seems to be expected of people in other cultures, Asian cultures in particular. Software developers who are afraid to experiment with new coding techniques, what is sometimes referred to as defensive coding, may not end up learning the techniques and methods needed for the profession in the future. We may become easily embarrassed by our missteps and while I agree that making mistakes on a regular basis may be an embarrassment and must be avoided, occasional experimentation made in the confines of our development environment can provide pivotal learning opportunities. If one is intimidated to further explore these techniques with their colleagues, because they are overly concerned about making mistakes and appearing incompetent, they may unnecessarily limit their career growth.

It's seems somewhat ironic to me that in a culture that upholds the individual, as we do in America, we have so little tolerance for those who make mistakes. Wouldn't you rather be renowned for your hard work and persistent nature than your genetic borne skills and abilities? I once had a teacher who mocked my tennis playing skills because I had acquired them principally due to the fact that I lived near my town's tennis facility. In America certain people may be more impressed with your natural talents versus your accomplishments due to effort and hard work.

Americans have become very self-conscious, as we have a culture that exploits many people who make mistakes. We are made out to be failures rather than risk takers searching for a new and better way. This culture of villainizing those who fail has become exasperated by the web and sites like YouTube. Do something silly or embarrassing and you could end up a national story, at least for a few minutes until the next victim is uploaded.

MITIGATION STRATEGIES

All of these cultural challenges just portrayed can seem a bit daunting and overwhelming. How does one even begin to address all these issues, especially when they are unique for every situation? Fortunately for us the research, both academic in nature and cases studies, yields several practical approaches for addressing these fragile situations.

Bridging

Several studies mention the possible use of a cultural liaison, also known as bridging techniques. This is where one person from each country is designated as the official go-between when there are problems or misunderstandings. Liaisons may also prevent certain problems from arising in the first place by coaching and from their prior experiences in multi-cultural settings. Having discussions on a peer-to-peer basis, as cited earlier in Chapter 8, is a reasonable approach to reducing and preventing communication gaffes.

Language Usage

Defining common terms and using them consistently will help reduce language barriers. It's important that native English speakers be especially patient with non-native speakers. Showing noticeable frustration in others' language abilities may end up shutting them down. This may be particularly true for technical people, of whom many are highly sensitive to criticism. Working in a multi-cultural environment is not the place to be featuring your mastery of the English language and your extensive vocabulary. It's important to speak slowly and clearly using common words while also avoiding slang and colloquialisms.

Understanding Other Cultures

Many Americans just parachute into other cultures completely oblivious to their nuances. Huang and Trauth highlight an example where Chinese hosts were attempting to build a personal relationship with their American software guests by showing them the local attractions. The next weekend the Americans, trying to be sensitive to the time spent by their gracious hosts, said that they would provide their own entertainment. This ended up offending the Chinese hosts and they became confused. Did they do something wrong? Did the Americans dislike them? The Chinese prefer to build personal relationships with their business counterparts, something referred to as "Guanxi." This is part of their culture and it is very important to them.

One way of better understanding another culture is to review the Hofstede research mentioned earlier in this chapter. An even better way is to speak with others who have previously worked in the same country. Personally, I've found that attempting to speak some of the native language demonstrates your commitment to establishing a positive relationship.

Staff Adjustments

From a management standpoint, selecting the proper staff at the outset of a project is critical. It's also important to make staff modifications quickly if things aren't working well during the course of the project. This reflects management's commitment and sensitivity to the project. As was highlighted in the Virtual Teams section, choosing staff members with high levels of conscientiousness is prudent, particularly for liaison roles.

GENDER

Gender is closely related to culture in that different cultures view the two gender roles differently, as was just briefly highlighted in the section on Indian culture.

For many of the recent decades it was taboo to discuss the differences between men and women. After all, women were desperately trying to gain equality with men in the workplace (at least in many Western countries), so to discuss differences was, in many instances, severely frowned upon. "Anything a man can do a woman can do better" was a common tongue in cheek saying among people supportive of the women's movement. Now, after many decades, researchers are again interested in discovering the differences between males and females in how they think, act, interpret sensory information, and so on. This is actually a fascinating topic when one discovers how many physiological disparities actually exist among the genders.

Gender Data

According to the 2009 figures from the U.S. Bureau of Labor Statistics (BLS), women comprised about 20% of all computer programmers. The BLS monitors a variety of employment figures across several business sectors. Several different categories are encompassed within the software field. These include programmers, software engineers, database administrators, system analysts and some additional roles – mainly those in the network and support areas. Here is the data for the specified roles and the percentage of women in each:

Programmers:	**20.2**
Software Engineers:	**20.2** (same as programmers, it's not clear if it's the same data or not)
Systems Analysts:	**26.9**
DBAs:	**35.3**

So it's relatively clear from the BLS data that men constitute the bulk of programmers, at least in the U.S. I would expect that these numbers would be closely mirrored in other Western countries. They could possibly be different in Asian countries, but I would be somewhat surprised. Discussions of the possible reasons for this discrepancy follow.

Social Expectations vs. Biological Differences

Differences between the sexes becomes evident at a very early age, partly because of the different ways in which society treats, and reacts to, young children. Boys learn to be more rough, tough and independent while girls are learning to be more dependent and conforming (Statt pg. 328). Just as many jobs in our society, such as construction for example, have become gendered as male, so too has the field of technology. There may be one or two exceptions, however. The area of Quality Assurance and Business Analysts, the field I have worked in since 2002, seems to be breaking the mold a bit. My unscientific determination is that there is a higher percentage of women working in the QA and BA fields than in other areas of software development. The U.S. Bureau of Labor Statistics does not break out the computer and software industry data this granularly, so this is only my educated guess.

As far as socialization is concerned, it is not entirely certain whether male brains are actually wired more optimally for software development or whether they have been socialized in favor of development by parents, teachers and other influential adults as a result of their gender. There are numerous studies and test results indicating that males are more adept in math and science while females are more proficient in language related skills, such as reading and writing (Berry, et al, 2002). While there is still a debate about why this difference exists, it seems to be rather clear that males do have a slight advantage in the spatial problem solving area whereas women have more language and emotional processing abilities. It is especially important to note that while these differences may exist, it is across large populations and any one particular group may reveal a great diversity in spatial and verbal abilities between men and women. To complicate matters further, there appear to be gender differences in mathematical problem solving across cultures too (Gifted Child Quarterly, 2008). This would lead one to expect socialization to have a larger impact on whether one excels at mathematics versus an innate biological difference.

Men generally exhibit more intellectual extremes than women. Slightly more men are typically found at the higher end of the intelligence scale, but also on the bottom end as well. It's as though the bell shaped curve for men is flattened somewhat on both ends. There are more men in prison, on the streets homeless, and more men with lower IQs than women (Baumeister, 2007). Baumeister goes on to say that men seem to specialize in many relationships, building their social network basically, while women prefer to have fewer, but deeper relationships. What that tells us about women and men in software development is not perfectly obvious, but we can make some reasonable guesses. Since there are fewer women in the profession and they prefer closer relationships, it would make some sense that these women might tend to band together with each other to nurture these relationship tendencies. There may also be a very small tendency to disengage from the men when the going gets tough. Therefore PMs and other managers must be on the lookout for such behavior and help to mitigate these situations. On the other hand, since there are fewer women involved in many projects, they may work extra hard to be included in the group and become accepted by the team. It's also quite possible that women who are attracted to the software field are those whose social traits more closely resemble that of men, where they prefer to have more social contacts but at a more superficial level.

Yet another possible reason for women avoiding careers in programming may be the lack of authentic role models. Others suggest that the women who do become programmers leave the profession earlier than most men, thereby leaving a shortage of qualified role models for incoming younger women. The data on this topic consists primarily of comments found in various blog posts from women within the industry, with little or no research data; hence this is only a weak prospective theory at best.

Two Brains – Male & Female

As researchers and neuroscientists discover and understand more deeply how our brains function, the difference between male and female brains is becoming more apparent. Overall intelligence does not seem to vary considerably between males and females even though brain usage patterns of males are distinct in several ways from those of females. That doesn't mean that there aren't differences at the extremes, as just mentioned earlier. Women have more white matter and men more gray matter as determined by analyzing brain functioning related to intelligence (Haier, 2007). There are various other parts of the brain that are either larger or smaller or more developed or undeveloped in the two brains. Clearly we are recognizing that male and female brains work somewhat differently, right from conception.

One of the more striking differences seems to be in the connection between brain hemispheres. The **Corpus Callosum** is a set of fibers which connects the two brain halves and it is here where women appear to have a significant advantage over men. This is the communication highway, as it is commonly referred to, that allows right brain activity to interact with left brain information and vice versa. There are various studies, some disputed, which show that the corpus callosum in women has more connections and is able to transmit more information between the two hemispheres. Whether it is larger or not is debatable but many studies seem to indicate that it functions more effectively in female brains. This is possibly what allows women to better verbalize what they're thinking and viewing, as these two functions primarily operate in different hemispheres. In addition, it appears that the corpus callosum is larger in some musicians and left handed people as well. There does appear, at least to me, to be a greater percentage of left handed people in the software development field in contrast to the general public. However, whether this is actually true or not is difficult to determine as I have yet to uncover any reliable data. Some research studies link left-handedness to higher levels of creativity, but there is no real scientific consensus at the moment. I tend to believe it though, but only because I'm left-handed.

Male Strengths and Weaknesses

Men seem nearly perfectly wired for software development and that's almost certainly why men tend to dominate the field. Their abstract thinking capabilities and task focused orientation combined with curtailed verbal skills make software development an almost ideal discipline for many men. However, the team component of development is where some men have tendencies to struggle, both in meetings and building fruitful, longstanding relationships with the business side and sometimes fellow technical people too. Some men may also flounder with the more verbal or "fuzzy" aspects of software engineering such as system requirements and management. Introverted men, all things being equal, would much rather work with other men. So the male gendered world of technology is unmistakably a comfortable setting for many men, especially as programmers.

Female Strengths & Weaknesses

There is a substantial body of evidence that has been accumulated and is still being compiled today that indicates, beyond a reasonable doubt, that women have superior communication skills. This is evident shortly after birth as girls learn to speak earlier and accumulate a larger vocabulary than most boys. Boys' brains develop more spatial processing capabilities from an early age while girls' brains are developing added verbal and emotional regulation proficiencies. Data also show that women are capable of processing language effectively in both hemispheres of their brain which doubtless improves their communication skills compared to men who tend to rely primarily upon the left hemisphere.

Women also spend more time tending to and building deeper personal relationships with their work peers. This helps them create and establish social capital which they can rely upon when they need it most, during those stressful negotiation meetings with the business or other co-workers.

Working Together

While it's clear that there are noticeably more men than women in our field, it's important to understand the implications when the two sexes work together. I would suggest that the differences between the sexes may be more extreme in software engineering than in most other professions except perhaps police work and firefighting. Since the profile of technically oriented males is more introverted, and men typically have slightly diminished verbal skills, you can readily find conditions where communications between the two is strained. Men would much rather focus on their task accomplishments whereas females prefer to highlight personal relationships (Sias, 2009). One might naturally surmise that this represents a fairly hefty disconnect between the two sexes.

Earlier it was highlighted that women seem to have (at least from my experience) gravitated towards certain well defined roles within software engineering. These include primarily BA, QA and PM roles. From what neuroscientists and cultural psychology researchers have determined this seems to be a rather pragmatic application of their unique skills.

Supervisor-Subordinate Relationships

While people generally prefer to report to people of the same gender, this scenario is less likely in an industry dominated by men. In many ways women are better equipped for management roles as long as they resist the temptation to operate too much like they believe men would act. This temptation can be strong in a field which has become gendered as male. Women are more intuitive and can detect social contextual cues and respond to them in more emotionally appropriate ways (Marano, 2003) which are ideal traits for managers. My personal experience, in several instances, was that women who became technical managers would sometimes react like they assumed men would react. This was more likely the case when women first started managing technical professionals decades ago. I'm presuming that this situation has mostly resolved itself by now but, I'm somewhat certain that some women, especially newly appointed supervisors, are convinced they must strive to act like their male counterparts in order to conform and be fully accepted by the other males.

Competitiveness

There's little dispute among researchers that men are much more competitive than women within the general public. However, I have witnessed little evidence of this within software development. Perhaps the women attracted to our field have adapted during the course of their lives to compete effectively with men. It's possible that Western women have become accustomed to competing with boys while growing up during sports and other types of activities so that entering the professional world of work is not a major adjustment for them. One thing is overwhelmingly clear from a vast amount of research and that is that men are much more aggressive than women, particularly younger men. It's therefore reasonable to expect that younger men may exhibit more competitive behaviors in the workplace, regardless of profession.

AFTERWORD

So where do we go from here? You've hopefully discovered at least a few new concepts or techniques that are pertinent to your unique situation. Or maybe you've been reminded of some you've already known about. Or perhaps I've made some linkages you hadn't before considered. Either way, the ball is now in your court. The challenge with all new information is how to best put it into practice. Most of the information presented here will not do you much good if you don't make a move to leverage it. Start with prioritizing your needs or problems and focus there first. Reviewing some of the referenced materials found in the bibliography is a great way to get started. Many times just starting is the biggest inertia people must overcome. For me personally, I've learned that I just need to take the first step on a project and then it doesn't seem so dreadful and daunting. A good percentage of project delays are due to languishing early on in the process. I'm not in any way proposing haphazard approaches, but getting behind before you start is not a realistic answer either. The planning may not be enjoyable but it still needs to be done so why not get started on it now?

I didn't start out trying to prove any specific points, as I really didn't know where the research in this endeavor would lead. It does appear to me now though that Agile development has some real merits and should be seriously considered by more organizations. My position in software consulting at SWAT Solutions allows me access to several project approaches from many different organizations and the Agile methodology is clearly becoming more and more prominent, albeit somewhat modified from the original manifesto.

From a research perspective there is much yet to be done within our discipline. Many of the studies I cite may or may not apply equally as well to developers and other technical staff. More large scale studies on technical people and organizations would be of great value, assuming that they can be conducted properly and pragmatically. I'd love to hear your stories, comments and suggestions at jfox@analogdevelopment.com.

AUTHOR
Bio

John R. Fox is Chief Operating Officer at SWAT Solutions. He joined the firm in 2002. He has acquired over 25 years of experience in the software industry while working for several prominent Twin Cities companies such as Unisys, Young America Corp, and Wilson Learning. John was also a co-founder of Boomerang Marketing, an Internet-based incentive company.

Fox launched his career as a systems programmer in the 1980s with Sperry Univac Defense Systems (now Lockheed Martin) where he focused on operating system and compiler development. All told, he has developed a well-rounded technical knowledge base by holding nearly every job within the software development field at one time or another.

As COO at SWAT Solutions, Fox envisions the company's mission as enhancing the quality, stability and performance of software usage, thereby preventing costly failures and unnecessary downtime.

Fox is a graduate of Gustavus Adolphus College in St. Peter, MN and holds a B.A. degree in Psychology with a minor in Computer Science. He lives in the Minneapolis, Minnesota area with his wife and two sons.

John may be reached, via email, at jfox@analogdevelopment.com.

BIBLIOGRAPHY

Abelson, Robert P., Kurt P. Frey, and Aiden P. Gregg. (2004). *Experiments with People: Revelations from Social Psychology*. Mahwah N.J.: L. Erlbaum.

Adamczyk, P. D., & Bailey, B. P. (2004). If Not Now, When?: The Effects of Interruption at Different Moments Within Task Execution. *CHI, Association for Computing Machinery, Inc.*

Albrecht, Karl. (2006). *Social Intelligence: The New Science of Success*. San Francisco: Jossey-Bass, A Wiley Imprint.

Arden, John B. (2010). *Rewire Your Brain: Think Your Way To A Better Life*. Hoboken, NJ: John Wiley & Sons.

Ariely, Dan. (2008). *Predictably Irrational: The Hidden Forces That Shape Our Decisions*. New York: Harper.

Arkes, H. R., Ayton, P. (1999). The Sunk Cost and Concorde Effects: Are Humans Less Rational Than Lower Animals? *Psychological Bulletin*, Vol. 125, No. 5, 591-600.

Aronson, Elliot, Timothy D. Wilson, and Robin M. Akert. (2007). *Social Psychology*. Upper Saddle River, NJ: Pearson Prentice-Hall.

Barrick, M. R., Stewart, G. L., Neubert, M. J. & Mount, M. K. (1998). Relating member ability and personality to work-team processes and team effectiveness. *Journal of Applied Psychology*, Vol 83(3), 377-391.

Baumeister, R. F. (2007). American Psychological Association, Invited Address.

Baumeister, Roy F., and Brad J. Bushman. (2011). *Social Psychology and Human Nature*. Belmont, CA: Wadsworth, Cengage.

Baumeister, R. F., Vohs, K. D., DeWall, C. N., & Zhang, L. (2007). How Emotion Shapes Behavior: Feedback, Anticipation, and Reflection, Rather Than Direct Causation. *Personality and Social Psychology Review*, Vol. 11 No. 2, 167-203.

Beach, Lee Roy, and Terry Connolly. (2005). *The Psychology of Decision Making: People in Organizations*. Thousand Oaks, CA: SAGE.

Berry, John W., Ype H. Poortinga, Marshall H. Segall, and Pierre R. Dasen. (2007). *Cross-Cultural Psychology: Research and Applications*. Cambridge: Cambridge Univ.

Blake, R.R., and Mouton, J.S. (1964). *The managerial grid*. Houston: Gulf Publishing Co.

Blanton. H., Pelham, B. W., DeHart, T., & Carvallo, M. (2001). Overconfidence as dissonance reduction. *Journal of Experimental Social Psychology*, 37, 373-385.

Brafman, Ori, and Rom Brafman. (2008). *Sway: The Irresistible Pull of Irrational Behavior*. New York: Doubleday.

Brett, J., Behfar, K., & Kern, M. C. (2006). Managing Multicultural Teams. *Harvard Business Review*.

Brizendine, Louann. (2010). *The Male Brain: A Breakthrough Understanding of How Men and Boys Think.* New York: Broadway.

Brooks, Frederick P., Jr. (2010). *The Mythical Man-Month: Essays on Software Engineering Anniversary Edition.* Boston: Addison-Wesley.

Brunnermeier, M. K., Papakonstantinou, F., & Parker, J. A. (2008). An Economic Model of The Planning Fallacy.

Bryant, S., Romero, P., & du Boulay, B. (2008). Pair programming and the mysterious role of the navigator. *International Journal of Human-Computer Studies 66* (2008) 519–529.

Buehler, R. Messervey, D., & Dale Griffin, D. (2005). Collaborative planning and prediction: Does group discussion affect optimistic biases in time estimation? *Organizational Behavior and Human Decision Processes* 97 47–63.

Buehler, R., Griffin, D., & Ross, M. (1994). Exploring the "Planning Fallacy": Why People Underestimate Their Task Completion Times. *Journal of Personality and Social Psychology Vol. 67*, No. 3.366-381.

Buehler, R. & Griffin, D. (2003). Planning, personality, and prediction: The role of future focus in optimistic time predictions. *Organizational Behavior and Human Decision Processes 92* 80–90.

Burmistrov, I. & Leonova, A. (2003). Do Interrupted Users Work Faster or Slower? The Micro-analysis of Computerized Text Editing Task. *Proceedings of HCI International.*

Cameron, J., Banko, K.M., & Pierce, W. (2001). Pervasive Negative Effects of Rewards on Intrinsic Motivation: The Myth Continues. *The Behavior Analyst 24*, 1–44, No. 1.

Capretz, L. F. (2003). Personality types in software engineering. *International Journal of Human Computer Studies 58* 207-214.

Carnegie, Dale. (1998). *How to Win Friends & Influence People.* New York: Pocket.

Cialdini, Robert B. (2007). *Influence: The Psychology of Persuasion.* New York: Collins.

Collett, J.L., Kelly, S., Sobolewski, C. (2010). Using Remember the Titans to Teach Theories of Conflict Reduction. *Teaching Sociology* 38(3) 258–266.

Collins, James C., and Jerry I. Porras. (1997). *Built to Last: Successful Habits of Visionary Companies.* New York: Harper Business.

Cooper, Joel. (2007). *Cognitive Dissonance: Fifty Years of Classic Theory.* Los Angeles, CA: SAGE.

Costa, P. T., & McCrae, R. R. (1992). Multiple uses for longitudinal personality data. *European Journal of Personality,* 6, 85–102.

Deci, Edward L., and Richard Flaste. (1995). *Why We Do What We Do: Understanding Self-Motivation.* New York: Penguin.

DeFranco-Tommarello, J. & Deek, F. P. (2002). Collaborative Software Development: A Discussion of Problem Solving Models and Groupware Technologies. Proceedings of the 35th Hawaii International Conference on System Sciences.

Deshpande, S., Richardson, I., Casey, V., Beecham, S. (2009). Culture in Global Software development – a Weakness or Strength? *Lero – the Irish Software Engineering Research Centre.*

Dickinson, D. L., & Oxoby, R. J. (2007). Cognitive Dissonance, Pessimism, and Behavioral Spillover Effects. *Institute for the Study of Labor* (IZA), Bonn, Germany.

Dollard, J., & Miller, N.E. (1950). *Personality and Psychotherapy: An analysis in terms of learning, thinking, and culture.* New York: McGraw-Hill.

Domino, M. A. (2004). Three studies of problem solving in collaborative software development.

DuBrin, Andrew J. (2009). *Political Behavior in Organizations.* Los Angeles: SAGE.

Erven, Bernard L. (2001). *Becoming an Effective Leader through Situational Leadership*, Department of Agricultural, Environmental and Development Economics, Ohio State University Extension, Columbus.

Ewusi-Mensah, Kweku. (2003). *Software Development Failures: Anatomy of Abandoned Projects.* Cambridge, MA: MIT.

Eysenck, Michael W., and Mark T. Keane. (2010). *Cognitive Psychology: A Student's Handbook.* Hove, Eng.: Psychology.

Falkenstern, M., Schiffrin, H. H., Nelson, S. K., Ford, L., & Keyser, C. (2009). Mood over matter: can happiness be your undoing? *The Journal of Positive Psychology* Vol. 4, No. 5, 365–371.

Feldman, Robert S. (2002). *Understanding Psychology.* Boston: McGraw-Hill Higher Education.

Felps, W., Mitchell, T. R., & Byington, E. (2006). How, when, and why bad apples spoil the barrel: Negative group members and dysfunctional groups.

Forgas, Joseph P., and Kipling D. Williams. (2001). *Social Influence: Direct and Indirect Processes.* Philadelphia, PA: Psychology.

Franklin, B. (1900). *The autobiography of Benjamin Franklin.* (J. Bigelow, Ed.). Philadelphia: Lippincott. (Originally published 1868).

Funder, David C. (2007). *The Personality Puzzle.* New York: W.W. Norton.

Geister Udo Konradt, S., Hertel, G. (2006). Effects of Process Feedback on Motivation, Satisfaction, and Performance in Virtual Teams. *Small Group Research*, SAGE Vol. 37 No. 5 459-489.

Gilovich, Thomas, Dale Griffin, and Daniel Kahneman. (2002). *Heuristics and Biases: The Psychology of Intuitive Judgment.* Cambridge: Cambridge UP.

Goldberg, L. R. (1990). An alternative "Description of personality": The Big-Five factor structure. *Journal of Personality and Social Psychology,* 59, 1216-1229.

Goleman, Daniel. (2006). *Social Intelligence: The Revolutionary New Science of Human Relationships.* New York: Bantam.

Goleman, Daniel. (2000). *Working with Emotional Intelligence.* New York: Bantam.

González, V. M. & Mark, G. (2004). "Constant, Constant, Multi-tasking Craziness": Managing Multiple Working Spheres. CHI Paper, Vienna, Austria.

Gottman, J. M. (1995). *Why marriages succeed or fail: And how you can make yours last.* New York: Simon & Schuster.

Gray, John. (1992). *Men Are from Mars, Women Are from Venus: A Practical Guide for Improving Communication and Getting What You Want in Your Relationships.* New York: HarperCollins.

Gross, J. J., & John, O. P. (2003). Individual differences in two emotion regulation processes: Implications for affect, relationships, and well-being. *Journal of Personality and Social Psychology,* 85, 348–362.

Guynes Clark, J., Walz, D. B., & Wynekoop, J. L. (2003). Identifying Exceptional Application Software Developers: A Comparison of Students and Professionals. *Communications of the Association for Information Systems* Vol. 11, No. 1.

Haier, R. (2007). Reference from article: Brain Network Related To Intelligence Identified. *ScienceDaily.*

Hallinan, Joseph T. (2009). *Why We Make Mistakes: How We Look Without Seeing, Forget Things in Seconds, and Are All Pretty Sure We Are Way Above Average.* New York: Broadway.

Hastie, Reid, and Robyn M. Dawes. (2010). *Rational Choice in an Uncertain World: The Psychology of Judgment and Decision Making.* Los Angeles: SAGE.

Hazzan, O. & Dubinsky, Y. (2005). Empower Gender Diversity with Agile Software Development. Israel Institute of Technology.

Hellige, J.B. (1990). Hemispheric asymmetry. *Annual Review of Psychology,* 41, 55-80.

Hillier, A., Alexander, J. K., & Beversdorf, D. Q. (2006). The Effect of Auditory Stressors on Cognitive Flexibility. *Neurocase* 12, 228–231.

Hofstede, Geert H., Gert Jan Hofstede, and Michael Minkov. (2010). *Cultures and Organizations: Software of the Mind: Intercultural Cooperation and Its Importance for Survival.* New York: McGraw-Hill.

Hogan, R., & Kaiser, R. B. (2005). What We Know About Leadership. *Review of General Psychology,* Vol. 9, No. 2, 169–180.

Hogan, Robert. (2007). *Personality and the Fate of Organizations.* Mahwah, NJ: Erlbaum.

Hornsey, M. J., Grice, T., Jetten, J., Paulsen, N., Callan, V. (2007). Group-Directed Criticisms and Recommendations for Change: Why Newcomers Arouse More Resistance Than Old-Timers. *Personality and Social Psychology Bulletin,* Vol. 33, No. 7 1036-1048.

Huang, H., Trauth, E.M. (2007). Cultural Influences and Global Information Systems Development Work: Experiences from Chinese IT Professionals. *ACM SIGMIS Computer Personnel Research Conference.*

Huff, R. A., & Prybutok, V. R. (2008). Information Systems Project Management Decision Making: The Influence of Experience and Risk Propensity. *Project Management Journal _ DOI: 10.1002.*

Humphrey, Watts S. (1997). *Managing Technical People: Innovation, Teamwork, and the Software Process.* Reading, MA: Addison-Wesley.

Isaksen, Scott G., K. Brian. Dorval, and Donald J. Treffinger. (2011). *Creative Approaches to Problem Solving: A Framework for Innovation and Change.* Los Angeles: SAGE.

John, O. P., & Srivastava, S. (1999). *The Big-Five Trait Taxonomy: History, Measurement, and Theoretical Perspectives.*

Jones, Morgan D. (1998). *The Thinker's Toolkit: Fourteen Powerful Techniques for Problem Solving.* New York: Times Business.

Jørgensen, M. & Moløkken, K. (2004). Eliminating Over-Confidence in Software Development Effort Estimates. University of Oslo, Norway.

Kavanagh, J., (1981). Stress and performance: a review of the literature and its applicability to the military.

Keil, M., Mann, J., Rai, A. (2000). Why Software Projects Escalate: An Empirical Analysis And Test of Four Theoretical Models. MIS Quarterly Vol. 24 No. 4, 631-664.

Keil, M. (1995). Pulling the Plug: Software Project Management and the Problem of Project Escalation. *MIS Quarterly.*

Keil, M. & Robey, D. (1999). Turning Around Troubled Software Projects: An Exploratory Study of the Deescalation of Commitment to Failing Courses of Action. *Journal of Management Information Systems*, Vol. 15. No. 4, 63-87.

Knox, R. E., & Inkster, J. A. (1968). Postdecision dissonance at post time. *Journal of Personality and Social Psychology,* 8(4), 319-323.

Konrad, Alison M. (2006). *Cases in Gender and Diversity in Organizations.* Thousand Oaks, CA: SAGE.

Kram, K. E., & Isabella, L. A. (1985). Mentoring alternatives: The role of peer relationships in career development. *Academy of Management Journal,* 28, 110-132.

Kraut, R. E. (2002). Applying Social Psychological Theory To The Problems Of Group Work. *Theories in Human-Computer Interaction.* J. Carroll (Ed.). New York: Morgan-Kaufmann Publishers, 325-356.

Kruger, J., Epley, N., Parker, J., Ng, Z. (2005). Egocentrism over e-mail: Can we communicate as well as we think? *Journal of Personality and Social Psychology,* Vol . 89(6) 925-936.

Larsen, Randy J., and David M. Buss. (2008). *Personality Psychology: Domains of Knowledge About Human Nature.* Boston: McGraw Hill.

Levi, Daniel. (2007). *Group Dynamics for Teams.* Los Angeles, CA: SAGE.

Levinson, Steve, and Pete Greider. (2007). *Following Through: A Revolutionary New Model for Finishing Whatever You Start.* Bloomington, IN: Unlimited.

Lewin, K. (1948). *Resolving Social Conflicts.* New York: Harper and Row Publishers.

Lichtenstein, S. and B. Fischhoff. (1977). Do those who know more also know more about how much they know? *Organizational Behaviour and Human Decision Processes.*

Locke, E.A., & Latham, G.P. (1990). *A theory of goal setting and task performance.* Englewood Cliffs, NJ: Prentice-Hall.

Lojeski, Karen Sobel, and Richard R. Reilly. (2008). *Uniting the Virtual Workforce: Transforming Leadership and Innovation in the Globally Integrated Enterprise.* Hoboken, NJ: John Wiley & Sons.

Lopp, Michael. (2007). *Managing Humans: Biting and Humorous Tales of a Software Engineering Manager.* Berkeley, CA: Apress.

Marano, H. E. (2003) *Psychology Today Magazine*, Jul/Aug.

Maravelas, Anna. (2005). *How to Reduce Workplace Conflict and Stress: How Leaders and Their Employees Can Protect Their Sanity and Productivity From Tension and Turf Wars.* Franklin Lakes, NJ: Career.

Mark, G., Gonzalez, V.M., Harris, J. (2005). No Task Left Behind? Examining the Nature of Fragmented Work. CHI Paper, Portland, Oregon.

Martin, C. (2007). The Importance of Face-to-Face Communication at Work. *CIO Magazine.*

Matsumoto, David R., and Linda P. Juang. (2008). *Culture and Psychology.* Belmont, CA: Wadsworth/Thomson.

May, Matthew E. (2009). *In Pursuit of Elegance: Why the Best Ideas Have Something Missing.* New York: Broadway.

McConnell, Steve. (1996). *Rapid Development: Taming Wild Software Schedules.* Redmond, WA: Microsoft.

McConnell, Steve. (2006). *Software Estimation: Demystifying the Black Art.* Redmond, WA: Microsoft.

McDermott, R., Fowler, J. H., & Smirnov, O. (2008). On the Evolutionary Origin of Prospect Theory Preferences. *The Journal of Politics,* Vol. 70, No. 2, 335–350.

McNeil, B.J., Pauker, S. G., Sox, H.C., Tversky, A. (1982). On the elicitation of preferences for alternative therapies. *New England Journal of Medicine,* 306(21):1259-62.

Meyer, Cheryl. Software Testers and Myers-Briggs Type Indicator Personality Types. University of Colorado at Colorado Springs.

Mitroff, I. (1974). *The subjective side of science.* Amsterdam: Elsevier.

Montague, Read. (2006). *Your Brain Is (Almost) Perfect.* New York: Penguin Group.

Moon, H. (2001). Looking Forward and Looking Back: Integrating Completion and Sunk-Cost Effects Within an Escalation-of-Commitment Progress Decision. *Journal of Applied Psychology Vol. 86.* No. 1 104-113.

Moore, D. A., & Healy, P. J., (2008). The Trouble With Overconfidence. *Psychological Review Vol. 115,* No. 2, 502–517.

Moskowitz, Gordon B., and Heidi Grant. (2009). *The Psychology of Goals.* New York: Guilford.

Muraven, M., Tice, D. M., & Baumeister, R. F. (1998). Self-Control as Limited Resource: Regulatory Depletion Patterns. *Journal of Personality and Social Psychology*, Vol. 74, No. 3, 774-789 0022-3514/98.

Nicholson, Nigel, David C. McClelland, David H. Burnham, and J. Sterling Livingston. (2003). *Harvard Business Review on Motivating People.* Boston: Harvard Business School.

Nicholson, N., Fenton-O'Creevy, M., Soane, E., & Willman, P. (2001). Risk Propensity and Personality. London Business School, Regent's Park, London NW1 4SA, UK.

Nickerson, R. S., (1998). Confirmation Bias: A Ubiquitous Phenomenon in Many Guises. *Review of General Psychology* Vol. 2, No. 2, 175-220.

Norem, J. (2002). *The Positive Power of Negative Thinking: Using Defensive Pessimism to Harness Anxiety and Perform at Your Peak.*

Parnin, C. & DeLine, R. (2010). Evaluating Cues for Resuming Interrupted Programming Tasks. *CHI '10- Proceedings of the 28th international conference on Human factors in computing systems. Association for Computing Machinery, Inc.*

Peng, K., & Nisbett, R. E. (1999). Culture, dialectics, and reasoning about contradiction. *American Psychologist,* 54, 741-754.

Preckel, F., Goetz, T., Pekrun, R., & Kleine, M. (2008). Gender Differences in Gifted and Average-Ability Students. Comparing Girls' and Boys' Achievement, Self-Concept, Interest, and Motivation in Mathematics. *Gifted Child Quarterly* Vol. 52 No. 2 146-159.

Rancer, Andrew S., and Theodore A. Avtgis. (2006). *Argumentative and Aggressive Communication: Theory, Research, and Application.* Thousand Oaks, CA: SAGE.

Reid, S. A., Palomares, N. A., Anderson, G. L., & Bondad-Brown, B. (2009). Gender, Language, and Social Influence: A Test of Expectation States, Role Congruity, and Self-Categorization Theories, *Human Communication Research.*

Restak, Richard M. (2006). *The Naked Brain: How the Emerging Neurosociety Is Changing How We Live, Work, and Love.* New York: Three Rivers.

Restak, Richard M. (2009). *Think Smart: A Neuroscientist's Prescription for Improving Your Brain's Performance.* New York: Riverhead.

Rink, F., & Ellemers, N. (2006). What Can You Expect? The Influence of Gender Diversity in Dyads on Work Goal Expectancies and Subsequent Work Commitment. *Group Processes & Intergroup Relations,* Vol. 9(4) 577–588.

Rozek, C. (2006). The Effects of Feedback and Attribution Style on Task Persistence. *Journal of Gustavus Undergraduate Psychology.*

Ryan, M. J. (2006). *This Year I Will: How to Finally Change a Habit, Keep a Resolution, or Make a Dream Come True.* New York: Broadway.

Sample, Steven B. (2002). *The Contrarian's Guide to Leadership.* San Francisco, CA: Jossey-Bass.

Schwartz, B., Ward, A., Monterosso, J., Lyubomirsky, S., White, K., & Lehman, D. R. (2002). Maximizing Versus Satisficing: Happiness Is a Matter of Choice. *Journal of Personality and Social Psychology,* Vol. 83, No. 5, 1178–1197.

Seligman, Martin E. P. (2002). *Authentic Happiness: Using the New Positive Psychology to Realize Your Potential for Lasting Fulfillment.* New York: Free.

Seligman, Martin E. P. (1998). *Learned Optimism: How to Change Your Mind and Your Life.* New York:Simon & Schuster.

Siakas, K. V., Balstrup, B., Georgiadou, E., Berki, E. (2005). Global Software Development; The Dimension of Culture. IADIS Virtual Multi Conference on Computer Science and Information Systems.

Sias, Patricia M. (2009). *Organizing Relationships: Traditional and Emerging Perspectives on Workplace Relationships.* Los Angeles: SAGE.

Siebdrat, F., Hoegl, M., & Ernst, H. (2009). How to Manage Virtual Teams. *MIT Sloan Management Review.*

Smith, H. J., Keil, M., & DePledge, G. (2001). Keeping Mum as the Project Goes Under: Toward an Explanatory Model. *Journal of Management Information Systems* Vol. 18 No. 2,189-227.

Sodiya, A. S., Longe, H. O. D., Onashoga, S. A., Awodele, O., & Omotosho, L. O. (2007). An Improved Assessment of Personality Traits in Software Engineering. *Interdisciplinary Journal of Information, Knowledge, and Management Volume 2.*

Solomon, C. (2003). Transactional Analysis Theory: the Basics. *Transactional Analysis Journal.* Vol. 33, No. 1.

Sonnentag, S. (2001). High Performance and Meeting Participation: An Observational Study in Software Design Teams. *Group Dynamics: Theory, Research, and Practice* 5, 1, 3-18.

Spencer-Rodgers, J., Peng, K.& Wang, L. (2010). Dialecticism and the Co-occurrence of Positive and Negative Emotions Across Cultures. *Journal of Cross-Cultural Psychology* 41(1) 109–115.

Spolsky, Joel. (2007). *Smart and Gets Things Done: Joel Spolsky's Concise Guide to Finding the Best Technical Talent.* Berkeley, CA: Apress.

Stafford, Tom, and Matt Webb. (2005). *Mind Hacks: Tips & Tools for Using Your Brain.* Sebastopol, CA: O'Reilly.

Stanovich, K. E., & West, R. F. (2008). On the relative independence of thinking biases and cognitive ability. *Journal of Personality and Social Psychology,* 94, 672-695.

Stasser G., & Titus W. (1985). Pooling of unshared information in group decision making: Biased information sampling during discussion. *Journal of Personality and Social Psychology,* 48, 48–1467.

Statt, David A. (2004). *Psychology and the World of Work.* New York: Palgrave Macmillan.

Stillman, T. F. Baumeister, R. F., Vohs, K. D., Lambert, N. M., Fincham, F. D., & Brewer, L. E. (2010). Personal Philosophy and Personnel Achievement: Belief in Free Will Predicts Better Job Performance. *Social Psychological and Personality Science* 1(1) 43-50.

Storti, Craig. (2007). *Speaking of India: Bridging the Communication Gap When Working with Indians.* Boston: Intercultural, a Nicholas Brealey Pub.

Tanner, M. (2009). Communication and Culture in Global Software Development: The Case of Mauritius and South Africa. *Journal of Information, Information Technology, and Organizations Volume 4.*

Tavris, Carol, and Elliot Aronson. (2007). *Mistakes Were Made (but Not by Me): Why We Justify Foolish Beliefs, Bad Decisions, and Hurtful Acts.* Orlando, FL: Harcourt.

Thaler, Richard H., and Cass R. Sunstein. (2009). *Nudge: Improving Decisions About Health, Wealth, and Happiness.* New York: Penguin.

Trope, Y. & Fishbach, A. (2000). Counteractive Self-Control in Overcoming Temptation. *Journal of Personality and Social Psychology,* Vol. 79, No. 4, 493-506.

Tuckman, B. W. & Jensen, M.C. (1977). Stages of Small-Group Development Revisited. *Group & Organization Studies,* 2, 419-427.

Tversky, A. & Kahneman, D. (1981). The Framing of Decisions and the Psychology of Choice *Science,* 221, 1124-1131.

Twenge, J. M., & Campbell, S. M. (2008). Generational differences in psychological traits and their impact on the workplace. *Journal of Managerial Psychology*, 23: 862-877.

Venners, B. (2003). Writing Better Code: How to Interview a Programmer.

Vohs, K. D., Baumeister, R. F., Schmeichel, B. J., Twenge, J. M., Nelson, N. M., Tice, D. M. (2008). Making Choices Impairs Subsequent Self-Control: A Limited-Resource Account of Decision Making, Self-Regulation, and Active Initiative. *Journal of Personality and Social Psychology,* Vol. 94, No. 5, 883–898.

Wheelan, Susan A. (2010). *Creating Effective Teams: A Guide for Members and Leaders.* Los Angeles: SAGE.

Wilmot, William W., and Joyce L. Hocker. (2011). *Interpersonal Conflict.* New York: McGraw-Hill.

Wittmann, M. and Paulus, M.P. (2007). Decision making, impulsivity and time perception, *Trends Cogn. Sci.*, doi:10.1016/j.tics.2007.10.004.

Won Yoon, S. & Johnson, S. D. (2008). Phases and patterns of group development in virtual learning teams. *Educational Technology, Research and Development.*

Wood, Samuel E., Ellen Green. Wood, and Denise Boyd. (2005). *The World of Psychology.* Boston: Pearson.

Wright, L. (1988). The Type A behavior pattern and coronary artery disease. *American Psychologist, 43*, 2-14.

INDEX

18626142R00142

Made in the USA
Lexington, KY
15 November 2012